Big Blue Nation

Kentucky Basketball's
Native Sons & Daughters

Russell Rice

Library of Congress Control Number: 2012950456

13 - digit International Standard Book Number 978-0-615-70316-9

Cover design by Still Publications
Cover photo provided by the University of Kentucky Athletics
Book layout by The Harrodsburg Herald

Manufactured in the United States of America

All book order correspondence should be addressed to:
Still Publications
11891 North Highway 27
Eubank, Kentucky 42567

or

valeriestill1@gmail.com

Acknowledgments

Adolph Rupp always credited his success to the fact that he surrounded himself with good people. He also refused to name his All-Time UK Basketball team, which he said would make a few happy and many not so. I subscribe to that thinking, so I beg forgiveness for omissions.

First and foremost, this book is a family effort, dating back to when son Rusty assisted in research, and culminating with the much appreciated efforts of daughters Sandy (power of attorney) and Judy (editing and proofing).

The published authors who went along for the ride were Danny Breeden ("The Hard Choice," and "Just Call Me Buck"; Janet Conley (Minnie Bailey Conley: A woman among Women") and Leanna Conley ("War Stories: A Father Talks to His Daughter). Sean Breeden who again contributed his computer expertise.

Oscar Combs also is a published author and fellow east Kentucky native whose advice and friendship I treasure dearly.

Thanks to the publishers, Valerie Still and Bob Todd

The Big Blue Nation:
Kentucky Basketball's Native Sons And Daughters
TABLE OF CONTENTS

1941-42 Van Lear Bank Mules (front, left to right): Richard Sparks, James Vaughn, Clyde Groves, Clifford Honaker, Tony Clifton; back: Hondell Adams, Russell Rice, Sebert Wells, Leonard Meade, Oral Trimble

Introduction

Grandfather Rice built the shoe-shine box. Grandfather Bowe supplied the brushes. Mother donated the rags. I hoed corn for 50 cents (script) a day for enough money to buy three shades of polish.

Father said, "Son, always shine the heel."

*I've tried to live with that...**Russell Rice***

Ours was a sports-oriented family of five boys and two girls born to Russell Ganes Rice and Alpha Bowe Rice in Johnson County, Ky., and reared during the Great Depression. Our father began working in the Van Lear coal mines at age fourteen. He lied about his age; Consol needed workers for the five mines the company then operated up and down Millers Creek.

A mine foreman taught my father the multiplication tables on pieces of slate by carbide light, deep inside the mines. Ganes eventually became a union secretary and for his own satisfaction, a keeper of UK statistics. His sons inherited their father's love of sports.

I earned letters in three sports at Van Lear High School and played briefly on the Kentucky Wesleyan baseball team. Brother Randy and I often took turns announcing imaginary UK games. Brother Jim played on the Garrett High School team that lost to Shelbyville in the 1948 KHSAA basketball tournament. Brother Clarence Darrell was captain of his Pikeville College basketball team. He later coached basketball at the middle and high school levels. Brother Bob still plays pick-up games at the Indianapolis, Ind., YMCA.

I was four years old when our father brought home two **BIG** batteries and a radio to our non-electric home in Wittensville. Those two items were a wagon-load. He attached a radio antenna to the tallest tree on the hill behind our house. It pulled in much static. That was seven years before WLAP-Radio in Lexington aired UK's first basketball game vs. Xavier in 1935.

We soon moved to Van Lear. We would gather around the radio and listen to prize fights, Lum & Abner and church music. We welcomed the arrival of the Grand Old Opry and high school basketball on the airways.

I was a 5-foot-8½ inch, 150 pound center/linebacker on our football team. I started most of the time, not because I was a good player, but due to a lack of depth on our team. Of the 18 students in our senior class (1942) there were only nine boys. When the United States entered WW-II, we voted on whether to field a football team that year. Two of us voted to continue playing the game, which was certainly unrealistic.

The company constructed a football field in the lower end of Van Lear, near the Levisa Fork of the Big Sandy River. It was approximately 1½ miles from the gymnasium. That was a long walk after a hard scrimmage session. Practically no one owned a car.

The C&O railroad and the main highway bordered one side, and Millers Creek ran on the other side of the field. A set of bleachers sat at one end behind what served as home plate during baseball games. The other end consisted of a corn field. The only room (standing) for spectators, other than the baseball bleachers, was on the railroad side of the field.

Due to poor roads and restricted travel, we played practically all our games close to home. That meant regular series with Inez, Meade Memorial, Paintsville, Prestonsburg, Jenkins and Pikeville, and occasional games with Kermit and Chattaroy, W.Va. We didn't win many of those games.

Van Lear once had a proud football tradition. That was prior to the 1940s, before the five coal mines began playing out. When I was growing up, the town had a population of 4,000, largest in the county. However, with the area's population diminishing and war clouds looming, we said goodbye to football and hello to basketball.

The first basketball game that I saw was a loss to Paintsville on a muddy court in the corner of our schoolyard. Spectators stood on the sidewalk that split the yard and continued uphill to the school.

In 1935, the Works Progress Administration (WPA) constructed a gym across the creek from our home. When not involved in school, gardening, or other chores, I eagerly watched the gym go up.

Two rooms flanked a stage on one side of the gym playing floor. Participating teams occupied benches at their respective ends of the stage. Substitutes climbed up and down the stage. There was a large coal-burning stove located on each end of the bleachers on the other side of the floor. Those two monsters emitted enough heat to roast persons nearest them. The back-rows spectators wore extra clothing, usually sheepskin jackets. Although warmer than the others in attendance, those persons nearest the stoves also had to dodge tobacco juice sailing overhead and spewing onto the stoves. Most men chewed tobacco; many smoked roll-your-own cigarettes in those days.

Our love affair with the Wildcats began when we finally were able to get their games on the radio. The Ashland Daily Independent kept us informed of the antics of Wallace Jones and other UK stars during the "Fabulous Five" era.

I was just out of the Marine Corps in 1946 when UK freshman guard Ralph Beard sank a free throw that gave UK a 46-45 win over Rhode Island in the 1946 NIT championship game. I turned off the radio and had my best night's sleep in years.

Throughout my 16 years as a newspaperman, and 22 years with UK sports information, I followed closely the progress of the mountain boys who played for the Blue & White. Johnny Cox was an eighth-grader at Fleming-Neon when I first interviewed him in 1951. Cox led Hazard to the 1955 KHSAA championship, and UK to the 1958 NCAA title. I was present at both events.

It saddened me when such east Kentucky high school stars as Wayland's Kelly Coleman and Corbin's Frank Selvy took their talents elsewhere. I worked in four coal banks in the Garrett-Lackey-Wayland area during Coleman's high school years at Wayland. I remember that he liked to play cards and drink, which many of us boys did in those days.

Making an all-state team was great for a mountain lad, but it took a back seat to being selected on a high school All-America team. As Rupp said, "Winning is everything; if not, why keep score?" We adhered to that philosophy while waiting patiently for another Wah Jones or Johnny Cox to come along.

What set me off on this current project was the Bible-quoting Rupp, who paraphrased the Psalm, "I shall lift up my eyes unto the hills, from whence cometh my help." He spoke mostly of the white, Anglo-Saxon Protestants who peopled the east Kentucky area. They were mostly the point-guard or shooting-guard types. We didn't grow any 7-footers.

The influx of mountain boys at UK began to wane in the 1950s when integration and school mergers changed the Kentucky high school sports scene. The number of native sons on UK rosters, like the old soldier, soon began to fade away. That was grist for the mill in writing a book, asking, "What happened to the mountain boys?"

I first submitted the book to a regional publisher. He said no. Bob Todd and Valerie Still, both longtime acquaintances and recent newcomers in the publishing business, were more receptive. They suggested that perhaps it might be better to include all in-state players.

The fact that Bob and Valerie are associated with McClanahan Publishers was just icing on the cake. I remembered Ed McClanahan from our early days at UK, when Playboy published his feature on Carlos "Little Enis" Toadvine. Enis was a left-handed, upside-down guitar player who was our answer to Elvis. Ed used that article in one of his books.

I had broken down Kentucky into what some consider five sections–Appalachian, Bluegrass, Pennyroyal, Western Coal Fields, and Purchase. I eliminated the Knobs because Appalachia includes most of those counties under its umbrella.

I led off the book with a listing of the players, their counties, county seats and home towns, accompanied by short bio's and appropriate quotes and anecdotes.

A final decision was to begin the book with an abbreviated history of Kentucky Basketball. I would emphasize the contributions of Kentucky boys, especially those from Appalachia, and retain that section of the book in its original state; then insert the other sections between Appalachia and the remaining chapters of the book. That would be the peg that I hung it on in other words.

There has been so much written about UK Basketball that I sought to approach the subject from a different angle with less emphasis on scores and stats.

Chapter I
An Humble Beginning

Walter W.H. Mustaine did not pose with the UK basketball team in 1904, but he was more than happy to surround himself with members of his fine gym squad. Indian clubs and tumbling were more important to the father of UK basketball than was the roundball.

*A simple game. And more. It gets in your heart. Maybe in Kentucky more than anywhere, maybe because basketball success energized hundreds of small towns as it did big towns, the game became a source of pride shared by people with few other things to share, certainly few so happy...***Dave Kindred.**

Walter Mustaine was the new physical director at Kentucky State College (forerunner of the University of Kentucky). He awakened to a busy schedule on Friday, February 4, 1903. In addition to his well-attended morning classes, Mustaine would oversee "a volunteer army of indoor athletes" that afternoon in the new gym.

As he approached the KSU campus, Mustaine thrilled at the sight of Barker Hall, which the school had erected with no specific purpose such as basketball in mind. The structure was three stories high in the center with broad lower wings on each side. The south wing housed the Armory, where cadets drilled on a dirt floor. The other wing contained the gym, which the school annual described as "a splendid room with all the apparatus necessary for complete gymnastic training." Spectators sat on folding chairs on the circular mezzanine track on game days.

Mustaine had the preps participating in graceful movements with Indian clubs; freshmen and sophomores doing stunts on bars and mats; juniors boxing, wrestling, or fencing, and seniors "adding the final embellishments to their bodies as well as to their minds."

Lean, Hawk-faced with protruding ears and black hair parted in the middle, Mustaine was described by the local press as an athlete of no mean ability. His hang-up was gym work. Interest in that phase of the curricula was the best in KSU's brief history. Mustaine eagerly looked forward to the day, March 12, when he would manage the school's first annual Gym Tournament. But on this February morning, he also was concerned with the Eighth Annual Intercollegiate Contest, which he considered of more importance than UK's first ever basketball game to be played in two days against Georgetown in the new gym.

The school officials told him that when football ended its 1902 season, some of the players, seeking to relieve the upcoming winter boredom, had turned their attention to basketball The new game was on the agendas of the local YMCA and the cross-town campus of Kentucky University (now Transylvania). It also was "creeping" onto the KSC campus.

The late Dr. Cronley Elliott, a retired Lexington dentist, was a member of the 1902 student group. They played for fun, without coach, captain, or a schedule, although they did play a couple of games with a team representing the Lexington YMCA.

When the athletics council asked Mustaine to organize a basketball team, he called together some students interested in playing the game.

The respondents included eastern Kentuckians George C. Montgomery, of Liberty; Joseph Coons, of Mt. Sterling; Charles Alberts, of Winchester; and Don Branson, of Yosemite. All except Branson were football players. Also present were future members of the school's first basketball team, J. White Guyn, H. J. Wurtele, Lee Andrus, Conrey Elliott, and R. H. Arnett. All were native Kentuckians.

Guyn was the acknowledged leader by virtue of his position as quarterback of the State football team. He served as the team grid captain in 1904 and later as

This 1904 photo from Kentucky's second season of basketball is one of the earliest known: (left to right) R. H. Arnett, J. White Guyn, Joe Coons, C. P. St. John, H. J. Wurtele, and H. H. Downing with the ball.

coach (1907, '08) of the Cadets, which was their name at the time.

Mustaine took up a collection totaling $3 for a ball. He told them to elect a captain, furnish their own shoes and uniforms and start playing. They scheduled an opening game on Feb. 6 with Georgetown.

A movement was underway to organize a Blue Grass Basketball League that would include teams from the YMCA, KU, KSC, and Georgetown as its charter members. It was just a matter of time before the game would sweep the state and the nation.

I had never seen a football or a basketball game when I entered the University (in 1903). I attended all the football games in the fall and became interested. When time came for basketball, I went out for it. I was given the ball; I ran the length of the court and pitched a goal. Naturally I received a razzing. I was fast and active, and had played baseball all my life. Basketball was in its infancy at the University and there were never many candidates. I studied and worked hard and made the team. I was made Captain the third year.

Basketball was a rough game at that time. There was never more than ten on the squad. The boys elected the Captain and he was coach and directed the play. In 1906, the year I was Captain, the five first stringers were as follows: Dick Barbee, Stanley Bair, J.M. Wilson, Terry (Tommy) Bryant and I. Wiley B. Wendt was manager. We won no national acclaim, and were most satisfied to break even during the season.

Thomson "Tommy" Bryant enrolled in the KSC prep school in 1903. At six-foot, they considered him a big boy at the time. His basketball experience consisted of some unorganized and somewhat crude games in high school at nearby Nicholasville.

"I remember chipping in to help buy the ball," he said in 1975. "It was one of those you inflated with a foot pump and then laced. If something had happened to the ball, we could not have played.

"None of us knew much about the game. We knew what jump-center was and that's about all. Mustaine was a prince of a fellow. He had a wonderful team of tumblers and taught a class in swinging Indian clubs, but he didn't know or care much about basketball. He came to see us practice twice during the season, and let us preps cavort with the varsity, but we weren't allowed to play on competing teams."

The first official uniform, suggested by the Spalding Co. in 1901, consisted of knee-length padded shorts or tights, sleeveless or quarter-length shirts, and long, woolen stockings. The suction-cup rubber-soled shoes appeared in 1903; knee guards were soon deemed a necessity.

"We didn't have fancy uniforms," Dr. Elliott said. "We wore

gym suits, which we bought ourselves. But the school provided us with a ball and hung iron hoops at each end of the gym."

The school eventually paid for complete uniforms and two basketballs.

The opening basketball game with Georgetown on February 6, 1903, held no special significance to Mustaine. His concern was that the sport would take much student time away from glee club practice and the Eighth Annual Intercollegiate (Debate) Contest scheduled that same day in the school chapel. State lost its first game to Georgetown, 17-6, which rated a short article in the Herald.

GEORGETOWN
Defeated State College In
Basketball Match

The basketball game between Georgetown College and State College, played in the gym of the latter college yesterday afternoon, resulted in a decisive victory for Georgetown, the score being 17-6.

The players for Georgetown were Stockton, center; Parrigan, guard; Abernathy, guard; Lovelace, forward. (The newspaper omitted a player named Browning.) State College players were (J. White) Guyn, guard; (Joe) Coons, forward; R. H. Arnett, guard; (Lee) Andrews (Andrus), guard; (H. J.) Wurtle (Wurtele), center.

Rooters for both teams reportedly packed the gym and applauded the 'brilliant' play of their respective colleges. However, the big story in both newspapers was about State's Allan Higgins Rhodes winning the Intercollegiate Contest amid the flaunting of banners and the deafening roar of college cheers before the largest and most enthusiastic audience ever in attendance at such a meet. Supporters carried Rhodes away on their backs.

The State basketball boys defeated the local YMCA, 11-10, and closed their season with a 42-2 loss to KU. As part of a double bill, the KSC girls defeated the KU girls in the first basketball game between girls from those two schools.

State defeated the Lexington YMCA and lost to Transylvania for a 1-2 record. They finished 1-4 the following two years.

Wendt was all things to all people in the KSC basketball camp in 1906. A slender, 6-foot-1 engineering student, he cut his basketball teeth in a playing arena located on the top floor of the Newport, Kentucky, city hall, just over the jail. Although he was a good player, he chose to serve as manager of the KSC team.

While entertaining a visitor in his room at Wesley Manor in South Louisville in December, 1974, the 89-year-old retired teacher of engineering let his mind travel back to those pioneer days of basketball at KSC.

"No, there was no such thing as a coach back then", he said. "We just practiced. I was a one-man operation. I made the schedule, printed the tickets, collected money, paid the bills, and was also in charge of the team on the road. I sometimes swept the floor.

"We printed our own cards to advertise the games. Classmates took care of the ticket sales. We charged 25 cents a game. The school allowed u s $25 expenses on the road. That included overnight rooms and meals. We tried to sleep as many in a room as we could, sometimes all eight of us that made the trips. Still, we always seemed to be running out of money. I made a little playing trap drums at the Opera House and I sometimes made up the basketball deficit with that.

"I was referee for all our games away from home and some of them at home. It was a custom for the visiting manager to referee while the home team had the umpire. The umpire was the one who controlled the game, the one who threw people out."

Wendt was the first person connected with basketball at KSU to purchase a scorebook. He also talked the Faculty Athletic Committee into purchasing jerseys for the team and arranged the school's first out-of-town trip.

Wendt led a contingent of basketball players that paraded at the dedication of a new Capitol building in Frankfort. Then they played a game in Louisville. Their new blue and white jerseys arrived that day.

The original school colors of blue and yellow were chosen in 1891. Blue and white officially became their colors in 1910. They adopted the "Wildcats" cognomen a year earlier after Commandant Phillip Corbusier, then head of the school's military department, said at chapel that their football team "fought like wildcats" in defeating Illinois, 6-2, in Urbana. They had previously been called "Cadets", "Colonels", "Corn-Crackers", and "Thoroughbreds". Each newspaper or periodical seemed to have a different name for the team.

After three straight losses at home in midseason, the 1906 team went on the school's first road trip.

They lost to the New Albany YMCA, and defeated Vernon College and Moores Hill in Indiana. They next lost to Christ Church and the YMCA in Cincinnati and Miami at Oxford. At Moores Hill they played by the light of lamps placed up and down both sides of the court.

In 1908, the team center was H. H. Downing, who later served as a UK astronomy professor.

"We didn't bother with set plays", Downing said in 1941, "There was no need for signals. Mustaine came in to see us practice twice during the season. He remained a few minutes each time."

The opposing centers jumped after each field goal. There was no limit to the number of fouls a player could make. Furthermore, the team captain designated the foul shooter before each game and that man did the foul-shooting.

The school won only 22 of 54 games played during its first six basketball seasons. Due to a poor record and an overcrowded gym, the University faculty committee on athletics passed a resolution in November 1909 abolishing basketball at the University. They rescinded the resolution the following month and installed a wooden floor and new lighting in the Armory. The college appointed head football coach E.R. Sweetland as its first paid basketball coach. That year, the team went 5–4.

Sweetland contacted a mysterious illness prior to the 1910 basketball season. During his hospitalization, Prof. R. E. Spahr coached the team. Sweetland returned in midseason, but the team was in the midst of a six-game losing streak and finished 4-8.

While Sweetland took a year's absence, Harold Iddings coached the State boys to a 5-6 record. Sweetland returned the following season and guided them to the school's first undefeated season, out-scoring their nine opponents, 281-134.

The victims were Georgetown, Central, Lexington YMCA, Miami, Central, Tennessee, Vanderbilt (twice on successive nights to inaugurate the series), and Georgetown. It would be 42 years before a UK team would experience another undefeated season.

Earning varsity letters that year were east Kentucky natives Brinkley Barnett and William Tuttle, both of Somerset; Henry L. Farmer, of Harlan; R. C. Preston, of Inez, along with J. H. Gaiser, D. W. Hart, W. C. Harrison, and manager Gils F. Meadors.

Due to travel difficulties, the trend of playing teams close to home continued through most of the early years of UK basketball. Here is how the leading scorers ranked:

1912-1913 (5-3)–R. C. Preston (9.1 ppg), Brinkley Barnett (8.4), Ralph Morgan, of Covington, (4.0); Henry Farmer (3.9), and William Tuttle (1.0).

1913-1914 (7-5)–R. C. Preston (6.1); Tom Zerfoss (6.0), and Karl Zerfoss (4.7), both of Ashland; William Tuttle of Somerset, (3.9), and Herschel Scott (3.2), of Madisonville.

1914-1915 (7-5)– Morgan, (8.3); Jim Server (5.3), of Henderson; William Tuttle (3.8), George Zerfoss (3.7), of Ashland, and Herschel Scott (2.9).

1915-1916 (8-6)–Derrill Hart (13.3), of Pisgah, Jim Server (5.7), Robert Ireland (5.6), of LaGrange; George Zerfoss (3.3), and George Gumbert (2.4), of Richmond.

1916-1917 (4-6)–C. C. Schrader (7.1), of Philadelphia, Pa.; Robert Ireland,(5.4); Lawrence Longsworth (4.4), Pat Campbell (4.2), , and William Rodes (1.3), all of Lexington. During the first 14 years of basketball at UK, the starting fives were all products of Kentucky high schools.

Schrader was the first out-of-state player to rank among UK's leading scorers. He came to UK on a football scholarship.

1917-1918 (9-2-1)–Henry C. Thomas (10.8), Arthur Bastin (4.0), A. P. Shanklin (3.5), and Pat Campbell, all from Lexington, and George Zerfoss (2.8).

1918-1919 (6-8) - Thomas (7.1), J. C. Everett (6.6), of Maysville; Bob Lavin (5.0), of Paris; Tony Dishman (3.3), of Henderson and EdParker (3.3), of Maysville.

1919-1920 (15-7)–Basil Hayden(10.8), of Paris; William Blakey (Blakeley?) (7.0), of Beattyville; J. C. Everett (5.5), Lavin (4.1), and Jim Wilhelm (3.6). After finishing that season, coach George Buchheit began preparing his Wildcats for the inaugural SIAA Tournament, which would be held in Atlanta the following Year.

1920-21 (13-1)–William King (11.4), Hayden (9.6), Paul Adkins (8.5), Lavin (2.50) and Fred Fest (1.3).

Chapter II
Champions of the South

The 1921 Wildcats are (front row, left to right): Sam Ridgeway, Paul Adkins, Basil Hayden, Bill King and Bobby Lavin. (back), Coach George Buchheit, Jim Wilhelm, Bill Poyntz, Gilbert Smith and Athletic Department Director S. A. Boles.

*The initial move in assembling a basketball team or any other undertaking is to understand the problems involved. Then it is necessary to get the right kind of material for the purpose and to instill a winning complex. Never talk about defeat. This simply breeds defeat.**Adolph Rupp.**

Tuesday, March 1, 1921, was one of those mild Kentucky winter days that gives just a hint of spring while at the same time threatening to dump rain, snow, or even hail on a populace long accustomed to the unpredictable.

The thermometer began a slow rise to a peak of 62 degrees by mid-afternoon and then dipped slowly to 50 degrees, enough to make the sap rise and start Lexington out of its cold-weather doldrums.

In addition to the first sign of upcoming spring, the city was still astir over events of the preceding night. President-elect Warren G. Harding had stopped in Lexington en route via the northbound Royal Palm to his home in Marion, Ohio.

Tanned by the Florida sun and clad in dark suit and leather cap, Harding was to be inaugurated on Friday. He stepped from the

Southern Railway System's crack passenger train and greeted the local gathering with such stock questions as: "How big is Lexington? This is where all the horses come from, isn't it? And whisky? How's the tobacco this year?"

They informed him that Lexington was a growing city of 40,000 patriotic folks. The thoroughbreds were still in the the Bue Grass, hearty and hale as ever. Probation had taken its toll on bourbon whisky. Burley tobacco was in such short demand that "a lot of us are trying to give it away, and can't."

After Harding's departure, the town's sporting element gathered at the Phoenix Hotel on East Main Street. Their thoughts turned to basketball, which someday would take its name among horses, Bourbon and Burley as a trademark of the Blue Grass.

The big news was Kentucky's 18-13 victory over Mississippi A&M in the semifinals in Atlanta. An air of anticipation permeated the city during that long and exciting Tuesday, when the final game would be played on a rattling, temporary court in the Atlanta Auditorium.

Making the trip South with Coach George Buchheit were the allotted eight players, all Kentuckians. The play-making captain, Basil Hayden, and defensive guard Robert Lavin had been teammates at nearby Paris High School. Forward William King was a product of Lexington Senior High. Paul Adkins, of Williamsburg, attended Cumberland College two years before joining the Wildcats as a center. Sam Ridgeway, outstanding guard from Shepherdsville, completed the starting five. The substitutes were guard Gilbert K. Smith of Lexington, center James E. Wilhelm of Paducah and forward William L. Poynz of Covington.

Buchheit came to Kentucky the preceding school year from the University of Illinois. He was an All-Western end and star of the Illini basketball and track teams. He served as football assistant at State in the fall of 1919. Buchheit began a five-year basketball stint in rather unimpressive fashion, winning only six of 14 games as influenza took a toll of the squad in late season.

He took to Atlanta an offense described by the Georgia press as one of the most peculiar attacks yet uncovered on a basketball court. Baffling the Southerners was the switching of guards to forwards by the Kentuckians. In addition, King, Hayden, and Adkins immediately impressed the Atlanta fans with their shooting.

Possibly half a dozen persons from Kentucky followed the team to Atlanta. Their spirits soared when Kentucky opened with a 50-28 victory over Tulane and then routed Mercer, 49-24. By the time the Wildcats defeated Mississippi A&M, the unorthodox shots of Adkins and the fine all-round play of the Wildcats were the talk of the basketball South.

In Lexington, hundreds of University students, alumni, and rooters crowded the balcony, the mezzanine and the street in front of the Phoenix Hotel, where a telegraph operator stood by to receive news of the game.

Shortly before tip-off, Albert E. Hukle, flushed face matching his red hair, stretched his slender 6-foot-5 frame, looked down at the crowded lobby, took a deep breath, raised a megaphone, and read the first message:

"Game ready to start. Boys in fine shape."

As tension mounted, the noise built to a crescendo and then suddenly stopped. Hukle once again spoke from the balcony. It was 9:40 p.m., and the first news of game action dot–dashed into the hotel:

"Adkins makes first goal. King second. Outclassing the Georgians. Adkins repeats. Georgia scores three on fouls; score 6 to 5 in favor of Kentucky."

Once again the Kentuckians cheered and shouted; then, at 9:50 p.m., a final wire came through on the first half:

"Georgia substitutes forward. Adkins makes goal. Georgia scores. Score end of first half Kentucky 9 Georgia 7."

During a long 30-minute wait for more news, Hukle announced plans for a welcoming celebration, including a parade and banquet.

"Ridgeway shoots foul. So does Georgia. Georgia makes another on foul. Score Kentucky 11 Georgia 10."

The shouts drowned out Hukle's excited voice. After a couple of minutes he finished the message:

"King makes goal on foul. King makes long goal."

"King makes goal. Georgia makes goal. Georgia makes another score. Kentucky 17 Georgia 16. Georgia makes goal. Georgia scored on foul."

Here is how "Fuzzy" Woodruff described the remaining action in the Atlanta Journal:

More red-blooded stuff was crowded into one brief minute last night, when Kentucky State University defeated the University of Georgia, 20 to 19, for the Southern Collegiate Athletic Association's first basketball championship of the South.

"There's less than a minute left to play. Georgia is leading by the scant margin of 19-17. Both teams are desperate. The Kentuckians are fighting with the courage born of despair. The throng watching the Homeric struggle is raving. Men are shouting in the hoarse combativeness of the struggle in which no mercy is expected or desired. Women are screaming in the fierce staccato battle-cry of motherhood defending its young. The athletes on the broad floor have aged a lifetime in a few brief minutes. They are no longer carefree, clean-limbed college boys. They are fighting the grim fight that men wage when their backs are against the wall, when hope seems just a mirage, fooling weary travelers into useless exerting of already-spent bodies, but they still fight."

The score was tied at 19-19 when "Buck" Cheeves, Georgia's captain, fouled KSU's Adkins as the final buzzer sounded. William King is State's designated shooter. He steps to the line with no time left on the clock.

The telegraph in the Phoenix Hotel received the news: King scores one point. Final score Kentucky 20 Georgia 19. Bring home cup tomorrow.

Few heard Hukle's final report: "Greatest game we ever played."

A large delegation of students met the team and paraded them from the train station to the Phoenix Hotel. During a celebration dinner in an over-crowded ballroom, plans were made for a new arena to be known as Alumni Gym.

The new gym seated 2,800 patrons. Kentucky completed it in time for the 1924-25 season. The basement contained UK administrative offices. Critics said it was a white elephant that basketball would never fill.

1922 (10-6)–Adkins (8.8), King (8.3), Lavin (5.2), Hayden (5.0), and Poynz (2.9). Hayden became Kentucky's first All-American in 1921. His game suffered when he received a knee injury prior to the first game in 1922.

1923 (3-10)–Carl Reifkin (10.2), Fred Fest (7.2), William Poynz (3.3), Gilbert Smith (1.5), and W. G. Williamson (1.2.)

1924 (13-3)–Jim McFarland ((9.9), Will Milward (6.3), Lowell Underwood (4.9), Reifkin (4.3), and King (2.9).

1924-25 (13-8)–McFarland (7.1), Underwood (6.3), Milward (6.2), Foster Helm (3.7) and Charles Alberts (2.5). The Wildcats opened Alumni Gym with a 28-23 win over Cincinnati. They lost six in a row before getting back to winning. They lost to Mississippi State after whipping VMI and Georgia in the Southern Conference tournament.

1925-26 (15-3)–Gayle Mohney (11.1), Paul Jenkins (3.7), McFarland (3.7), Lowell Underwood (3.7) and Henry Besuden (2.1).

1926-27 (13-13)–Jenkins (6.1), Edwin Knadler (4.4), Van Buren Ropke (3.4), Frank Phipps (3.4), and Helm (2.5).

Chapter III
A New System

The 1929-30 Wildcats are (front, left to right): Mgr. Leonard Weakley, Stanley Milward, Cecil Combs, Paul McBrayer, Lawrence (Big) McGinnis, Carey Spicer; Middle row, left to right: Coach John Mauer, Jake Bronston, Ercel Little, Bill Trott, George Yates; Back row, left to right: Hays Owens, Larry Crump, Milton Cavana, William Kleiser, and Louis McGinnis.

That uniform is not just a uniform; it's a sacred piece of cloth. It demands our best--all our sweat and tears--because of the great players who came before us. And there are many. No, it's not just another jersey. It's a matter of the heart.. John Pelphrey ((UK '92).

An air of secrecy shrouded the entire University of Kentucky basketball operation in the winter of 1927 as new coach John Mauer wasted no time indoctrinating his charges into an intricate new system.

Neville Dunn of the Herald told a curious public, "The Illinois system is the same in basketball as it is in football-drive and hard work, topped with a line of chatter that would make a pack of monkeys hide their faces behind coconuts in shame. No Illinois coach thinks much of a player who goes about his work with tight lips and tied tongue."

There was no mistaking the Illinois influence throughout the

Wildcat athletic operation. Harry Gamage was football coach. Bernie Shively was line coach. Fred Major coached the freshmen in basketball and football. Mauer coached varsity basketball, freshman baseball, and the football backfield.

Mauer brought to UK a five-man offense with guards as important to the attack as centers and forwards. The slow-break attack featured a steady procession of bounce passes that had the players operating from bended positions and working persistently for the good shot. He was one of the first coaches to popularize the bounce pass as an element of basketball offense.

Mauer received his basketball indoctrination at Batavia High. He was an All-Western Conference forward at the University of Illinois.

Mauer played halfback in the same backfield with the immortal Red Grange. Just under six feet, with a shock of dark, wavy hair, he was a taciturn individual who was very set in his ways.

Mauer inherited a Wildcat squad that included Paul Jenkins, the captain, and Lawrence McGinnis, Paul McBrayer, Stanley Milward and Cecil Combs. There were also some football players, guys like Elmer "Baldy" Gilb, Leonard Miller, Clair Dees, June Lyons and Ray Ellis. Mauer used the football crew as substitutes, which most teams did in those days.

At the time there was much skepticism throughout the South about his "submarine" attack. The disbelievers began to take notice after the Wildcats defeated South Carolina and Georgia and lost only to Mississippi in the 1928 tournament. Ed Danforth of the Constitution called them "just about the sweetest bit of basketball mechanism of the age." One year later, Ben Cothran of that newspaper described the offense as a "weird sort of dribble-pass that keeps the ball from rolling on the floor." Mauer started five sophomores–Combs, Owens, Milward, McGinnis, and McBrayer, all native Kentuckians, in 1927-28. They had their good and bad moments as they sought to master his intricate system of passing and feinting. They opened with a 33-17 win over Clemson before one of the largest crowds up to that time.

The Wildcats fumbled away a game with Miami of Ohio. They defeated Centre in a game cited for the referee's knack for ignoring football tackles and wrestling. They defeated Vanderbilt 43-23. They lost to the Naval Academy on an asphalt playing surface in Annapolis; Maryland's five-man defense so confused them the following day at College Park that they scored only one field goal in 48 attempts en route to a 37-7 loss.

Mauer inserted Irvine Jeffries, of Louisville, into the lineup. He responded with 22 points and they beat Tennessee rather easily, 48-18. They beat them again later in the season at Knoxville. They also beat Vanderbilt on the road, 54-29.

Among those joining the varsity in 1928-29 was Louis McGinnis, nicknamed "Little" because he was one inch shorter and three years younger than his brother, Lawrence "Big" McGinnis.

They opened with a 35-10 win over Eastern Normal. Next came a three-overtime victory, 43-42, over Miami. They lost to a North Carolina team, 26-15, that had won four southern championships in six years. Neville Dunn of the Herald called the Tar Heel offense "that flip and run stuff that nearly makes you crazy with the sheer speed and excitement of it."

Kentucky finished that season with a 12-5 record after defeating Tulane and losing to Georgia in the SIAA tournament.

Combs, McBrayer and "Big" McGinnis returned as starters the following year. Milward and "Little" McGinnis, both of Lexington, filled the other two spots. By season's end, Carey Spicer was the fourth-leading scorer. Hayes Owens was a chief substitute. McBrayer was from Lawrenceburg. He was the only non-Lexington boy in the group.

That 1929-30 UK team was a sensation wherever it played. They had a floor game polished to the finest degree and a defense hard to penetrate. In victories over Georgetown, Miami, Berea and Clemson, the Wildcats utilized what the local newspapers called "legal blocks" to spring men open time and time again for easy chip shots.

The biggest event of the season was a two-night series with Creighton. The visitors featured 6-foot-7 center Brud Jensen, considered a giant in those days. When Willie Worthing scored from 50 feet in the closing seconds of the first game to put the Blue Jays ahead by one point, Jensen rushed into the game, got the tip, and preserved the victory for Creighton. UK won by four points the following night.

The other team to beat them that year was Tennessee, which took a 29-26 decision in Knoxville to avenge a 23-20 loss in Lexington. The Wildcats closed the regular season with an exciting 28-26 overtime victory over Washington & Lee.

In Atlanta they defeated Maryland, 26-21, doubled the score, 44-22, on Sewanee, and lost to Duke, 37-32. Ed Danforth of the Constitution called the Duke game "one of the most brilliantly played games the conference has ever produced and was a neck-to-neck race down to the final wire."

Although they lost the championship, the Wildcats received a royal welcome upon their return to Lexington. A mob of boosters shoulder-carried them through the railroad terminal.

The school newspaper described Mauer as the "Moses" of Kentucky basketball, a round ball prophet who had led the game out of its slam-bang hit-and-miss style of former years and developed it along the lines of the machinelike precision of football. Mauer had changed the Wildcats from doormat to drawing card. His influence was felt throughout the South, where coaches had begun to develop his style of play. He seemed destined to go down in Southern annals as the pioneer of a new system, the father, so to speak, of Dixie Basketball.

Less than two months later, the UK Athletic Council refused him a pay raise. Mauer resigned as UK coach and accepted a similar position at Miami University in Ohio.

More than 70 persons applied for the job. The university chose Adolph Rupp, who had coached Freeport (Ill.) High School to a four-year record of 59-21.

Chapter IV
Rupp Arrives

I would not care to live in a society unless it is competitive. I think our sports teach that better than most other phases of education. If it matters not who wins or loses, why keep score?...A. Rupp.

Adolph Rupp 's first team, the 1930-31 Wildcats: (front row, left to right) Ercel Little, George Yates, Carey Spicer, Aggie Sale, and Bud Cavana. Second row, George Skinner, Allan Lavin, Bill Trott, Jake Bronson, Louis McGinnis, Cecil Bell, Morris Levin, mgr.; (Back row, Left to right) Rupp, Bill Congleton, Bill Kleiser, Ellis Johnson, Charles Worthington and Darrell Darby.

Born on a 120-acre homestead near Halstead in central Kansas, Adolph Rupp was the fourth of six children of Heinrich Rupp and Anna Lichti. The parents came to this country from Austria and Germany with the first wave of Mennonites who homestead in frontier Kansas in the 1880s.

After the father died of stomach cancer in 1910, the oldest son, Otto, dropped out of school and took over the farming operation. The other children–Henry, Theodore, Adolph, Elizabeth, and Albert–assisted Anna with the chores. They attended District 33 elementary school and Halstead High School.

Theirs was the usual story of hardships, dawn-to-dusk toil in the fields and a close family relationship that resulted from the battle for survival on the prairie.

After graduating from Halstead High School, Rupp played on two national championship basketball teams coached by Dr. Forrest "Phog" Allen at Kansas University. When the UK job came open, he viewed it as a step upward in prestige, not in salary.

"Kentucky offered me exactly the same salary as I was making at Freeport," Rupp said. "I felt it was a golden opportunity to get into college coaching, so I accepted."

One of Rupp's duties at UK was helping Birkett Pribble coach the freshman football team. "I saw right then that the University considered basketball a poor cousin to football," Rupp aid. "It was a situation that I planned to change."

Aggie Sale, a high school All-American from Harrodsburg, was among a record 50 candidates who reported for Rupp's first practice session. Carey Spicer, Jake Bronston and Ellis Johnson were among the football players who joined them later.

Rupp's offensive system consisted of a set of 10 plays centered around the pivot-post. He instructed his players to run and fast break whenever the opportunity afforded itself.

He cut the squad by more than half and relentlessly stressed fundamentals, particularly goal-shooting. His impatience with anything less than perfection resulted in a verbal barrage against the varsity for letting the freshmen score so many points in their first scrimmage, which the varsity won, 75-21. After long hours of work on defense, the varsity won the next scrimmage, 75-9.

"Fans don't appreciate good defensive players, but you must have them," Rupp said. "It's just like on a farm. Fertilizer must be spread. Nobody likes to spread it, but it just has to be done. That is the way with defense. A lot of boys just want to shoot, but you have to have defense."

He used five or six standard plays based on outside screening.

"They were very kind to us because the South still had not caught onto the screen," he said. "We didn't use the inside screen until five or six years later. We discovered it in spring practice. We won 48 consecutive games in the conference before they knew what we were doing.

In Rupp's first game as coach, Capt. Harry Lancaster of Georgetown started the scoring with a field goal. Johnson scored the first goal for Rupp. The Wildcats won, 67-19.

Wildcats who saw action in the opening game against Georgetown were Jake Bronston, Bill Congleton, Bill Kleiser, Louis McGinnis, George Skinner, and Carey Spicer, all of Lexington; Allan Lavin and Cecil Bell, of Paris; Aggie Sale, of Harrodsburg; Ercel Little, of Tolu; Paul McBrayer, of Lawrenceburg; Ellis Johnson; of Ashland, Bud Cavana, of Bellevue, and Bill Trott, of Evansville, Ind..

With a lineup of Combs, Spicer, Milward, McGinnis and McBrayer, the Wildcats lost only to Georgia and Clemson in back-to-back games on the road. They closed Rupp's initial campaign (15-3) with a loss to Maryland, 29-27, in the Southern Conference Tournament.

Despite the defeat the Wildcats were the talk of Atlanta. Spicer broke the tournament scoring record. They placed him on the All-Tournament team with McGinnis and Yates. After the final game, Rupp wired the Herald:

Getting away to a bad start and fighting an uphill battle all the way then forging to the front only to be denied by a long shot from mid-court with ten seconds to go, was a little too much for the Wildcats tonight.

The boys from old Kentucky staged the greatest comeback of the tournament, and their loss to Maryland is no disgrace. I only wish that the people at home could have seen the battle, for the fight they put up in the last half will live in my memory forever.

While other Southern schools searched for football talent, Rupp made a concentrated drive for basketball players. As late as 1941, there were no basketball scholarships given at Mississippi, only two at Tennessee, and a few at the other conference schools. Lack of playing space was also a big handicap in the South. Secondary schools, which nurtured the game, played their games on outdoor courts.

"The South did not have big places to play in," Rupp said. "As a result I did not like to go there. When I was coaching high school at Freeport, every school had a nice place to play. I came to Kentucky and we would go to Georgia Tech and play in that old wooden building. It finally burned down. They blamed me. But they didn't even fill those little shacks."

The coaches in the North felt that Southern basketball just wasn't up to par. When they took on a Southern team, the North expected to win. Rupp wasn't going to put up with that attitude. Notre Dame beat them seven times in a row before UK finally beat them.

"I kept going back, because if they were better than we were I was going to find out what made them better," he said. "I found out some of the answers by getting beat by those teams."

It was obvious that the other teams had better players. Since the Athletic Department had no money set aside for recruitment, Rupp combed the state for talent.

"We did not go out and recruit where we stayed overnight," Rupp said. "If we went somewhere we went on our own. My assistant coach would look over some boys, naturally, and we'd see the boys play in the State Tournament."

Rupp considered the tournament his personal hunting ground. It was a reservoir of talent ripe for plucking. Beginning as an invitational affair at Danville in 1916, the tournament moved to Lexington in March 1918, under the auspices of the KHSAA. The university managed the event until 1938. It paid the bills, and turned the remainder over to the KHSAA for division among the teams.

The tournament remained in Lexington a few years after the KHSAA assumed management responsibilities, moved it to Louisville, back to Lexington, and again to Louisville as each city built a bigger arena.

However, it was on the UK campus that the tournament developed its character. The big "Dribble Derby" gained much of its flavor from a steady procession of fine players and teams from little-known hamlets in all reaches of the commonwealth.

The game that gave the tournament nationwide exposure occurred in 1928, when Ashland defeated Carr Creek, 13-11, in four overtimes, and both teams participated in the national high school tournament in Chicago.

Starters on James Anderson's Ashland team were Jim Barney, Darrell Darby, Ellis Johnson, Jack Phipps and Gene Strother. Other team members were Bill Hemlepp, Bud Fullerton, Eck Allen, Kermit Riffe, and Manager Gordon Kershner.

Gurney Adams, Ben Adams, Gillis Madden, Shelby Stamper and Zelda Hale started for Carr Creek. Substitutes Willard Johnson, Lot Francis, Hermit Adams and Carson Cornett completed the roster. Oscar Morgan, a faculty member with no basketball background, coached the team.

Carr Creek finished the regular season undefeated. School officials accepted an invitation to the regional tournament. They rode a log wagon to Sassafras, a boat to Jeff, and then to Richmond on their first train ride. Friends and relatives chipped in enough money to purchase uniforms for seven of the eight players making the trip. After Carr Creek won the regional, Richmond fans purchased a set of uniforms for the team.

Carr Creek played Lawrenceburg in a semifinal game. Both teams ran on the floor attired in white uniforms. UK athletic director S. A. Boles loaned the Creekers eight blue Wildcat jerseys. He seated the Ashland band on one end of the floor, the UK band on the other.

Ashland fans occupied almost half the 2,800 seats available. Carr Creek's home section consisted of eight players, the coach, and a school benefactor. The remaining fans rooted for Carr Creek. Both teams accepted invitations to the national high school tournament held on the University of Chicago campus.

After the Creekers defeated the U. S. Indian School, almost

4,000 fans filled Bartlett Gymnasium; an equal number lined the street to see the "team from nowhere." Carr Creek defeated Bristol, Connecticut, 22-11, and lost to a veteran team from Vienna, Georgia. Ashland won the tournament. Kentucky held the distinction of having the best and most colorful teams in the country.

A team of sportswriters selected Ellis Johnson captain of the National Interscholastic Basketball All-American team. Carr Creek's Stamper also made the first team. Ashland's Darby and Phipps were on the second team. Johnson, Darby and Phipps cast their lot with UK. Strother signed with Ohio State. The Carr Creek boys signed with Eastern.

In addition to Carr Creek, the Kentucky tournaments featured teams from such small locales as Lynn Grove, Heath, Betsy Layne, Brewers, Corinth, Garrett, Tolu, Cuba, Inez, and Hindman.

"When Rupp coached UK, it was his custom to grant a virtually automatic scholarship to the most valuable player of the 'Sweet Sixteen,'" Lonnie Wheeler wrote in his book, *Blue Yonder*. "In a time when many mountain schools were isolated by virtue of road conditions, many Western Kentucky schools were isolated by virtue of distance, and the media was not nearly as electronic or nimble as we know it today; countless Kentucky stars were undiscovered until the state tournament."

While Rupp got the cream of the crop, so to speak, from the tournament, his hold on the mountain boys began to wane in the mid-1950s, when some good players either signed elsewhere or transferred to other schools after a brief stay at UK.

"When I first came to UK, I heard about this boy from Walton named 'Frenchy' DeMoisey," Rupp said. "He was about 6-6 and had scored 50 points in a game against Butler High and 45 in a regional game against Paris.

"I visited Frenchy at Walton. He was working on a road gang. We sat in the shade on a creek bank. I asked if he would like to attend UK. He told me he was making plans to attend Trinity College (now Duke University) because he was a minister's son and entitled to free tuition there. They also promised him a job.

"When I visited Frenchy again, I told him that tuition for the first semester was $31.50 and that I would find someone to pay for that and for the second semester, or find him a job."

Birkett Pribble and Rupp drove to Corinth where Dave Lawrence was digging a ditch under a railroad track. Rupp told him a painting job awaited at UK. That sounded good to Lawrence.

Rupp did not know Jack Tucker was in school until the boy from Cynthiana came out for basketball.

Joe "Red" Hagan starred at both Male and Manual high schools in Louisville. He went out for basketball at UK without an invitation from Rupp.

Hagan earned three basketball and two football letters. He was captain of both teams. His son Tom later earned All-Conference basketball honors at Vanderbilt.

Warfield Donohue of St. Xavier was an excellent tennis player. He went out for basketball at UK on his own. Donohue became a three-year starter. He served as team captain in 1937.

Andy Anderson of Covington played in the State Tournament.

Bill Davis, of Hazard, was a product of the tryouts.

Before the NCAA banned the tryouts, many outstanding high school players from Kentucky and elsewhere beat a path to Rupp's door. He chose the pick of the litter, then sent others to schools mostly in-state. He gave Chuck Connors a dollar and told the future TV "Rifleman" to catch a bus home.

Other names that were familiar to Wildcat fans during those years preceding World War II were Russell Ellington (1935, 36), and Jim Goforth (1935,36, 37), both of Louisville; Layton "Mickey" Rouse (1938, 39, 40), of Ludlow; Walter Hodge (1937), of Paris; Homer "Tub" Thompson (1937, '38, '39) of Jeffersonville, Ind.; Jim Goodman (1938, '39) of Paris, Marion Cluggish (1938, '39, '40) of Corbin; Carl "Hoot" Combs (1940) of Hazard; Waller White (1940, 41, 42) of Lawrenceburg, and Milt Ticco (1941, '42, '43) of Jenkins.

Lee Huber (1939, 40, 41) was the best schoolboy tennis player in the state. He was a member of the St. Xavier basketball team that lost to Midway in the finals of the 1937 State Tournament. Huber attended UK on a partial scholarship. It consisted of tuition and food. He made All-America in 1941.

When Carr Creek won its second KHSAA tournament in 1956, Rupp signed E. A. Couch and Bobby Shepherd to UK scholarships. Shepherd transferred to Pikeville College after his freshman year at UK. Couch failed to earn a letter.

From 1940 to 1956, eastern Kentucky basketball was the standard of excellence for the state. During that time, mountain teams won seven of the 17 state tournament championships: Hazel Green in '40, Inez in '41 and '54. Hindman in '43; Harlan in'54, Hazard in '55, and Carr Creek in '56.

Rupp ventured into Indiana and Ohio so often on recruiting trips that Big Ten coaches called him a "Carpetbagger".

Rupp was the featured speaker at a banquet in Ohio. The chairman asked what he would talk about. Rupp replied, "My text will be, 'A Carpetbagger in the Holy Land'."

The UK rosters of today are a melting pot, with many fine Kentucky high school players looking elsewhere for basketball fame and glory.

"The experience of the eastern Kentucky player in general was that Rupp didn't like them," E. A. Couch told Lonnie Wheeler. "Everybody always thought he did and he recruited a lot of them, but when we got there he talked about our area in a bad manner. It destroyed the confidence of the eastern Kentucky boy."

Couch and Shepherd played on the Carr Creek team that defeated Wayland in a semifinal game of the 1956 state tournament.

The Wasps featured 6-foot-4 Kelly Coleman, undoubtedly the best high school player of that era.

Rupp quit recruiting Coleman after the player's involvement with West Virginia resulted in an NCAA investigation. Many other mountain boys failed the UK basketball test.

John Lee Butcher, Pikeville, 1955, transferred to Pikeville College after his freshman year.

Mickey Gibson, Hazard, 1964, transferred to UNC-Charlotte after a disagreement with UK trainer Joe Brown.

Bob Tallent, Langley (Maytown), 1967, transferred to Georgetown after a disagreement with Rupp.

Alvin Ratliff, Williamsport (Meade Memorial) (1967), entered military service after his freshman year at UK.

Donnis Butcher, Meade Memorial, failed to go to class at UK. He transferred to Pikeville College. He later played for and coached Detroit.

Bobby Slusher, Lone Oak, (1959), transferred to Cincinnati after earning a letter at UK.

Todd May, Virgie, (1983), transferred to Wake Forest after his freshman year at UK.

Grady Wallace of Betsy Layne signed with South Carolina and led the nation in scoring.

Frank Selvy and Darrell Floyd of Corbin both went to Furman and each led the nation in scoring twice.

Phil Cox of Cawood made All-SEC three times at Vanderbilt. The conference bestowed the honor twice on Danny Schultz of Middlesboro, who chose Tennessee over Kentucky.

Harry Lancaster, Rupp's longtime assistant, when asked why he failed to sign Selvy, replied, "You lose some, win some; we won an NCAA championship and had an undefeated season without him."

The KHSAA integrated its tournaments in 1957. During the next 19 years, Louisville teams won 11 championships and finished second six times. Not a single mountain team made it to the championship game. Integrated teams had been dominant during those years.

The last all-white team to win the tournament was Shelby County, which defeated Louisville Male 62-57 in 1966.

From 1970 through 1975 the tournament champions did not have a white player on a starting team. Jock Sutherland, whose Lexington Lafayette team won the 1979 tournament, declared that the day of the small schools was over in Kentucky:

"The black element has changed the game–black quickness. black endurance, and the black athlete's ability to be uninhibited," he told Dave Kindred. "Whether anyone wants to admit that or not, it's so, especially in the metropolitan areas.

"Soon there will be very few small schools," Kindred predicted. "Cinderella's time has passed."

Chapter V

Unto These Hills

The Fabulous Five: Front row; Ralph Beard, Adolph
Rupp, Kenny Rollins. Back row: Wah Jones, Alex
Groza and Cliff Barker.

When a Kentucky baby is born, the mother has two wishes for him: to grow up to be like another native son, Abraham Lincoln, and to play basketball for Adolph Rupp at the University of Kentucky...
Rupp.

When Adolph Rupp said he would "lift up mine eyes unto the hills, from whence cometh my help," he was not referring to the Book of Psalms, but to the eastern Kentucky mountain boys that he recruited for his UK basketball teams.

However, that noted scholar of the Holy Scriptures could have included all of Kentucky under his recruiting umbrella.

A list of leading scorers each year attests to that fact.

1930-31 (15-3)–Carey Spicer, Lexington (10.6), Louis McGinnis, Lexington (9.6), George Yates, Elizabethtown (7.0), Aggie Sale, Harrodsburg (5.6), and Jake Bronston, Lexington (3.9).

1931-32 (15-2)–Sale (13.6), John DeMoisey, Walton (10.0), Darrell Darby, Ashland (8.4), and Howard Kreuter, Newport (3.9).

1932-33 (21-3, 8-0 SEC)–Sale (13.8), DeMoisey (12.0), Bill Davis, Hazard (7.0), Darby (4.0), and Ellis Johnson, Ashland (3.8).

1933-34 (16-1, 11-0 SEC)–DeMoisey (12.5), Davis (8.3), Dave Lawrence (7.9), Garland Lewis, Jefferson, Ind. (4.9), and Jack Tucker, Cynthiana, (3.0).

1934-35 (19-2, 11-0 SEC)–Leroy Edwards, of Indianapolis, Ind., (16.3), Lawrence (9.1), Lewis, (5.8, Tucker, (3.7), and Warfield Donohue, of Louisville (3.5).

It is significant that two starters on that team, Garland and Edwards, were from Indiana. Edwards was Rupp's prime player up to that time.

"I don't know about the standards at Purdue or those other Indiana schools but none of them seemed interested in Edwards," Rupp said. "Perhaps it was because he was so happy-go-lucky that they thought he wasn't interested in higher education.

"George Keogan, my friend who was coaching at Notre Dame, told me Ed was big and tough as they come, if we could just get him in school and keep him there. Recruiting wasn't a problem in those times. They didn't have to sign anything. I visited him one time, and he agreed to come down here."

Edwards made All-America in his only year of varsity action at UK. His most memorable game was a 23-22 loss to NYU in Madison Square Garden.

"It has been reported as the roughest game ever played," Rupp said. "NYU knew that Edwards was big, strong, and a deadly shooter under the basket, and they were determined that he would not get there.

"The way those two centers kicked each other around, shoving, pushing, holding, and all those things, both should have been thrown out of the game in two minutes."

With eight seconds to go and the score tied at 22-all, an official called Edwards for setting an illegal screen. NYU made the free throw to win the game.

The Rules Committee put in a three-second rule to force the pivot man away from the basket.

Edwards went home at season's end, married his high school sweetheart, and went to work for a rubber company. He eventually became an All-Pro player.

Remembering NYU: *I really don't know what happened. Riding back on the train yesterday I turned on the radio. A broadcast came from one of the churches in New York. The minister used as his text, He was a stranger and they took him in...***Adolph Rupp.**

Dear Coach Rupp:

The boys on the basketball team here at State have asked me to write you and compliment you and your team upon the splendid exhibition of sportsmanship which you displayed during our game here Feb. 13 (1935).

We want you to know that we are proud to have played against as fine an aggregation as you. We sincerely believe that we are expressing not only our own opinion but that of the entire student body and the hundreds of fans who watched your team play.

"Our mid-western basketball is usually a case of "dog-eat-dog," and it is a real treat to play as cleanly a fought game as was ours. We begin to understand much better the expression "Southern gentlemen."

We are extremely sorry that Mr. Tucker was hurt in our game, and hope that his services will not be lost to the team for long. We would like to express our admiration for Anderson, who, we under-

stand, played the entire game with a painful toe injury. In conclusion it is our opinion that your team is the finest in every respect we have seen in action this year, and believe that in Edwards you have a true All-America.

R. C. Herrick (Michigan State star guard)

1935-36 (15-6, 6-2 SEC)–Ralph Carlisle, Lawrenceburg, (11.5), Joe Hagan, Louisville (8.0), Lewis, (7.5), Donohue (3.0), and J. Rice Walker, Lexington (2.4).

1936-37 (17-5, 5-3 SEC)–Carlisle (9.9), Hagan (7.3), Homer Thompson, Jeffersonville, Ind.(4.9), Walter Hodge, of Paris (3.7), and Bernie Opper, of Brooklyn, N. Y. (3.5).

Opper was a high-scoring guard at Morris High in New York and later at a New York prep school. He wanted to attend school away from home and to play for a strong team. "I knew Rupp always had a good record," he told Tev Laudeman of the Courier-Journal and Louisville Times. "I saw Kentucky play in 1935 against NYU in Madison Square Garden. I didn't talk to Rupp at the time, but I wrote him a letter and told him I'd like to attend UK. I had recommendations from Clair Bee (LIU coach) and Nat Holman (CCNY coach). Rupp wrote back and said to come on down." Opper was the first Jewish boy and the first New Yorker to play for Rupp. He made All-America in 1939.

1937-38 (13-5, 6-0 SEC)–Hagan (10.1), Fred Curtis, of Nashville (6.3), Opper (5.6), Thompson (4.9), and Mickey Rouse, Ludlow (4.4).

1938-39 (16-4, 5-2 SEC)–Curtis (9.2), Thompson (6.7), Keith Farnsley, New Albany, Rouse (5.4), and Marion Cluggish, Corbin (5.3).

Dear Bernie:
In the mad scramble following the game (UK 36-UT 34, 2 OT's) I did not get a chance to express to all the Kentucky boys my con-

gratulations on their fine victory. You have a fine team and one that adds further prestige to our fine type of ball played in the SEC.

Your own performance in the tournament was the best I have seen, and you have been a fine leader and player. I hope that all future games between Kentucky and Tennessee are as well played and that the keen rivalry and good feelings between the boys will continue in years to come.

I hope that you will convey these sentiments to all members of the squad, coaches and friends of Kentucky, and that you continue to be as successful in whatever you do as you have been in basketball. **Johnny Mauer (Basketball Coach University of Tennessee March 5, 1939)**

1939-40 (15-6, 4.4 SEC)–Rouse (8.3), Cluggish (7.2), Lee Huber, Louisville (5.4), Bill King, Lexington (3.9), and Carl Combs, Hazard (3.9).

1940-41 (17-8, SEC 8-1)–Jim King, Sharpe (6.0), Huber (5.9), Farnsley, New Albany, Ind. (5.8), and Mel Brewer, New Albany, Ind. (5.1), Milt Ticco, Jenkins (4..8)

1941-42 (19-6, 6-2 SEC)–Marvin Akers, Jeffersonville, Ind. (7.6), Brewer (7.0), Ticco (5.8), Ermal Allen, Morristown, Tenn. (4.9), and Ken England, Campbellsburg, (4.9).

(Please note: three of the five are from out-of-state).

1942-43 (17-6, 8-1 SEC)–Ticco (10.1), Brewer (8.3), Akers (7.1), Milford Davis (7.1), and Kenny Rollins, Wickliffe (5.3).

1943-44 (19-2), Bob Brannum, Winfield, Kan. (12.1); Jack Tingle, Bedford (8.4), Jack Parkinson, Yorktown, Ind. (7.0); Wilbur Schu, Versailles (6.2), and Tom Moseley, Lexington (4.2).

1944-45 (22-4, 4-1 SEC)–Alex Groza, Martins Ferry, Ohio (12.1), Tingle (8.4), Parkinson (7.0), Schu (6.2), and Campbell (8.3).

1945-46 (28-2, 6-0 SEC)–Parkinson (11.3), Wallace Jones, Harlan (9.7), Ralph Beard, Louisville (9.3), Tingle (9.2), and Schu (7.7).

1946-47 (34-3, 11-0 SEC)–Beard (10.9), Groza (10.6), Rollins (8.4), Joe Holland, Benton (8.2), Jones (5.9).

1947-48 (36-3, 9-0 SEC)–Groza (12.5), Beard (12.5), Jones

(8.3), Jim Line, Akron, Ohio, (6.9), and Rollins (6.6).

1948-49 (32-2, 13-0 SEC)–Groza (20.5), Beard (10.8), Jones, Cliff Barker, Yorktown, Ind. (7.3), and Dale Barnstable, Antioch, Ill. (6.1)

1949-50 (25-5, 11.2)–Bill Spivey, Warner-Robbins, Ga. (19.3); Line (13.1), Hirsch; Chicago, Ill. (8.9); Bobby Watson, Owensboro (7.5), and Barnstable (5.9).

The 1947 All SEC Team members, all Kentuckians are (left to right): Wah Jones, Jack Tingle, Joe Holland, Ralph Beard and Kenny Rollins.

Chapter VI
The Glory Years

*When I get this business organized properly, you'll see something. I'll have a squad of ten centers, twenty-six guards and thirty forwards. I'll have a coach for the guards, one for the centers and one for the forwards, and a scout to go around and look over the opposition. I'll be the head coach. We'll have two ball teams-one for home games and one for the road. We'll pack the field house every night at two dollars a head. At the end of the season, we'll win the NCAA tournament with one team and the Metropolitan Invitational with the other. Then we'll throw the two together at Soldiers Field in Chicago for the national championship. That'll draw eighty-seven thousand people at ten dollars a head....*__Adolph Rupp, BBM.__

Collegiate basketball's "Era of the Wildcats" had its beginning in the 1946 season. It   coincided with the arrival on campus of

Kentuckians Wallace "Wall Wah" Jones of Harlan, Ralph Beard of Louisville and Joe Holland of Benton.

Jones was a true "mountain boy" from an area that spawned the Hatfields and McCoys of feuding infamy. A 6-foot-5 tower of strength, he scored a national scholastic record 2,398 points during his career at Harlan High. Jones was also a two-year All-State football choice and a fine baseball player.

Called "Wah Wah" by a baby sister who could not pronounce his name, Wallace and his brother Hugh led Harlan to the state tournament in 1942 and 1943. After Hugh was graduated and in the Navy, Wah Wah led Harlan to the state tournament two more years.

Jones planned to attend the University of Tennessee. Thanks to his future wife, Edna Ball, of Middlesboro, who was a sophomore at UK, he cast his lot with Rupp.

By the third game of that season, Jones was UK's starting center. Rupp teamed him with Beard and Parkinson at guard, and Holland and Tingle at forward. That combination won their first seven games before losing to Temple, 53-45, in Philadelphia. They won six more games; they lost to Notre Dame in Louisville. They won their remaining games, including a 54-43 decision over Temple in Louisville.

After breezing through the SEC Tournament, they disposed of Arizona and West Virginia and advanced to the NIT championship game in Madison Square Garden. Beard hit a free throw with time expiring to give UK a one-point victory over Rhode Island and UK its first national championship.

Rupp predicted there would never be another Kentucky basketball team that would equal the record of that 1945-46 squad: 28 victories in 30 games, conference and National Invitational titles and a new team scoring record of 1,821 points. The secret was a reserve squad on par with the starters.

Returning the following season was the finest group of basketball players assembled at UK up to that time. Lettermen Tingle, Davis, Holland, Campbell, Malcolm McMullen, Beard, Parker, Jones, and Rudy Yessin were joined by military veterans Groza and Brannum, who were teammates on the Camp Hood, Texas, team; Jim Jordan, a two-time All-American at North Carolina Pre-Flight; Cliff Barker, who had spent 16 months in a German prison camp, and Kenny Rollins, who was elected team captain in midseason.

There were so many fine players reporting to Alumni Gym that Rupp divided them into two squads, with 19 on the "A" squad and 23 on a "B" squad. Lancaster coached the B squad. Later in the season, Rupp promoted four members of the B squad. He told the others to pursue their studies uninterrupted by basketball.

Starters the following year were Beard and Rollins at guard, Groza at center, and Holland and Tingle at forward.

Barker was the No. 1 substitute. Freshmen Jim Line and Dale Barnstable started the half of the opener against Indiana Central with Brannum, Rollins and Beard. Kentucky won that game, 78-36. They won 10 more games before losing to Oklahoma A&M, 37-31, in the Sugar Bowl. Beard's free throw as time expired gave them a 46-45 win over Rhode Island on the NIT. It was Rupp's first national title.

Kentucky opened the 1946-47 season with an easy conquest of Indiana Central. Rupp started Beard and Rollins at guard, Groza at center, and Tingle and Holland at forward. Barker was the No.1 substitute. Freshmen Jim Line and Dale Barnstable started the second half, along with Bob Brannum, of Winfield, Kan; Rollins, and Beard. Others seeing action were Parker, Davis, Malcomb McMullen, of Hamilton, Ohio; Jim Jordan, of Chester, W. Va.; Kenton "Dutch" Campbell, of Newark, Ohio, and Al Cummins, of Brooksville.

After they defeated St. John's, 70-50, in the Garden for their 24th straight victory over a two-season span, Joe Lapchick called them the greatest team he had ever coached against. The Associated Press said they were "the greatest aggregation to visit the Eighth Avenue arena."

Both wire services ranked the Wildcats, No. 1 in the nation. They returned home from New York and defeated Baylor and Wabash before losing to Oklahoma State, 37-31, in the Sugar Bowl.

The Wildcats put together a 10-game winning streak, including a 60-30 victory over Notre Dame in Louisville.

Prior to the annual conference tournament, Rupp cut his squad to the 10-man limit. He chose Line and Barnstable ahead of Brannum and Jordan. They easily won the tournament and once again dominated the All-Tournament team, placing five native sons–Beard, Jones, Holland, Tingle and Rollins on the first team. Groza made second-team because of limited action due to an injury.

The Wildcats advanced to the semi-finals of the NIT, where they lost to Utah, 49-45.

Although Rupp was unhappy, he had to appreciate his team's 34-3 record and the fact that it had outscored the opponents, 2,536 to 1,416. Beard and Groza made All-America teams.

When the 1947-48 season began, the starting lineup consisted of Beard and Rollins at guard, Groza at center, and Barker and Holland at forward. Jones was in the process of making the change from football to basketball; in addition, he had received a foot injury in football.

The Wildcats had dispatched six foes in routine order. They stopped off at Philadelphia to play Temple while en route to meet St. John's in New York. The Owls won, 60-59. . Beard had an injured hip and played only 10 minutes as a substitute. Jones' sore foot kept him out of the game entirely.

Kentucky disposed of St. John's and Creighton before Jones broke into the starting lineup against Western Ontario. Beard was still ailing and did not start that game. Jack Parkinson started in his place.

Two nights later, on January 5, 1948, the Wildcats defeated Miami (Ohio) 67-53, as all the pieces fell together to form what was to be known as the "Fabulous Five"- Rollins and Beard at guard, Groza at center, and Jones and Barker at forward. They would become a yardstick by which all future UK teams would be measured.

That new combination took an 11-game winning streak into South Bend. A fine Notre Dame team and a vociferous student body proved too much for the Wildcats, who fell, 64-55. UK lost no more collegiate games that season.

A late season highlight came against Tennessee in Alumni Gym when Beard hit a shot from 52 1/2 feet in the first half. That beat the previous long shot of 48 feet, 2 inches set by Joe Hagan in 1938. Hagan's shot had beat Marquette in the closing seconds; Beard's shot was of no great significance in a 69-42 win over Tennessee.

The Wildcats swept their next schedule. They selected games and repeated as SEC champions. They defeated Columbia and Baylor for their first NCAA championship.

After defeating Louisville and Baylor again in the Olympic Trials, they lost to the Phillips Oilers, AAU champs, 53-49.

Calling that squad "the greatest team ever assembled in college sport," Rupp, eyes filled with tears, locked the UK dressing room door and said, "You've done everything you've been asked to do. You won your own SEC tournament, you won the NCAA championship. You've kept training and made many sacrifices to do these things and for all of it I thank you from the bottom of my heart."

The Olympic Committee named UK's five starters–Groza, Beard, Jones, Barker and Rollins to its Olympic squad. Barnstable, Holland and Line were alternates. The U.S. won the Gold in London.

On February 24, 1949, the Optimist Club honored Rupp as the outstanding citizen of the City of Lexington. Dr. A. D. Kirwan, University dean of students and former UK football coach, presented the award.

"Like Alexander the Great, Rupp can weep because he, too, has no more worlds to conquer," Kirwan said. "He's conquered them all in the basketball world-Southeastern, National Collegiate, and Olympics."

Dale Barnstable replaced the graduated Rollins in 1948-49. That gave Rupp a starting lineup that included three non-native Kentuckians (Barker, Barnstable and Groza), and Beard and Jones.

That combo won 32 of 34 games played and was 13-0 in the

SEC. They repeated as conference and national champions. The losses were to St. Louis, 42-40, in the Sugar Bowl and Loyola of Chicago, 67-56, in the NIT.

Rupp entered the Wildcats in both major tournaments that year. They lost to Loyola, 67-56, in the NIT. After Rupp put them through some hard practice days, they returned to New York and defcated Villanova, 85-72, and Illinois, 76-47, in the Eastern Regional.

The media billed the championship battle between Kentucky and Oklahoma as a contest between the contrasting styles of "Red Hot Rupp" and "Deep Freeze (Hank) Iba." Before a capacity crowd of 12,000 in Seattle, the Wildcats slowed the game down to the Aggie pace. They controlled the game so artistically that for one 12-minute stretch A&M failed to score a field goal. Groza fouled out with five minutes to go. His 25 points and fine all-around play kept UK in the lead. The Wildcats won, 46-36. It was Rupp's third NCAA championship.

The Wildcats set 22 NCAA team and individual records. Groza scored 82 points in three games and was again named Most Valuable Player. Groza, Beard, Jones, and Barker, billed as the "Fabulous Four" had led the team to such major marks as:

32 victories in 34 games, a percentage of .941, best in the modern history of the school.

Sixth straight SEC championship.

Number One ranking in the nation by the Associated Press.

First team ever to compete in the two major tournaments in one season.

Rupp retired the jerseys worn by Barker, Beard, Jones, Groza, and the departed Kenny Rollins, who was playing in the pros. Rupp still had such veteran performers as Barnstable, Hirsch and Line around which to build a new team as UK entered the 1950s.

1949-50, (25-5, SEC 11-2)–Bill Spivey, Warner-Robbins, Ga. (19.3); Jim Line, Akron, Ohio (13.1); Walt Hirsch, Chicago (9.9); and Bobby Watson, Owensboro. UK's sophomore "Mutt & Jeff" combination consisted of 7-foot Spivey and 5-foot-10 Bobby Watson. Other newcomers on the varsity team were guards Guy Strong of Irvine; Len Pearson of Chicago, Ill.; Lucian "Skippy" Whitaker of Sarasota, Fla.; and forward C. M. Newton, of Ft. Lauderdale; junior college transfers Shelby Linville, of Middletown, Ohio, and Read Morgan, of Milwaukee.

Trailing Vanderbilt by 12 points in the last game to be played in Alumni Gym, Rupp told his players at halftime:

*"Boys, a man spends a lifetime compiling a record, and in one given night a bunch of bums like you are about to tear it down. If it looks to me like we're going to go down in defeat tonight, I want you to know that I am personally going to do something to this facility before the game is over and before you get out of this gym...***A. Rupp**.

The Wildcats won that game, 70-66, preserving the gym record of 84 consecutive victories and ending an era that saw Wildcat teams win 262 games and lose only 25 times in the facility. In saying goodbye to Alumni Gym, the University left behind an antiquated structure that had served as the Wildcats' home floor from 1924-1950. Rupp's record was 201-8 in the 19-year-old building. That included 84 consecutive wins in Alumni, which also included 64 consecutive wins in the conference.

Those 1949-50 Wildcats won 25 of 30 games played and were Sugar Bowl and SEC champs (11-2).

Rupp felt that the Wildcats, with their 25-4 record and the conference championship, deserved to represent District 3 in the NCAA playoffs; however, the Selection Committee chose North Carolina State after UK stubbornly refused to play the Wolfpack for the honor.

The NCAA ended such internal squabbling by doubling the tournament field the following year, automatically including 10 major conference champions, and filling the other berths with members-at-large, a total of 16 teams.

The Wildcats accepted a bid to the NIT, meeting City College of New York for the first time. The CCNY team, which included superstar Ed Warner and two other black starters, defeated the Wildcats,

89-50, pinning on Rupp his worst defeat in 24 years of coaching.

1950-51 (32-2, 14-0, SEC)–Bill Spivey, (19.2), Shelby Linville (10.4), Watson (10.4), Ramsey (10.1), Hagan (9.2), and Hirsch (9.1).

1951-52 (29-3, SEC 14-0)--Spivey, (21.6), Ramsey (15.9), Watson (13.1) Tsioropoulos (7.9) and Whitaker (7.8).

The Wildcats moved into new Memorial Coliseum. The 11,500-seat structure cost $3,925,000. It was dedicated as a memorial to Kentuckians killed in World War II. The University later added the names of Kentucky's Korean War dead. The Wildcats defeated Kansas State for Rupp's third NCAA title.

An estimated 8,000 fans, second largest crowd ever to see a basketball game in Kentucky, attended the opening game in the new facility. They were subjected to a rather drab affair as UK swamped West Texas State, 73-43. The only sophomore in the starting lineup for UK was Ramsey. The other starters were Watson, Spivey, Linville and Hirsch. Cliff Hagan would not become eligible for varsity competition until late January 1951.

The next game, against Purdue, featured official dedicatory ceremonies. An estimated 11,000 persons heard Dr. Leo M. Chamberlain, UK vice president, urge that the building be the "home of true sportsmanship, and the source of men of exalted minds, of vigorous bodies, and of great character." The Wildcats won, 70-52.

Kansas came to town, focusing national attention on the matchup between Rupp and his old coach Phog Allen, and between Jayhawk center Clyde Lovellette and Spivey. Spivey outscored Lovellette, 22-10. Rupp took Spivey out of the game after Lovellette fouled out with more than 12 minutes remaining. UK won, 68-39.

Ramsey made a brilliant debut in New York and Linville scored six clutch points midway of the second half to lead the Wildcats over St. John's, 43-37. They then journeyed to New Orleans and the Sugar Bowl, where the UK football team also was part of the festivities, being matched against national champion Oklahoma.

Spivey broke a tie against St. Louis with less than two minutes remaining. The Wildcats lost possession out of bounds with 10 seconds left. St. Louis scored a 43-42 victory. Some gamblers claimed the game was so obviously suspicious that they could not get bets down.

The NCAA declared Hirsch ineligible for their tournament because he was in his fourth season of varsity play. Hagan replaced him in the starting lineup. Louisville led the Wildcats, 64-60, with less than 10 minutes remaining. "Skippy" Whitaker hit some clutch baskets to pace UK to a 79-68 victory.

Hagan was on the bench with the flu in the first half of the championship game against Kansas State in Minneapolis. Spivey had a cold. The Wildcats trailed, 29-27, at halftime. They took control of the game in the second half and won, 68-58. Spivey scored 22 points and had 21 rebounds. Hagan had 10 points.

1951-52 (29-3), 14, 0 SEC)–Hagan (21.6), Ramsey (15.9), Watson (13.1), and Whitaker (7.8).

1952-53–The NCAA and the SEC suspended UK basketball one year for some past UK players being involved in a point-shaving scandal. The Wildcats held some inter-squad scrimmages that were well-attended. Rupp vowed not to retire until the persons who were responsible handed him the NCAA championship trophy.

1953-54 (25-0, SEC 14-0)–Hagan (24.0), Ramsey 19.6), Tsioropoulos (14.5), Billy Evans, of Berea, (8.4), and Gayle Rose, of Paris (6.7).Kentucky defeated LSU, 63-56, in a playoff for the conference crown. The players voted to accept an invitation to the NCAA playoffs. Rupp told them:

I had hoped that you would not vote to go and not to put this record (25-0) in jeopardy. If we can't play with our full team, we will not allow a bunch of turds to mar the record established in a large measure by our three seniors. We are not going to Kansas City...
BBM.

The 1953-54 Wildcats are front row: Coach Adolph Rupp, Linville Puckett, Jess Curry, Gayle Rose, Clay Evans, Willie Rouse, Dan Chandler, Pete Grigsby, Assistant Coach Harry Lancaster; Back row: Student Manager Mike Dolan, Hugh Coy, Cliff Hagan, Lou Tsioropoulos, Jerry Bird, Phil Grawemeyer, Harold Hurst, Bill Bibb, Frank Ramsey, and Bill Evans

Chapter VII
Starting Over

It has always been my idea that there is reason for a golf course having par. I have thought my greatest team was the Hagan-Ramsey-Tsioropoulos team that won 25 games and was named National Champions. They finished with the highest rating of any team up to that date. I call that par for the course..A. Rupp.

Twelve thousand basketball-starved fans sat in hushed anticipation as the wall clock in Memorial Coliseum ticked off the final seconds before 7:30 o'clock on the night of December 5, 1953. The scoreboard signs spelled "KENTUCKY" and "TEMPLE".

Rupp and Cliff Hagan,

There was only room for two digits beneath the Kentucky sign, contrary to the published reports that Rupp, to make sure there was no shaving of points and to wreak his revenge, was going to run up the score in every game his team played. For that he would need at least three digits, they said.

At the player entrance to the floor, uniformed policemen shielded the runway from a pushing, surging group of youngsters while cheerleaders peered anxiously into the dim hallway. Promptly on schedule a group of tall, angry young men in scanty blue and white uniforms ran from the opening and onto the playing floor. The band struck up, "On, On, U of K," the cheerleaders jumped up and down, with pompons waving, and the fans clapped in unison.

It had been a year since they had witnessed that scene in the Coliseum. The cheers echoed throughout the arena and into the UK training room. Rupp was dressed in his best brown suit. He finished his silent pregame meditation, and prepared for a date with destiny.

As the players ran onto the floor, the team manager quickly tossed basketballs to co-captains Cliff Hagan and Frank Ramsey. They took the first warm-up shots. The other players automatically lined up in equal rows on each side of the basket for a series of pre-game drills that never varied.

Seconds later Rupp walked down the left side of the hallway as others in his entourage followed in a specific order: assistant coach, trainer, team doctor, and managers. He paused until the band quit playing. Then he entered the arena. He turned and waved to a lady seated over the entrance, as he had done in all those better years gone by. She returned the salute and remained standing until the game began.

A tremendous roar, followed by a "Hello, Adolph" from the student body, greeted him. He smiled, acknowledged the ovation, and sat in his chair. Manager Bobby Moore handed him two sticks of chewing gum and placed a damp towel, blue side up, on the floor, so the players could wipe their shoe soles and gain better traction. Before the second half, the white side would be up. Only Rupp was allowed to pick up the towel.

He sat, chin in hand, silently watching the players go through their warm-up paces. Five minutes before game time, players and the entire entourage automatically headed back to the dressing room, via the same route and in the same pecking order as when they entered. After they returned ("all steamed up", as Hagan put it), the band struck up the national anthem. Everyone faced the American flag. Player introductions, with the individuals spotlighted, were followed by the traditional pre-game huddle and crossing of hands.

That night Cliff Hagan turned in one of the finest performances ever witnessed in the Coliseum. He equaled Temple's output of 20 points in the first half. He added 13 more points early in the second half. The crowd realized a record was in sight. They began pulling for him to reach the SEC half-century mark held by Bob Pettit. Hagan made 17 consecutive free throws; the crowd groaned as he missed two with 43 seconds remaining. Eight seconds later Puckett stole the ball and threw a floor-length pass to Hagan. He caught it on the run and scored a layup for his 51st point. That record would stand until Dan Issel scored 53 in 1970 and Jodie Meeks 54 in 2009.

Remembering: I remember being carried off the floor. Jess Curry had hold of one leg and Linville Puckett the other...Cliff Hagan, BBM.

Lou Tsioropoulos, of Lynn, Mass., was the only "outsider" on a starting five that included   in-state boys Hagan, of Owensboro; Frank Ramsey, of Madisonville; Billy Evans, of Berea, and Gayle Rose, of Paris. Evans and Rose returned as starters the following year with juniors Jerry Bird, of Corbin; Phil Grawemeyer, of Louisville, and Bob Burrow, a graduate of Lon Morris Junior College, in Jacksonville, Fla.

1954-55 (23-3), 12-2 SEC)–Bob Burrow, of Wells, Tex. (19.0); Evans (13.9); Phil Grawemeyer, of Louisville (13.0); Jerry Bird, of Corbin (10.7); and Gayle Rose (7.4). They were rated No. 1 nationally when lowly Georgia Tech came to town.

To say that no one in Kentucky took the Georgia Tech basketball team seriously when the Yellow Jackets lined up to play UK on the night of January 8, 1955, would be putting it mildly. Coach John "Whack" Hyder's team had a 2-4 record to pit against a UK team with a national record of 129 straight wins over a 12-year span in Alumni Gym and Memorial Coliseum. Seventy of those victories were over Southeastern Conference teams.

Tech was so lightly regarded that only 8,000 fans turned out to see the game; UK coaches had not even bothered to scout the Yellow Jackets. They knew about Lenny Cohen and Dick Lenholt, who had played the season before in two lopsided losses to UK, and Bobby Kimmel, a little guard from Valley High near Louisville. Who could get serious about them and a team that had just lost to lowly Sewanee?

Tech was troublesome from the start. They held UK's high-powered offense in check and took a surprising five-point lead into halftime.

"Still no one really doubted the outcome," Dan Chandler said, "but our regulars would have to stop messing around or some of the lowly scrubs might miss getting into action."

Rupp and Johnny Cox

54

Tech built that lead to eight points, 38-30, with 15 minutes remaining. The startled Wildcats went into an all-court, pressing defense. Kentucky took the lead, 58-57. Joe Helms hit a 15-foot jumper. Tech won, 59-58.

Tevis Laudeman, beat writer for *The Courier-Journal*, called it "the night the mouse ate the cat." Rupp told his players to go out and purchase the newspapers containing the game write-ups because they undoubtedly would be collectors' items.

The Wildcats lost one other game in regular season, to Georgia Tech, 65-59, in Atlanta. They lost to Marquette, 76-61, in the Midwest Regional.

1955-56 (20-6, 12.2 SEC)–(Burrow (21.1), Bird (16.2), Vernon Hatton, of Lexington (13.3); Gerry Calvert, of Maysville (11.2), and Grawemeyer (8.4).

That team defeated Wayne, 84-64, and lost to Iowa, 89-77, in the Eastern Regional at Iowa City.

1956-57 (23-5, 12-2 SEC)–Johnny Cox, of Hazard (19.4); Calvert 15.2), Hatton (24.5), John Crigler, of Hebron (10.3), and Ed Beck, of Ft. Valley, Ga. (9.5). The back-ups were Earl Adkins, of Ashland; Don Mills, of Berea; Billy Ray Cassady, of Inez, and Lincoln Collinsworth, of Salyersville. After Cox scored 20 points against St. Louis, Billikens' coach Ed Hickey called him "the greatest sophomore in the country."

UK led Duke by 15 points at halftime in Durham. The Blue Devils narrowed that lead to five points with six minutes remaining and Adrian Smith on the foul line. Before the shot dropped through, qualifying Smith for a bonus shot, a Duke substitute ran onto the floor. ACC official Phil Fox ruled the goal no try because the shooter did not know that Duke had six men on the floor. Smith missed the next try. With one minute remaining, Rupp instructed his players to protect their slim lead. One of the officials ruled that John Brewer took too much time out-of-bounds. Duke scored on the toss-in and won, 85-84.

The Wildcats won 23 of 28 games, and were SEC and Sugar Bowl champions. They defeated Pittsburgh, 98-92, but lost to Michigan State, 80-68, in the Mideast Regional.

Remembering Officials*: It's a shame that the University pays* *me a pretty good salary, spends about $20,000 in scholarships, and then turns the game over to officials to butcher up the play. We work hard two hours every day and then everything we have worked for can be undone by an official in 40 minutes. Entirely too much authority is given officials. Something must be done. The fans don't come to ball games to see a free-throw contest, and that is what basketball has boiled down to. I'll finish my coaching career and train seeing-eye dogs for officials...* **Adolph Rupp BBM.**

1957-58 (23-6, 12-2 SEC)–Hatton (17.1), Cox (14.9), Crigler (13.6), Adrian "Odie" Smith, of Farmington (12.4), and Beck (5.6). On December, 7, 1957, Pearl Harbor day, Hatton hit a long set shot with one second remaining to send a game with Temple into the first of three overtimes. UK won, 85-83.

The Wildcats lost six games, a record for a loser entering the Final Four. They advanced to the championship game against Seattle by derailing Miami (Ohio), Notre Dame, and Temple (61-60).

Rupp thought Seattle coach Castellani would assign his All-American Elgin Baylor to guarding Beck, who was averaging 4.8 points a game. Since Crigler had gone scoreless against Temple, Castellani switched Baylor to guarding Crigler out on the floor. Rupp told Crigler to drive on Baylor. Crigler got a couple fouls on Baylor, and at the same time scored a couple of baskets. After Baylor committed a fourth foul, he could play only token defense. Hatton scored 30 points, Cox 24, and UK won, 84-72, presenting Rupp with his fourth NCAA championship.

Those boys certainly are not concert violinists, but they sure can fiddle....A. Rupp.

1958-59 (24-3, 12-2 SEC)–Cox (17.9), Billy Ray Lickert, of Lexington (13.5); Bennie Coffman, of Huntington, W.Va. (10.7); Don Mills (10.5), Sid Cohen, of Brooklyn N. Y. (8.1), and Dickie Parsons, of Yancey, (8.0). They lost to Louisville, 76-61, in the Mideast Regional.

After we beat Marquette, for third place, we sat behind the Louisville bench and cheered for them. It seemed the right thing to do... **Dick Parsons, BBM.**

1959-60 (18-7, 10-4 SEC)–Lickert (14.4), Mills (12.7), Cohen

(10.7), Coffman (10.2) and Ned Jennings, Carlisle, (8.8). Lickert and Mills were co-captains of a UK team that went nowhere.

1960-61 (19-9, 10-4 SEC)–Lickert (16.0), Roger Newman, Greenville, (14.1); Larry Pursiful, Four Mile, (13.4); Jennings (11.5) and Carroll Burchett, Flat Gap, (5.1). The Wildcats beat Morehead, 71-64, and lost to Ohio State, 87-74, in the Mideast Regional.

1961-62 (23-3, 13-1 SEC)–Cotton Nash, Lake Charles, La., (23.4); Pursiful (19.1), Burchett (11.2), Scotty Baesler, Athens, 10.9) and Roy Roberts, Atlanta (7.0) Sophomore Nash's 608 points led a

Rupp's Runts: Larry Conley, Tommy Kron, Thad Jaracz, Pat Riley and Louie Dampier.

Wildcat team that was SEC co-champion. They defeated Butler, 81-60, and lost to Ohio State, 74-64, in the Mideast.

1962-63 (16-9, 8-6 SEC)–Nash (20.6), Charles Ishmael, Mt. Sterling (11.1); Ted Deeken, Louisville (8.8); Baesler (9.7) and Roberts (9.0). In his 45th game vs. Florida on February 2, Nash became the earliest Wildcat to reach the 1,000 point scoring mark. Ohio University upset the Wildcats, 85-69, in the Mideast.

1963-64 (21-6, 11-3 SEC)–Nash (24.0, Deeken) 18.5), Larry Conley, Ashland, (12.2); Terry Mobley, Harrodsburg (9.4), and Randy Embry, Owensboro (7.2). The Wildcats were UKIT, SEC and Sugar Bowl champions. They defeated Ohio University, 85-69, and lost to Loyola, 100-91, in the Mideast.

Remembering the Sugar Bowl: *Terry Mobley scored only one point in a Sugar Bowl game vs. Loyola, but it was his field goal that tied Duke, 79-79, with less than two minutes to go. With 45 seconds*

remaining and UK in possession, Rupp instructed Mobley to feed the ball to one of the other players. Mobley dribbled around the keyhole, failed to see an open man, and banked in the winning goal. **BBM.**

1964-65 (15-10, 10-6)–Louie Dampier, Indianapolis (17.0); Pat Riley, Schenectady, N.Y. (15.0); Tommy Kron, Jeffersonville Ind. (12.3); John Adams. Rising Sun, Ind. (11.8), and Conley (11.6). Rupp had a surprise in store for those who said the old man was slipping.

1965-66 (27-2, 15-1 SEC)–They were called "Rupp's Runts" because the two tallest starters–Tom Kron and sophomore Thad Jaracz–were only 6-foot-5. Conley and Riley were 6-3; Dampier was 6-0. Conley was a passing wizard. Dampier and Riley were excellent scorers.

Riley had a fine game against Notre Dame in Freedom Hall, scoring 36 points and holding Irish scoring ace Jim Monahan to seven points in a 103-69 UK win. Dampier's best game was against Vanderbilt in Nashville, where he sizzled the nets for 42 points.

Nearly everywhere UK played that year, fans who had booed and despised Rupp for years were giving him ovations. "I love those boys," he said.

The Runts lost only to Tennessee at Nashville in regular season and advanced to a national championship game against a Texas Western team that started five black players. The Miners won that game, 72-65, and marched into history.

Remembering the Runts: *Rupp began the 1965-66 season with an unlikely collection of smallish players who would become, perhaps, the most loved team in the history of Kentucky basketball...* **Cawood Ledford, 1966.**

1966-67 (13-13, 8-10 SEC). (Dampier (20.6), Riley (17.4), Jaracz (11.3), Cliff Berger, of Centralia, Ill. (11.3), and Phil Argento, of Cleveland (5.2). Without Conley and Kron, the Wildcats were a ship without a rudder.

1967-68 (22-5, 15-3 SEC)–Mike Casey, Shelby County, (20.1); Dan Issel, Batavia, Ill. (16.4); Mike Pratt, Dayton, Ohio (14.1), Argento (12.3) and Jaracz 11.3). With all starters in double scoring figures the Wildcats were an awesome team. They lost a heartbreaker to Duke, 82-81, in the Mideast regional, which was held in Memorial Coliseum.

1968-69 (23-5, 10-2 SEC)–Issel (26.6), Casey (19.1), Pratt (16.9), Argento (10.0), and Larry Steele, of Bainbridge, Ind., (8.6). The "Big Three" led UK to an SEC championship and No. 1 ranking. They lost to Marquette, 81-74, in a racially charged Wisconsin Field House in Madison. UK set school team records that year for most points (2,542), highest scoring average (90.8), and highest field goal percentage (49.0); Issel scored 746 points, beating the 698 scored by Alex Groza in 1949. His 26.6 points per game average set a record for most field goals. Pratt made a record 53.9 percent of his field goal attempts. Casey had a record 129 assists.**1969-70 (26-2, 17-1 SEC)**– Issel (33.9), Pratt ((19.3), Tom Parker, East St. Louis Ill., 10.4; Steele (8.8) and Terry Mills, Barbourville, (8.1). Kentucky's hopes of winning another national championship were shattered when Casey received a crushed leg in an automobile accident. The Wildcats repeated as SEC champs, but lost to Jacksonville, 106-100 in the Mideast.

Issel bowed out as the most prolific men's scorer in UK history. He scored 948 points that season. That brought his career total to 2,138 in 83 games. He broke seven individual records and two single game records, and he put eight career offensive records on the books.

Remembering the Accident: *Once again, I think fate dealt us a cruel blow. That was another time we could have won it all. Destined to be an All-American, no doubt about it, Casey was never able to come back...****Adolph Rupp. BBM****.*

1970-71 (22-6, 16-2 SEC)–Parker (17.6), Casey (17.0), Tom Payne, Louisville (16.9); Kent Hollenbeck Knoxville, (14.0), and Steele, (13.1). The Wildcats repeated as SEC champs and lost to Marquette 91-74, in the Mideast.

1971-72 (21-7, 14-4 SEC)–Jim Andrews, Lima, Ohio (21.5); Parker (18.0), Ronnie Lyons, Maysville (13.2); Stan Key, Hazel, (12.5); and Larry Stamper, (10.3). Adolph Rupp bowed out reluctantly with an all-white team that gave him another SEC championship, but lost to an integrated Florida State team, 73-54, in the Mideast Regional at Dayton. Rupp retired as the winningest coach in NCAA history with an 876-190 record.

Chapter VIII

New Sheriff in Town

Coach Hall and Coach Rupp.

You can take a boy to the Coliseum, sit him down for five minutes, and if he doesn't want to play at Kentucky, after just looking at the place he's too dumb to go to college anyway... ***Rupp, 1952.***

Rupp's chief recruiter during his last seven years as UK basketball coach was Joe B. Hall. Hall was a Cynthiana native who played briefly for Rupp during the "Fabulous Five" era.

Hall's father was a former postal worker, two-time sheriff of Harrison County, and dry cleaning plant operator. The mother grew up on a farm in Harrison County. They raised championship horses that her brother, Ray Harney, showed in the international ring.

Joe B. was captain of both the basketball and football teams at Cynthiana. He tried out for both sports at Eastern State. Then he attended one of Rupp's tryouts.

"I think I was more surprised than anyone when I made the final cut," Hall said. "There were more than 100 boys there, many of whom had been All-State from many parts of the country."

The 1947 Wildcats were so talented that Bob Brannum, an All-America center at UK in 1944, Jim Jordan, a two-time All-America at North Carolina Pre-Flight, and .Jack Parkinson, a UK All-America in 1946, failed to make the starting five.

World War II interrupted Rupp's march to immortality, but many of his former stars were returning as mature combat veterans, along with a wealth of new talent.

"I was out there when all those veterans were returning," Hall said, "There was a backlog of about four years of high school graduates entering college. I played on a squad with seven returnees, guys like Jordan, Parkinson, Holland, Groza, and Barker. That made it pretty rough. I felt like I was young enough to be the son of some of  them, or definitely a younger brother. I never quite gained the confidence necessary for a top performance by being on a squad with so many older people and nobody my age."

During Hall's sophomore year, Rupp put together his "Fabulous Five". Hall made the traveling squad. That included a trip to Boston for a game with Holy Cross and to Madison Square Garden for a game with St. John's. Still he was not satisfied with his lot.

"I was a sophomore and I wasn't playing much," Hall said. "I felt that I was not helping the team. They had brought in about 18 freshmen that year, including Bill Spivey and nine guards. They were also returning Dale Barnstable and Johnny Stough. I felt like my playing opportunities were going to be very little because it looked pretty pat who was going to be in the lineup my junior year."

Hall transferred to Sewanee. He scored a school record 26 points against Millsaps his first game there.

After coaching two years at Shepherdsville High School in Kentucky, Hall accepted the position of head basketball coach at Regis College in Denver, Colorado. His first announcement there was the signing of Lewis Stout, a black All-State player from Cynthiana.

Regis won 51 of 105 games during Hall's five years as their coach. His star player was Cozel Walker, who followed Hall to Central Missouri (19-6, 1964-65).

Hall returned to UK in 1965 as an assistant to Rupp, who placed him in charge of recruiting. Rupp assured him he definitely would take black players. That was fine with Hall. He never coached a team that did not have a black player; he had never shown any signs of racial prejudice or discrimination.

While at Regis, Hall recruited several black players, including Kentuckians Lewis Stout of Cynthiana, James Ray Jones of Shepherdsville and Alan Thomas of Lexington Dunbar.

He later asked Cozel Walker if he might be interested in going to Kentucky with him. Walker said he did not want to fight "that battle" throughout the South.

1972-73 (20-8, 14-4 SEC)–Jim Andrews (20.1), Kevin Grevey, Hamilton, Ohio, (18.7); (Jimmy Dan Conner, Lawrenceburg (11.2); Lyons (9.2) and Mike Flynn, Jeffersonville, Ind., (9.1). .Joe B. Hall's first UK team won an SEC championship. They defeated Austin Peay, 106-100, and lost to Indiana, 72-65, in the Mideast.

1973-74 (13-13, 9-9 SEC)–Grevey (21.9), Bob Guyette, of Ottawa, Ill., (12.7); Conner (12.0), Flynn (11.5) and Lyons (7.8). The Wildcats struggled to a break-even season, defeating Mississippi State, 108-69, to avoid UK's first losing season since 1927.

1974-75 (26-5, 15-3 SEC)– Grevey (23.6), Conner (12.4), Rick Robey, of New Orleans; (10.4); Jack Givens, of Lexington, (9.4); Flynn, (9.0), and Guyette (8.6). Kentucky bounced back with a conference co-championship, a get-even win over Indiana in the Mideast and a loss to UCLA in the NCAA championship game.

1975-76 (20-10, 11-7 SEC)–Givens (20.1), Phillips (15.6), Larry Johnson, (11.2); James Lee, of Lexington, (9.3); Robey15.6), and Reggie Warford, of Drakesboro (6.5). The Wildcats played without an injured Robey most of the season. They were 10-10 when they put together a 10-game winning streak that ended with an NIT championship.

Remembering Knoxville: *The bizarre became routine. The simple became complicated. The sidelights became highlights...Tennessee defeated Kentucky 92-85 here yesterday in what was supposed to be a basketball game. It was, instead, an experiment in pressure for all concerned. Any resemblance of sanity was purely coincidental..*.**Rick Bailey, The Herald-Leader, 1976.**

Remembering Grevey: *After a long bus trip from Starkville, everyone was tired. I came back from the airport to the Coliseum, where we put up the equipment. I went to the dorm to make sure everyone was all right and that we didn't have any sick or anyone needing any attention. After an hour and 45 minutes, I called my wife and told her I would just wait and see if I could find out where Kevin went and why he was late. I laid down on his bed and went to sleep. Kevin never showed up. They called me "Papa Bear" after that, said I was sleeping in Baby Bear's bed.* ***Joe B... BBM.***

1976-77 (26-4, 16-2 SEC)–Givens (18.9), Robey (14.2), Phillips (12.2), Johnson (10.7), Jay Shidler, of Lawrenceville, Ill., (7.8), and Truman Claytor, of Toledo, Ohio, (6.6). That team was SEC co-champion. They lost to North Carolina, 79-72, in the East Regional.

1977-78 (30-2, 16-2 SEC)–Givens *(*18.1), Robey (14.4*)*, Kyle Macy, of Peru, Ind. 12.5); James Lee, (11.3), Phillips (10.2), and Claytor (6.9). Macy transferred from Purdue, laid out a required year, and led the Wildcats to SEC and national championships in 1978. Givens scored 41 points in the championship win over Duke.

As UK was defeating Kansas on "Adolph Rupp Night" in Allen Field House in Lawrence, Rupp lay dying in Lexington. "Just say I did the best I could," he said.

1978-79 (19-12, 10-8 SEC)–Macy (15.2), Dwight Anderson, of Dayton, Ohio, (13.3); Lavon Williams, of Denver, Col., (11.5); Fred

Cowan, of Union County, (9.4), and Claytor (8.7). They lost the NIT to Clemson, 68-67, in Memorial Coliseum.

Remembering LaVon: *His carvings have been acquired by several prominent national collectors, including a member of the Museum of Folk Art's Board of Trustees and a Director of a fine museum.*

1979-80 (29-6, 15-3 SEC)–Macy (15.4), Sam Bowie, of Lebanon, Pa., (12.9); Cowan (12.5), Williams (7.5) and Shidler (6.2). Despite the presence of 7-foot-Sam Bowie, the defending SEC champions had a heart-breaking loss to Duke, 55-54, in the Mideast Regional, which was held in Memorial Coliseum. Macy bowed out with a career high 1,411 points. His 470 assists were a school record at the time.

1980-81 (22-6, 15-3 SEC)–(Bowie (17.4), Dirk Minniefield, of Lexington (10.4); Derrick Hord, of Bristol, Tenn. (8.9), Cowan (8.2), and Chuck Verderber, of Lincoln, Ill. (7.5).UAB upset the Wildcats, 69-62, in the Mideast.

1981-82 (22-8, 13-5 SEC)–Hord (16.3), Jim Master, Fort Wayne, Ind.,, (13.4); Melvin Turpin, of Lexington, (11.1); Minniefield (11.3), and Charles Hurt, of Shelbyville, (6.6). The Wildcats won another SEC title and advanced to the NCAA first round, losing to Middle Tennessee, 50-44, in Nashville.

1982-83 (23-8, 13-5)–Turpin (13.1), Master (12.5), Hord (8.9), Minniefield (8.6), and Hurt (8.2). The Wildcats repeated as SEC champs, beat Indiana, 64-59, but lost to Louisville, 80-68, in overtime in the Mideast final. It was the first meeting between UK and UL in 24 years. Minniefield's 181 assists gave him a school record of 646, which still stands.

1983-84 (29-5, 14-4 SEC)–Turpin (15.2), Kenny Walker, of Roberta, Ga., (12.4); Bowie (10.5), Master (9.6), and Winston Bennett, of Louisville, (6.5). Georgetown outscored UK, 23-2, at the start of the second half to defeat the Wildcats, 53-40, in an NCAA semifinal game in Seattle.

1984-85 (18-13, 11-7 SEC)–Walker (22.9), Ed Davender, of Brooklyn, (8.5); Bennett (7.2), James Blackmon, of Marion, Ind., (5.4), and Roger Harden, of Valparaiso, Ind., (5.3). After the Wildcats lost to St. John's, 86-70, in the West Region in Denver, Joe B.

Hall resigned as UK coach.

Hall expanded the UK recruiting base, bringing in such fine out-of-state players as Dan Issel, Mike Pratt, Larry Steele, Tom Parker, Jim Andrews, Mike Flynn, Kevin Grevey, Mike Casey, Mike Phillips, and Rick Robey. All except Casey, a Shelby County native, were from out-of-state.

Chapter IX
Date With Destiny

Joe B. Hall sauntered Into the Wildcat locker room at Dayton, Ohio, shortly before the tipoff for the 1975 NCAA Mideast Regional championship basketball game against arch-enemy Indiana. He walked to the chalkboard. The players took off their warm-up jackets, drank some water, sat down on their benches, ready for a brief discussion about defensive assignments and offensive strategy. Seated before the ambitious young coach was a group of players that he had personally recruited during and after the retirement three years earlier of his old former coach and mentor Adolph Rupp.

During Rupp's hopeless battle to beat UK's mandatory retirement age, Hall had gone quietly on his way, coaching the freshmen to an undefeated season. Rupp resented the fact that the freshmen were better than some of his varsity players. The NCAA was only a year away from making frosh eligible for varsity.

The promising freshmen, now seniors, were Kevin Grevey, of Hamilton, Ohio, Mike Flynn, of Jeffersonville, Ind.; Jerry Hale, of New Albany, Ind.; Bob Guyette, of Ottawa, Ill., and Kentuckians Jimmy Dan Conner, of Lawrenceburg, and G. J. Smith, of London.

Rounding out the roster were Rick Robey, of New Orleans; Mike Phillips, of Akron, Ohio, and Kentuckians Larry Johnson, of Morganfield; Reggie Warford, Jr., of Drakesboro; Merion Haskins, of Campbellsville; Jack Givens and James Lee, both of Lexington, and Dan Hall, of Betsy Layne.

Dickey Beal

As sophomores, the seniors had posted a 20-8 record after losing to Indiana, 72-65, in the Mideast Regional. They fell to 13-13 in their junior year. One of the losses was to Indiana, 77-68, in Louisville.

The Wildcats lost only three more games during that regular season and tied Alabama for the conference championship. They were

24-4 going into the NCAA Region championship at Dayton.

With his players properly seated in the Dayton facility, Hall went to the blackboard and wrote: NETS! BUS! POLICE! COLISEUM!

The confused players looked at each other and then back to the board. Hall explained:

"NETS-I want you to be careful that no one gets cut or falls off the ladder as we cut down the nets after the game.

"BUS-We will all ride back on the bus to Lexington.

"POLICE-We will pick up the Kentucky State Police escort as we cross the Ohio River.

"COLISEUM-We will go to the Coliseum for a victory celebration."

The Wildcats that afternoon faced a Hoosier team that had annihilated (74-98), and embarrassed them in Bloomington in December. The Hoosiers had finished the regular season undefeated and ranked No. 1 nationally. They had a winning margin of better than 23 points over all foes and were a solid 12-point choice over the Wildcats.

Kentucky advanced to the regional final by defeating Marquette in Tuscaloosa and Central Michigan in Dayton. Meanwhile, Indiana easily disposed of Texas El Paso in Lexington and Oregon State at Dayton.

The UK players had looked forward to a rematch with Indiana ever since the IU fans and their coach Bobby Knight had given them a rough time in Bloomington.

Indiana took an 8-2 lead and increased that to 38-31. Kentucky tied the score, 44-44, at halftime. Flynn hit six of six in the second half for a team-high 22 points. UK upset the mighty Hoosiers, 92-90.

The Wildcats later lost to UCLA 92-85, in the NCAA championship game in San Diego. On the eve of that game, veteran Bruin coach John Wooden announced his retirement. Grevey bowed out with 34 points for a career high 1,801, which ranks seventh on UK's all-time list.

Remembering Wooden: *Upon hearing that John was retiring, I felt like somebody had stuck a pin in me and let all of the air out…* **Joe B. Hall.**

Remembering the Game*: I had 34 points, and it meant nothing to me. The agony. The pain. It's hard to even talk about it…Coach Wooden and I were on a plane together 10 years later. I told him I really believed we would have won the game had he not announced his retirement. And Coach Wooden said, Kevin, you would have won the game if you had played better defense…* **Kevin Grevey.**

Remembering the Incident: *Bobby was yelling at the officials from in front of my bench, in front of me. As he turned to go back to the bench, I said, 'Way to go, Bob, give 'em hell.' Good-naturedly, because this was a friend of mine."*

"He turned and broke down, almost like an attack position, and he screamed at me, 'Don't ever talk to me during a game! Why don't you coach your own m…..f…… team?

*I turned to walk away and he popped me with an open hand at the back of the neck. Pretty strongly. And I turned in response, and he again broke down in attack mode and he said, 'I didn't mean anything by that, eithe*r**….Joe B. Hall, BBM.**

Remembering the Incident: *When we got back to Lexington, I was summoned to the office of the Athletic Director, Harry Lan-caster. When he tells me to sit down, "I think, 'Oh crap, I'm going to get fired before I even get started."*

*"He says to me, 'I reviewed that incident at Indiana. You had a chance to hit that son of a bitch. If you ever get a chance like that again, and you DON'T hit him, I'm firing your ass.'"…***Lynn Nance, assistant coach, 1985**.

The following year, the Wildcats played Mississippi State in their 25th and final season in Memorial Coliseum. State brought to town a 13-12 record that included a 77-73 victory over UK in Starkville. The Wildcats had struggled to a 10-10 record and then won 10 in a row before meeting the Bulldogs again. They had earned a Trip to the NIT.

The Wildcat squad consisted of nine players from Kentucky, two from Ohio, and one each from Michigan and West Virginia. The Kentucky natives were senior Reggie Warford, juniors Larry Johnson and Merion Haskins, sophomores Jack Givens, James Lee and Dan Hall, and freshmen Dwane Casey. Joey Holland, a sophomore from Charleston, W.Va., was a son of former Wildcat Joe Holland (1946, 47, 48). Mike Phillips, of Akron, and Truman Claytor, of Toledo, were from Ohio. Bob Fowler was a freshman from Dearborn Heights, Mich. Never again would Kentucky natives so dominate a UK roster.

Kentucky tied the game at 85-85 with seven seconds remaining. Mississippi State missed the final shot and the game went into overtime. Johnson made two free throws to give UK a 94-91 lead. State got an unchallenged layup and that was the game, UK 94, MSU 93.

Thus the Wildcats said goodbye to Memorial Coliseum, where they had compiled a record of 306 wins and only 38 losses. Thirty-seven years later, the Wildcats "re-christened" the ancient structure with a 70-60 win over UNLV.

In 1978, Givens, Lee, Robey, Claytor and Phillips were starters with Kyle Macy, of Peru, Ind., on a UK team matched against Duke in the NCAA championship game in St. Louis. Five members of that UK squad were Kentucky natives, six were black. The non-starters were Dwane Casey, Morganfield; Jay Shidler, of Lawrenceville, Ill.; Tim Stephens, of Revelo; Fred Cowan,

Governor Wendell Ford and Coach Joe B. Hall.

of Morganfield; Scott Courts, of Arvada, Colo.; Chuck Aleksinas, of Morris, Conn.; LaVon Williams, of Denver, Colo., and Chris Gettelfinger, of Knoxville.

That team won 30 games and lost only to Alabama and LSU, both on the road.

Givens' 41 points in a championship win over Duke gave him a career total of 2,038 points, third on UK's all-time list. Kyle Macy (1,411 points) Rick Robey (1,395), and Mike Phillips (1,367) also are members of the 1000 Point Scorers Club.

During his 13 years (1973-85) as UK head coach, Hall successfully recruited the following black in-state players who would at one time or another start for him: Jack Givens (1975-78), James Lee (1975-78), and Dirk Minniefield (1980-83), all of Lexington; and Paul Andrews (1984-87), of London; Larry Johnson (1974-77) of Morganfield; Reggie Warford 1976), of Drakesboro; Charles Hurt (1980-83), of Shelbyville, Winston Bennett (1984, 85, 86, 88), of Louisville; Fred Cowan (1978-81), of Morganfield, and Melvin Turpin (1981-84), of Lexington..

The other Kentucky boys who played either briefly for Hall or long enough to earn a letter at UK were Merion Haskins (1975, 76, 77), of Campbellsville; Robert Mayhall (Fr. 1974), of Middlesboro; Ernie Whitus (Fr. 1974), of Louisville; Dan Hall, of Betsy Layne (1975); Dwayne Casey, of Morganfield (1976-79); Tim Stephens, of Stearns (1976-79); Bo Lanter, of Versailles, (1980- 82); Troy McKinley, of Independence, (1982-85), and LeRoy Byrd, (1984-86), of Lexington. Haskins, Casey and Byrd were black.

Hall coached seven All-America players and nine All-SEC first-team choices. Jack Givens (A-A) and Melvin Turpin (All-SEC) were the only Kentuckians in the group.

Chapter X
In Like a Lion

Present at UK's hiring of Eddie Sutton were Dr. Otis Singletary, left, Athletic Director, Cliff Hagan, seated, Sutton and Hank Iba.

They're getting the best coach in America. He'll dedicate his entire life to maintaining the quality of that program. The players won't be cheated. They'll be expected to excel academically and they'll be pushed to excel in basketball.. **Sidney Moncrief, former Arkansas All-American under Sutton***.*

*I would have crawled on my hands and knees all the way from Arkansas to coach at Kentucky...***Eddie Sutton***.*

Eddie Sutton succeeded Joe B. Hall and served four years (1986-89) as UK coach. He came to UK with glowing credentials, having won big at Creighton and Arkansas. Sutton favored a sticky defense and deliberate offense, which irritated some UK fans.

Sutton inherited from Joe B. Hall a team that usually started three guards, lacked a true center, and was short on depth. The senior leaders were All-America forward Kenny Walker of Roberta, Ga., and Roger Harden, of Valparaiso, Ind. The only Kentuckian who started was Winston Bennett, of Louisville, joined by Ed Davender, of Brooklyn, and James Blackmon, of Marion, Ind.

The roster contained the name of one freshman, Irving Thomas, of Miami, Florida.

Paul Andrews, of London, and LeRoy Byrd, of Lexington, were the only Kentucky boys in the group. They sat on the bench with Richard Madison, of Memphis; Rob Lock, of Reedley, Cal.; and Cedric Jenkins, of Dawson, Ga. Andrews served as a UK co-captain his senior year.

The team surprised everyone by winning 32 games and losing only to Kansas, Auburn, and North Carolina, all on the road, and to LSU, 59-57, in the East Regional.

Walker ended his two-time All-America career at UK with 2,080 points, second only to Dan Issel's all-time men's scoring total. The conference named him player of the year for the second straight time. Sutton garnered SEC and National Coach of the Year Honors.

"Sutton's first Wildcat team remains one of the most successful and most appreciated in UK hoops history," Tom Wallace wrote. "What that team accomplished far exceeded anyone's expectations."

Sutton's greatest coup at UK was the recruitment of Rex Chapman, a 6-4 prep All-America from Owensboro, Ky. Rex was a son of Wayne Chapman. Wayne transferred to Western Kentucky after his freshman season at UK. Rex's arrival at UK coincided with the three-point shot in college basketball.

Chapman was the first freshman ever to start for a Sutton-coached team. His presence helped offset the loss of Bennett, who sat out the season with a knee injury.

The heralded freshman started his UK career by scoring 18 points and six assists in a 71-69 win over Austin Peay. They defeated Texas Tech, 66-60, and lost to Indiana, 71-66. The Wildcats trailed IU by eight late in the game. Chapman wrapped two treys and an old-fashioned three around an IU basket to trim the margin to 60-59. The Hoosiers were led by Steve Alford's 26 points, which Chapman equaled.

The Cats were 5-1 when they met Louisville in a televised game in Freedom Hall. Chapman scored 26 points and UK won, 85-51. "He destroyed the Cardinals in every way imaginable–dunks, finger rolls and, of course, from the outside, (Chapman hit five of eight three-point attempts)," Wallace wrote. "It was a spectacular performance, one of the most memorable in UK history."

The Cats won only 10 of 18 SEC games the remainder of the season. They lost to Auburn, 79-72, in the SEC tournament opener, and to Ohio State, 91-77 in the NCAA tournament. Chapman's 16-point average made him the first freshman since Alex Groza to lead UK in scoring. He led the team in assists with 3.6 per game.

The 1987-88 UK team seemed headed for greatness, thanks to the presence of Chapman and such established stars as seniors Bennett, Davender, Lock and Jenkins. The bench, led by Derrick Miller, LeRon Ellis, and Reggie Hanson provided an excellent back-up at all positions.

Despite personality clashes between Sutton and Chapman, the 'Cats were 27-6 after losing to Villanova, 80-74, in the NCAA tournament. Chapman led the scoring with a 19-point average, becoming the first Wildcat sophomore to join the 1,000-point club.

Kentucky entered the 1988-89 season lacking significant talent in their lineup. The previous season's offensive and defensive stars, Davender, Lock and Bennett had graduated; All-SEC sophomore Rex Chapman left school early to enter the 1988 NBA Draft.

Additionally, the NCAA accused sophomore standout Eric Manuel of cheating on his college entrance exam. Manuel voluntarily agreed to sit out until the investigation was finished. Potential franchise recruit Shawn Kemp transferred out of Kentucky after signing with the school early that year.

Manuel did not play a game as the investigation dragged through the entire season. That essentially placed the Wildcats in the hands of the inexperienced sophomore LeRon Ellis and freshman Chris Mills. The two underclassmen struggled to fill the talent vacuum on the court. The Wildcats finished with a record of 13-19, the team's first losing record since 1927.

Ellis led all scorers with 16 points a game. Mills averaged 14.3 ppg. He scored UK's only triple double in an 85-77 win over Austin Peay. Reggie Hanson, the only east Kentuckian on the starting five, averaged 9.8 ppg.

Sutton's tenure at Kentucky ended after a scandal and a losing record tarnished the school's basketball program. The NCAA announced that its investigation into the basketball program found the school guilty of violating numerous NCAA policies.

The scandal broke when Emery Worldwide employees discovered $1,000 in cash in an envelope Kentucky assistant coach Dwane Casey allegedly sent to Mills' father. Kentucky was already on probation stemming from an extensive scheme of payments to recruits. The NCAA seriously considered hitting the Wildcats with the "death penalty", which would have shut down the entire basketball program for up to two years.

School president David Roselle forced Sutton and athletic director Cliff Hagan to resign. The NCAA slapped UK with three years' probation, a two-year ban from postseason play, and a ban from live television in 1989-90. They banned Manuel from playing again for any NCAA member school.

The NCAA committee completed its investigation in May. They forced UK to vacate three NCAA games and surrender the 1988 SEC regular-season title.

Mills transferred to Arizona, Ellis to Syracuse, and Sean Sutton to Purdue. Sutton later joined his father Eddie at Oklahoma State. Remaining were Reggie Hanson and three other native sons–Richie Farmer, of Manchester; Deron Feldhaus, of Mason County, and John Pelphrey, of Paintsville.

Hanson, Pelphrey, Farmer, Feldhaus, and Woods decided to remain at UK. That decision would reap unexpected benefits three years down the road.

Sutton coached the Wildcats for four years, leading them to the Elite Eight of the 1986 NCAA Tournament. Two seasons later, Sutton and the 25-5 Wildcats captured their 37th SEC title (which was later vacated by the SEC) and were ranked as the 6th college basketball team in the nation by the Associated Press and UPI . They lost to Villanova in the NCAA Tournament.

C.M. Newton, a Wildcat letterman who coached at Vanderbilt, replaced Hagan as athletic director on April 1, 1989. He immediately started searching for a new coach. Newton set his sights on Rick Pitino, coach of the New York Knicks. Pitino had rebuilt struggling programs at Boston College and Providence.

Pitino accepted the UK job on June 2, 1989. There were eight scholarship players available. Only Hanson and Miller had proven themselves capable Division I players.

"These were young men of unlimited character," Tom Wallace wrote. "It also didn't hurt that four of the players–Hanson, Feldhaus, Farmer and Pelphrey–were Kentucky kids who had grown up following the Big Blue. Wearing a Wildcat uniform had been a lifelong dream for them. Their drive to succeed was propelled by the winning tradition they were now part of."

1985-86 (32-4, 17-1)–Walker (20.0), Bennett (12.7), Davender (11.5), Blackmon (9.4) and Harden (6.8).

In his first year as Wildcat coach, Eddie Sutton led the Wildcats to 32 wins in 36 outings, including a 59-57 loss to LSU in the Southeast Region in Atlanta.

1986-87 (18-11, 10-8 SEC)–Chapman (16.0), Davender (15.7), Bennett (15.3), Rob Lock, of Reedley, Cal., (7.5). Eddie Sutton went from the penthouse to the outhouse, so to speak, as his Wildcats lost the SEC Tournament, 79-72, to Auburn the first round, and bowed to Ohio State, 91-77, in the NCAA.

1987-88 (25-5, 13-5 SEC)–Chapman (19.0), Davender (15.7), (Bennett 15.3), Lock (10.9).

1988-89 (13-19, 8-10 SEC)–LeRon Ellis (16.0), Chris Mills, of Los Angeles, Cal., (14.3); Derrick Miller (13.9), Reggie Hanson, of Somerset, (9.8), and Sean Sutton, Lexington (5.9). Kentucky finished the year with a 13-19 record. It was the first losing slate in 61 seasons. In the wake of an NCAA investigation, Eddie Sutton resigned.

Chapter IX
Big City Basketball

*I'm not trying to blow smoke at Kentucky. I just want people to realize that they may not see another team like them for a long time. They've got guys that can go play in the NBA, not just to wear the uniform and draw a salary...***Coach Nolan Richardson, Arkansas, 1996.**

During his eight years as Wildcat coach, Rick Pitino brought big-city, open-court basketball to the University of Kentucky. He inherited four native sons–Richie Farmer, of Manchester; Reggie Hanson, of Somerset; Deron Feldhaus, of Mason County, and John Pelphrey, of Paintsville–from the Eddie Sutton regime. They formed the nucleus of Pitino's first UK team, along with Sean Woods, of Indianapolis; Jeff Brassow, of Houston, Texas; Derrick Miller, of Savannah, Ga., and Jonathan Davis, of Pensacola, Fla.

"The first time I met with them, I kept waiting for the big guys to walk through the door, but there were no giants in this group," Pitino said. He felt that Hanson and Miller could play on that level, but that not everybody else belonged at Kentucky. He said Farmer made Billy Donovan look like Charles Atlas, while Pelphrey and Feldhaus seemed like a team's 11th and 12th men.

"None of our players was taller than 6' 7", and each one must have felt about two feet tall after the NCAA had embarrassed them (with sanctions and probation)," he said. "They were the end of the bench. Their self-esteem was at rock bottom."

Cawood Ledford told Pitino he should be named coach of the year if he won with that bunch; other "experts" and most UK fans echoed that opinion.

Dubbed "Pitino's Bombinos" by the media, the 1989-90 Wildcats, utilizing a pressing defense and the three-point shot, defeated Ohio, 76-73, in their home opener.

They lost to Indiana by only two points in Indianapolis. They pulled their biggest upset, a 100-95 win over an LSU team that featured 7-footers Shaquille O'Neal and Stanley Roberts, and All-America guard Chris Jackson. They were 3-1 when Kansas soundly trounced them, 150-95, in Lawrence. Pitino ignored Jayhawk coach Roy Williams' suggestion that he call off his full-court press. The Cats finished with a 14-14 record, which pleased practically every UK fan.

The three Kentuckians, Farmer, Feldhaus, and Pelphrey, combined with their other senior guard, Sean Woods of Indianapolis, and freshman Jamal Mashburn, of the Bronx, became the heart of the team that resuscitated Kentucky basketball. Mashburn was the first of a long line of "Big City" boys recruited by Pitino.

A high point came in 1992 when they won 29 games, captured the SEC championship, finished sixth in the final Associated Press poll, and reached the Elite Eight of the NCAA tournament.

They lost to Duke, 104-103, in overtime in the 1992-championship game of the NCAA Regional in Philadelphia. Experts considered it one of the best college basketball games ever played. Mashburn was All-NCAA Regional that year.

During a special awards ceremony held in Rupp Arena, the University honored the four seniors, dubbed the "Untouchables", by having a banner raised in their honor. Their names are enshrined in the UK Athletic Hall of Fame.

In 1996, Pitino presented a star-studded squad that listed four Kentucky-born among its 16 members. The Kentuckians were Cameron Mills, of Lexington; Derek Anderson,

The Unforgettables: John Pelphrey, Richie Farmer, Sean Woods and Deron Feldhaus.

of Louisville; Anthony Epps, of Lebanon, and Jason Lathrem, of Bowling Green.

Rounding out the squad were Tony Delk, of Brownsville, Tenn., Allen Edwards, of Miami, Fla.; Wayne Turner, of Chestnut Hills, Mass.; Nazr Mohammed, of Chicago; Jeff Sheppard, of Atlanta; Walter McCarty, of Evansville, Ind.; Mark Pope, of Bellevue, Wash., Antoine Walker, also of Chicago; Jared Prickett, of Fairmont, W. Va.; Ron Mercer and Oliver Simmons, both of Nashville. Nine of those players played pro basketball.

"If the 1996 championship restored the glory to Kentucky basketball, The Unforgettables restored its spirit," Lonnie Wheeler wrote. "Pride in the program was disproportionately swollen in the mountains, which had given the team both Farmer, the schoolboy whose famous name was placed on a boulevard in Manchester, and a reddish-haired Pelphrey, a former Mr. Basketball and an unlikely all-conference selection."

Despite the overachievers he inherited from Sutton, Pitino felt he could not return UK to its place atop the basketball world with the white boys that Rupp once recruited out of the mountains.

Pitino shocked the mountain folks when he failed to recruit J. R. VanHoose, of Paintsville. VanHoose was a 6-9 center who led the voting for both the Courier-Journal and Herald-Leader all-state teams. As a sophomore, he led Paintsville to the state championship and as a junior took them back to the Final Four.

"In another time, such credentials would have made VanHoose a shoo-in for UK," Lonnie Wheeler wrote." Bob VanHoose said that if UK had gone after his son hard, it would have been a no-brainer. J. R. would have been satisfied with a seat on the UK bench.

"There was a day when J. R. VanHoose would have been at Kentucky, no questions asked," Lonnie Wheeler wrote. "Now the best player in the state was on the outside, looking in at the new Kentucky. It was Rick Pitino's Kentucky, Derek Anderson's Kentucky, Tubby Smith's Kentucky, Souleymane Camara's Kentucky, and, even still, Kentucky's Kentucky."

"No longer is it the days of Pat, Jimmy Dan, Jack, Kyle, Sam, Rex, and Richie," observed Capt. Dan Armstrong on Chit Chat. "I'm cheering for Souleymane, Tayshaun, Jamaal, Heshimu, and Nazr. Times are a-changing."

The scholarship players who earned letters under Pitino were as follows:

Jamal Mashburn (1991-93), 6-8, C, Bronx, N. Y., was a Parade All-America who earned the title of Mr. Basketball in the State of New York in 1990. He was an All-SEC Freshman and a third-team All-SEC selection in 1991. He made All-SEC, All-Regional, and All-America teams in 1992 and 1993. His career total of 1,183 points ranks high on UK's all-time list. He also got 760 rebounds, 218 assists, 153 steals, and 53 blocked shots. Mashburn played 11 years in the NBA.

Carlos Toomer (1991, 92), 6-4, G, Corinth, Miss., saw brief action at UK before transferring to St. Louis.

Gimel Martinez (1991-94), 6-8, C, Miami, Fla., scored 719 points, pulled down 338 rebounds, dished out 137 assists, and blocked 58 shots during four years at UK.

Travis Ford (1992-94), 5-9, G, Madisonville, was a Parade All-America who transferred to UK after a fine freshman year at the University of Missouri. After laying out the required year of ineligibility at UK, he scored 951 points, 428 assists, and 201 rebounds as a starter at point guard.

Ford set a UK record with 15 assists against Eastern Kentucky in 1993. He was All-SEC Tournament MVP in 1993 and 1994, and Academic All-SEC each of his three years at UK. Ford is currently head coach at Oklahoma State University.

Aminu Timberlake (1992, 93), 6-8, C, Chicago, Ill., played in 39 UK games He transferred to Southern Illinois after his sophomore year at UK.

Chris Harrison (1992, 93, 94, 95), 6-3, G. Tollesboro, was the only eastern Kentucky boy that Pitino signed during his tenure at UK.

Tony Delk (1993-96), 6-1 G, Brownsville, Tenn. Tennessee's Mr. Basketball; in 1992, Delk enjoyed an All-America career at UK. He scored 1,890 points, pulled down 490 rebounds, dished out 210 assists, and got 201 steals as a Wildcat. He was the outstanding player of the 1996 NCAA championship game, with a record-tying seven three-pointers and 24 points. Delk was the SEC Player of the Year in 1996.

Rodney Dent, (1993, 94), 6-11, Edison, Ga., transferred to UK from Odessa (Tex.) Junior College. He averaged 5.1 rebounds and 6.4 points per game in 1992-93. He played in 11 games the following year before being sidelined by an injury. He scored 625 points and 460 rebounds at UK.

Jared Prickett. (1993-97), 6-9, F, Fairmont, W. Va., was "Gatorade State Player of the Year" and "Mr. Basketball" in West Virginia in 1992. He scored 300 points and 89 rebounds for UK's 1996 NCAA championship Wildcats. Prickett finished his UK career with 998 points and 777 rebounds.

Andre Riddick (1992-95), 6-9, C, New York, N. Y. was an All-America and Gatorade Player of the Year in New York, Riddick was All-SEC Tournament in 1993.He scored 625 points and 460 rebounds at UK.

Walter McCarty (1993-96), 6-9, F, Evansville, Ind., was a Parade All-America. He scored 946 points, got 522 rebounds, dished out 108 assists and blocked 108 shots during three seasons at UK. McCarty scored 23 points including four of seven three-pointers as UK erased a 31-point deficit to defeat LSU 99-94 in Baton Rouge. McCarty was All-SEC Tournament in 1996.

Anthony Epps (1994-97), 6-3, G, Lebanon, was a guard who scored 881 points and 544 assists at UK. He ranks second to Dirk Minniefield (646 assists) in UK annals. Epps was NCAA All-Regional on UK's 1996 NCAA championship team.

Jeff Sheppard, (1994, 95, 96, 98), 6-4, G, Peachtree City, Ga., was a Gatorade State Player of the Year and a Parade All-America. He was Academic All-SEC as a sophomore. Sheppard scored 1,091 points, 320 rebounds, and 288 assists at UK. He was All-NCAA Regional and Most Valuable Player on UK's 1998 NCAA championship team.

Scott Padgett (1995-99), 6-9, F, Louisville, scored 1,252 points and got 651 rebounds in 122 games played at UK. He was All-NCAA Final Four in 1997, Wooden All-American (1998), All-NCAA Final Four , All-SEC Regional (1998, '99), and Academic All-SEC, (1998, '99). He scored 17 points in UK's win over Utah in the 1998 NCAA championship game. Padgett is a member of John Calipari's staff at UK.

Allen Edwards (1995-98), 6-5, G-F, Miami, Fla., "Mr. Basketball" in the State of Florida, Edwards scored 819 points, pulled in 293 rebounds, dished out 285 assists, and blocked 19 shots during four years at UK.

Mark Pope, (1995, 96), 6-10, F-C, Bellevue, Wash., played two years at UK after transferring from the University of Washington. He scored 546 points, pulled down 458 rebounds, and blocked 82 shots in 69 games at UK. Pope was All-SEC Tournament and Academic All-SEC in 1995.

Antoine Walker (1995, 96), 6-8, F, Chicago, Ill., was Gatorade Player of the Year in Illinois He received All-America recognition by both Parade and McDonald's. Walker scored 806 points, 450 rebounds, 151 assists, 33 blocked shots, and 89 steals in two years at UK. He was All-SEC Tournament in 1995, All-America and All-SEC regular season and tournament in 1996.

Derek Anderson (1996, 97), 6-6, G, Louisville, played two years at UK after transferring from Ohio State. He scored 674 points, 199 rebounds, 155 assists, and 98 steals before a knee injury in midseason 1997 ended his UK career. He was All-NCAA Regional in 1996.

Wayne Turner (1996-99), 6-2, G, Boston, Mass., was a Parade and McDonald's All-America and Gatorade Player of the Year. He scored 1,170 points, 381 rebounds, 494 assists, 381 rebounds, and 238 steals during four seasons at UK. Turner was All-NCAA Regional with UK's 1996 NCAA champions, Most Outstanding Player on the 1998 championship team, and SEC Tournament MVP in 1998 and 1999.

Nazr Mohammad (1996-98), 6-10, C, Chicago, scored 814 points, 532 rebounds, and 135 blocked shots during three years at UK. He played on two NCAA championship teams. Mohammad was All-SEC and All-SEC Tournament in 1998. He declared early for the NFL draft after his junior season.

Ron Mercer (1996, 97, 98), 6-7, F, Nashville, was a two-time Mr. Basketball in Tennessee, and a Parade and McDonalds All-American. He played on two NCAA championship teams at UK. In three seasons, Mercer scored 1,013 points, 314 rebounds, and 100 steals. He was All-Final Four and All-America in 1998.

Oliver Simmons (1996, 97), 6-8, F, Nashville, was a Mr. Basketball who scored 37 points, 25 rebounds and four blocked shots in 21 games as a UK freshman. He transferred to Florida State after playing in one game (broken leg) as a sophomore.

When Pitino arrived on campus, four of the eight surviving scholarship players were black. Two years later, there were nine minority players on a team roster of 15. When he left UK, 16 of the 22 scholarship players who lettered for him were black. Chris Harrison, a reserve, was the only eastern Kentuckian in the group that included native sons Epps, Ford, Harrison, Padgett, Lathrem, and Anderson.

1989-90 (14-14, 10-8 SEC)–Miller (19.2), Hanson (16.4), Deron Feldhaus, of Maysville, (14.4); John Pelphrey, of Paintsville, (13.0), and Sean Woods, of Indianapolis (9.1).

1990-91 (22-6, 14.4 SEC)–Pelphrey (14.4), Hanson (14.4), Jamal Mashburn, of Brooklyn, (12.9); Feldhaus, (10.8), and Richie Farmer, of Manchester, (10.1). Kentucky defeated Auburn, 114-93, before 24,310 in Rupp Arena to claim the best record in the SEC and to celebrate the end of a two-year probation.

1991-92 (29-7, 12-4 SEC) – Mashburn (21.3), Pelphrey, 12.5), Feldhaus (11.4), Farmer (9.6), and Woods, 7.7). In what many called the best NCAA Tournament game ever, UK took defending champion Duke into overtime before losing, 104-103, in the East Regional in Philadelphia. A last-second shot by Christian Lattner sent Duke to the Final Four. It was Cawood Ledford's last game as "Voice of the Wildcats."

On the Tuesday night following the Final Four that year, a special night of celebration took place at Rupp Arena to honor a team that had earned the nickname "The Unforgettables." UK athletic director C. M. Newton told the four seniors, Farmer, Feldhaus Pelphrey, and Woods, "Many have scored more points than you have. They have won more individual honors, but no one can match what you've given us by putting your hearts into the wearing of the Kentucky jersey. Look to the ceiling." When the four looked up, they saw their jerseys hanging from the rafters...Denny Trease, 2002.

1992-93 (30-4, 13-3, SEC)–(Mashburn (21.0), Travis Ford, of

Madisonville, (13.6); Dale Brown, of Pascagoula, Miss., (9.4); Rodrick Rhodes, of Jersey, N. J.,(9.1), and Rodney Dent, of Edison, Ga., (6.4). Jamal Mashburn bowed out in an 81-78 overtime loss to Michigan in an NCAA semifinal game. He ranks sixth among UK career scorers with 1,843 points.

1993-94 (27-7, 12-4, SEC)–Tony Delk (16.6), Rhodes (14.6), Ford (11.3), Jared Prickett (8.2), and Andre Riddick (7.9). The Wildcats trailed LSU by 31 points with 15:34 remaining in Baton Rouge. They hit 11 three-pointers and outscored the Tigers, 62-27, for a 99-95 win. It was the greatest comeback in UK history.

1994-95 (28-5, 14-2, SEC)–Delk (16.7), Rhodes (13.9), Walter McCarty, of Evansville, Ind., (10.5), Jeff Sheppard, of Atlanta, (8.3) and Mark Pope, of Bellevue, Wash, (8.2).

1995-96 (34-2, 16-0 SEC)–Delk (17.8), Antoine Walker, of Chicago, (15.2), McCarty (11.3), Derek Anderson, of Louisville, (9.4), and Ron Mercer, of Nashville, (8.0). Kentucky defeated Vanderbilt, 101-63, in Rupp Arena, becoming the first team in 40 years to sweep the conference. After avenging an earlier loss to John Calipari's U-Mass team, UK defeated Syracuse, 76-67, for the national title.

1996-97 (35-5, 13-3 SEC)–Ron Mercer (18.1), Anderson (17.7), Padgett (9.6), Anthony Epps (8.9), and Edwards (8.6).

Chapter XII
Tubbyball

The University announced Tubby Smith as the Wildcats' 20th head coach on May 12, 1997. They charged him with the task of replacing Rick Pitino, who left to become head coach of the NBA's Boston Celtics. The Wildcats were at the top of the basketball world at the time. They had won a national title in 1996 and played in the national title game in 1997. The team Smith inherited sported seven players from the Arizona loss, and five from the 1996 championship team.

In his first season at UK, Smith coached the Wildcats to their seventh NCAA Men's Division I Basketball Championship. It was the only team in more than twenty years to win without a first-team All-American or future NBA lottery pick. (Smith's teams, known primarily for a defense-oriented slower style of play coined "Tubbyball", received mixed reviews among Kentucky fans who have historically enjoyed a faster, higher-scoring style of play under previous coaches).

In addition to the national championship, Smith's Wildcats compiled a perfect 16–0 regular season conference record in 2003 (as well as his being named national AP Coach of the Year), five SEC regular season championships (1998, 1999, 2001, 2003, 2005) and five SEC Tournament titles (1998, 1999, 2001, 2003, 2004), with six Sweet Sixteen finishes and four Elite Eight finishes (1998, 1999, 2003, 2005) in his nine seasons after the 1998 championship. He totaled 100 wins quicker than any other Wildcat coach except Hall of Fame member Adolph Rupp, reaching the plateau in 130 games.

The roster of his 1998 championship team included nine players who eventually would play pro ball. However, most were holdovers from Pitino. Smith's best year featuring Kentucky boys was probably 2005-2006, when six of the 16-man roster were from in-state. Only Sparks and Rondo were starters.

Sparks was from Central City. He transferred from Western Kentucky and averaged 11.0 in '05 and 9.7 ppg the following year. Rondo was a Louisville boy who averaged 8.1 ppg in '05 and 11.2 in '06.

Although some fans considered Smith a poor recruiter, he brought into the UK fold such noted performers as Tayshaun Prince and Keith Bogans, among others. His percentage of .760 ranks third behind only Rupp and Pitino. In his 10 seasons with Kentucky, he averaged more than 26 wins per season.

The only Kentucky natives to start for Smith were Scott Padgett, Patrick Sparks and Rajon Rondo. Padgett was a holdover from the Pitino era.

Sparks, Erik Daniels, Jason Parker, Marquis Estill, Chuck Hayes, Gerald Fitch, Randolph Morris, Patrick Patterson, Jodie Meeks and Rondo were Smith recruits.

1997-98 (35-4, 14-2 SEC)–Sheppard (13.7), Mohammad (12.0,

Padgett (11.5), and Edwards (11.2). Kentucky roared back from a 17-point deficit with 9:38 remaining to defeat Duke, 86-84, in St. Petersburg. They defeated Utah, 78-69, in the championship game.

1998-99 (28-9, 11-5 SEC)–Padgett (12.6), Heshimu Evans, (11.8), Turner (10.5), Michael Bradley (9.8), and Magliore (7.0).

1999-2000 (23-10, 12-4 SEC)–Tayshaun Prince, of Compton, Calif., (13.3); Jamaal Magliore (13.2), Keith Bogans, of Washington, D C. (12.5); Desmond Allison, of Tampa, Fla., (7.8), and Jules Camara, Dakar, (7.2).

2000-2001 (24-10, 12-2 SEC)–Bogans (17.0), Prince (16.9), Jason Parker, of West Charlotte, N, C., (8.8); Marquis Estill, of Richmond (7.3), and Saul **Smith,** of Lexington (6.8).

2001-2002 (22-10, 10-6 SEC)–Prince (17.5), Bogans (11.6), Estill (8.9), Gerald Fitch, of Macon, Ga., (8.9), and Cliff Hawkins of Dumfries, Va., (7.1).

2002-2003 (32-4, 16-0 SEC) – Bogans (15.7), Fitch (12.3), Estill (11.6) Erik Daniels (9.5), and Chuck Hayes (8.6).

2003-2004 (27-5, 13-3 SEC)–Fitch (16.2), Daniels (14.5), Kelenna Azubuike, of Tulsa, Okla., (11.1), Hayes (10.7), and Hawkins (10.3).

2004-2005 (28-6, 14.2 SEC)–Azubuike (14.7), Patrick Sparks, of Central City, (11.0); Hayes (10.9), Randolph Morris, of Atlanta, Ga., (8.8), and Rajon Rondo, of Louisville, (8.1). Rondo sets UK records for most steals (8 vs. Mississippi State) in a game and most per game (2.56).

2005-2006 (22-13, 9-7 SEC)–Morris (13.3), Rondo (11.2), Joe Crawford, of Detroit, (10.2); Sparks (9.7) and Ramel Bradley, of Manhattan, N. Y., (7.9)

2006-2007 (22-12, 9-7 SEC)–Morris (16.1), Crawford (14.0), Bradley (13.4), Jodie Meeks, of Norcross, Ga., (8.7), and Bobby Perry (8.4).

I like expectations. I like passion. That passion has enabled Kentucky to win the most games in college history, and hopefully that passion is going to help us win...Billy Clyde Gillispie, 2007.

At 12:45 p.m. on April 6, 2007, UK athletic director Mitch Barnhart announced Billy Clyde Gillispie as the new head coach of the Wildcats. During two years at Kentucky, Gillispie snagged numerous high profile recruits. These included three three-star recruits according to Scout.com: (Patrick Patterson, Daniel Orton & Dominique Ferguson).

Gillispie's first team got off to a rocky start, falling, 84–68, to unranked Gardner–Webb in Rupp Arena. The loss dropped the Wildcats from the AP Top 25 poll for the remainder of the season. They improved their record during conference play, achieving a 12–4 record The conference named Gillispie its Co-Coach of the Year along with Bruce Pearl of the Tennessee Volunteers.

Gillispie's Kentucky team opened the 2008–09 season with a loss to the Virginia Military Institute (VMI) Keydets, by a score of 111–103. Two weeks later, Gillispie led Kentucky to a 54–43 come-from-behind victory over West Virginia to win the Findlay Toyota Las Vegas Invitational championship. It was the first in-season tournament championship win for UK since the Great Alaska Shootout in 1996.

After a 5–0 start in the SEC schedule, Gillispie's team dropped three straight games to Ole Miss, South Carolina and Mississippi State. The latter two losses came at home. Some Kentucky fans booed Gillispie during the Mississippi State game.

Kentucky rebounded against the Florida Gators with a 68–65 victory at home. Jodie Meeks hit a contested fade-away three pointer with less than five seconds left to give Kentucky the lead.

The Wildcats also had two lopsided victories over SEC East regular season champion Tennessee. They defeated UNLV and Creighton before losing to Notre Dame in the NIT. Kentucky finished the year with an 8–8 record in conference play and 22–14 overall. They tied for the second-most losses ever in the program's history.

The University of Kentucky fired Gillispie on March 27, 2009. He listed Mark Krebs, of Newport; Kerry Benson, of Louisville, and Darius Miller, of Maysville as the only Kentucky boys signed during his two years in Lexington.

2007-2008 (18-13, 12-4 SEC)–Crawford (1.9), Patrick Patterson, of Huntington. W. Va., (16.4); Bradley (15.9), Meeks (8.8), and Perry Stevenson (5.9). The Wildcats lost to Marquette, 74-66, in the first round of the NCAA Tournament in Anaheim.

2008-09 (22-14, 8-8 SEC)–Meeks 23.7), Patterson (17.9), Stevenson (7.8), Ramon Harris, (5.5), and Miller, (5.3). The Wildcats defeated Drexel, 88-44, on Dec. 22nd to become the first college program to reach the 2,000-win mark. Jodie Meeks hit 15 of 22 shots and scored a school-record 54 points in a 90-72 win over Tennessee in Knoxville.

Chapter XIII

Coach Cal

*Kentucky's basketball program is in fact a tribute to a real-world system that works, preparing young people for a viable profession — in this case, professional athletics...***William C. Rhoden.**

On April 1, 2009, Mitch Barnhart introduced John Calipari as the new coach of the Wildcats. Calipari spoke at length about his relationships with former UK basketball players and coaches. He also expressed his difficulties in accepting the UK job, largely due to his deep emotional ties with both the city of Memphis and University of Memphis.

He referred to the University of Kentucky coaching position as his "dream job".

Calipari was the 22nd coach overall at Kentucky. He was just the 7th coach in the last 79 years for the Wildcats.

As a college coach, Calipari has 18 20-win seasons (17 official), eight 30-win seasons (7 official), and has been named National Coach of the Year three times.

He utilized a dribble-drive offense that emphasized speed and fine handling of the ball. His philosophy was that you win (1) with good players, (2) with good players, and (3) with more of the same.

Calipari inherited eight players from the previous year: Darius Miller, Darnell Dodson, Ramon Harris, Mark Krebs, Perry Stevenson, DeAndre Liggins, Patrick Patterson and Josh Harrellson. Krebs and Miller were the only in-state players in the group.

John Wall, a 6-4 point guard from Raleigh, N. C., headed Calipari's first crop of recruits. Many experts considered Wall the best high school player in the nation. Rivals.com ranked DeMarcus Cousins, 6-11, of Mobile, Ala., the second-best. Daniel Orton, 6-10, of Oklahoma City, ranked as third-best center. Rivals rated Eric Bledsoe, 6-1, of Birmingham, Ala., the nation's third-best point guard. Jon Hood, an All-State player from Madisonville, was the only Kentucky player Calipari signed.

That team finished 35-3, losing only at South Carolina and to Tennessee at Knoxville. They won both the season and tournament crowns and three NCAA games before falling to West Virginia, 73-66, in the NCAA Tournament.

John Wall became the first Wildcat named the No. 1 overall pick as Washington chose him in the NBA draft. UK had a record four other players drafted in the first round: DeMarcus Cousins, 5th by Sacramento; Patrick Patterson, 14th by Houston; Eric Bledsoe, 18th by Oklahoma City, and Daniel Orton, 29th by Orlando.

Calapari led the nation in recruiting for the second straight year in 2010-11. He brought Brandon Knight, Terrence Jones, Doron Lamb and Stacey Poole. Jr., into the UK fold. He also signed Jarrod Polson, of Nicholasville .

Knight was a 6-3 guard who averaged 32.5 ppg, 6.6 rebounds and four assists in his senior year at Pine Crest High in Ft. Lauderdale, Fla. He rated No. 4 overall in the nation. Jones was a 6-8 forward who averaged 30.0 ppg, 14.0 rpg and 6.0 assists at Jefferson High in Portland, Oregon. He was a member of the 2010 USA Team. Lamb averaged 23 points, six rebounds and four assists in his senior year at Oak Hill Academy in Mouth of Wilson, Va. Scout. com rated him third best shooting guard.

Knight led the 2010-2011 Cats in scoring with 17.3 points per game. They were SEC Tournament champs who finished 29-9 after losing to Connecticut, 66-65, in the Final Four.

Jones (15.7 ppg, 8.8 rpg) and Lamb (12.3 ppg) chose not to turn pro. They were joined by Calipari's third top recruiting class. It featured Anthony Davis, of Chicago; Marquis Teague, of Indianapolis; Michael Kidd-Gilchrist, of Somerdale, N. J., and Kyle Wiltjer, of Portland, Oregon. Other frosh signees were Brian Long, of Dumot, N. J.; Sam Malone, of Scituate, Mass, and Ryan Harrow, of Marietta, Ga.; They completed a roster that included Twany Beckham, of Louisville, who transferred from Mississippi State; Darius Miller, Jon Hood, Jarrod Polson, Stacey Poole, Jr. and Eloy Vargas. Hood sat out the season with an injury.

Davis was high scorer (14.2 ppg), rebounder (10.4) and shot blocker (186) on a 38-2 UK team that defeated Kansas for an eighth NCAA championship. The losses were to Indiana, 73-72, in Bloomington and to Vanderbilt, 71-64, in the SEC Tournament.

Davis was a 2012 NCAA Consensus First team All-American (unanimous).He was the 2011–12 NCAA Division I men's basketball season blocks leader. He established Southeastern Conference single-season blocked shots and NCAA Division I freshman blocked shots records.

Davis also earned the national Freshman, Defensive Player and Big Man awards. In addition, he was named the 2012 National Player of the Year by various organizations, earning the Oscar Robertson Trophy, the Adolph Rupp Trophy, the Associated Press Player of the

Year, Naismith Award, Sporting News Player of the Year and John R. Wooden Award.

He was the Southeastern Conference's player, freshman, and defensive player of the year. Davis helped lead Kentucky to an undefeated 2011–12 Southeastern Conference men's basketball season and was the NCAA Tournament Most Outstanding Player when Kentucky won the 2012 NCAA Men's Division I Basketball Tournament.

2009-10 (35-3, 14-2 SEC)–John Wall, of Raleigh, N. Car., (16.6); DeMarcus Cousins, of Mobile, Ala., (15.1); Patterson (14.3), Eric Bledsoe, of Birmingham, Ala., (11.3), and Darius Miller, of Maysville, (6.5).

2010-11)–(29-9, 10-6 SEC)–Brandon Knight (17.3), Terrence Jones (15.7), Deron Lamb (12.3), Darius Miller (10.9), and DeAndre Liggins (8.6). Calipari was the first coach to direct three different colleges to a No. 1 seed in the NCAA Tournament,

2011-12 (38-2, 16-0, SEC)–Anthony Davis, of Chicago, (14.2); Lamb (13.7), Jones (12.3), Michael Kidd-Gilchrist, of Somersdale, N. J. (11.9), and Marquis Teague, of Indianapolis (10.0).

2012-2013—Willie Cauley-Stein, Olathe, Kan.; Archie Goodwin, Little Rock, Ark.; Nerlens Noel, Everett, Mass., and Alex Poythress, Clarksville Tenn.

The contemporary style of Pitino and those who succeeded him–Tubby Smith, Billy Gillispie, and John Calipari–led many to wonder if Kentucky high school basketball would ever regain the type of national eminence it enjoyed when Rupp ruled the state.

Some partisan observers theorized that the time might come again when a team like Kentucky can stock its roster with small-town, in-state players.

"That's a pipe dream," Rick Pitino said.

Tradition

Chapter XIV

*What is it about basketball in Kentucky that endures from one generation to the next? A high school game lasts 24 minutes; a college game 40; players play for a few years and move on; coaches might last for a few more; but they all come and go. What lasts is the affection and the interests of fans, the ordinary Kentuckians whose hearts rise and fall a hundred times a season in perfect unison with their favorite team's fortune.…*From *Basketball in Kentucky: Great Balls of Fire..***Dave Kindred.**

Basketball succeeded in Kentucky partly because of the essentially rural nature of the state. Any hamlet large or small could afford a sport that equipped its players in scant uniforms, needing only a ball, a couple of goals, and a place to play. The early high schools, which played their state tournaments on the UK campus, played a major role in elevating the sport.

"Hoops were everywhere, fashioned from coat hangers, barrel rings, and bicycle wheels," Dave Kindred wrote after 11 years traveling through Kentucky, looking for basketball stories. *"They were nailed to trees, garages, telephone poles, work sheds, great white mansions, and a dog house in Hardinsburg. They came with new nets, no nets, ripped nets, nets of chain, nets of braided rope, red-white-and-blue nets, and just plain nets. Anyway, who needs nets? Ralph Beard, the greatest guard in Kentucky history, got his start by throwing a rubber ball into his potty chair."*

The obsession that Kentuckians have with basketball is a mystique that extends throughout all levels of life in the commonwealth. Early Wildcat rosters consisted mostly of Kentucky natives, due mainly to travel restrictions and the economics of the times. High school games provided a rallying point for communities throughout the state. Lexington fast became the Mecca of college basketball.

Basketball teams from small towns throughout commonwealth

beat a path to the tournaments in Lexington and Louisville before consolidation took its toll. UK was a prime beneficiary of this largesse, mining a wealth of talent and establishing a rich fan base.

Although the YMCA's and colleges established the early games, it was the rural Kentucky teams that gave it a flavor unique to the state. They turned the annual high school tournament into a ritual that featured a steady stream of basketball sharpshooters who would become modern-day heroes in the mold of the Daniel Boones, Davey Crockets, Jim Bowies, and other noted Kentuckians of pioneer days.

By the time Adolph Rupp arrived at the University of Kentucky in 1930, basketball already had replaced the long rifle as Kentucky's weapon of choice.

Although other colleges and universities played fine basketball and were building their own traditions, the

University of Kentucky emerged as "THE" state university, thanks to some fine early Wildcat teams that were composed mainly of Kentucky boys, and to the state high school tournament.

The tournaments attracted such little known schools as Carr Creek, Corinth, Kavanaugh, Tolu, Horse Cave, Nebo, Millersburg, Heath, Sharpe, Brooksville, Hazel Green, Hindman, Inez, and Dayton played in Alumni Gym.

The fear of losing the tournament to Louisville, which would happen a few times over the years, was a key argument for UK fans and officials seeking bigger and better arenas.

The arenas that the UK basketball teams have called home mirror the development of the game at the University of Kentucky and for a large part in the commonwealth, with each facility making its own unique contribution to the tradition. The Wildcats remained in their initial home-Buell Armory-12 years and then occupied Alumni Gym and Memorial Coliseum each for 26 years before moving to Freedom Hall and back to Rupp Arena.

In each instance, the demand for tickets was much greater than the available space as the popularity of the Wildcats and the game of basketball continued to grow.

Nowhere was the game more accepted than in eastern Kentucky, where UK Basketball reigns next to God and country in the hearts of most residents. It is a love affair started at an early age, and handed down from family to family.

Anyone familiar with the Appalachian culture can understand this phenomenon; basketball has been the main social outlet in towns throughout the area. Each small town and mining camp could afford the needs of a basketball team.

However, basketball in Kentucky is more than a rural game; it is one that expands to the cities and towns of all sizes. Wildcat basketball also knows no bounds, attracting fans as far as upstate New York, where tavern owner Bob Sherlock listened to broadcasts during the "Fabulous Five" era. He helped UK recruit Pat Riley from nearby Schenectady.

In 2011, Kentucky became the first program to post 2,000 basketball victories. The Wildcats have won eight NCAA and 45 SEC titles. They have produced 54 All-Americans, eight Olympians, and six members of the Basketball Hall of Fame. Kentucky holds records for the most NCAA tournament appearances and wins, most 30-win seasons. It has experienced just two losing season since 1927.

Kentucky leads the nation in home basketball attendance; its following of fans is legendary. When the Wildcats played in the 1997 Maui Classic, more than 1,000 fans joined them in Hawaii. They purchased every ticket available in the cramped gym

Thanks again to the Big Blue Nation for leading UK to its seventh straight attendance title and 16th in the last 17 years. Big Blue Nation has true meaning as an NCAA record total of 885,953 fans watched our 40 games this season, breaking Syracuse's record.

*I said it three years ago. During the season, it is about our team. You saw it in this year's team. They were about each other. It is about how we play together, how we share. When the season is over, it is about moments like this....***John Calipari.**

Wildcat fans embrace all wearers of the Blue & White. The players return in kind by continuing the steady flow of championships and All-Americans.

My genuine opinion of the Kentucky basketball program is that there is only one and it is top drawer, Park Avenue, and that all other basketball programs in the country think they are, but they are not. "The closest ones to get to it (Kentucky) are North Carolina, maybe Indiana, and UCLA. But at Kentucky, basketball is a type of religion, such a fanatical obsession that they expect to be national champion each year, and they live and die with each ball game.... Al McGuire, 1981

McGuire said he was not looking to throw a party for Kentucky. That was just the way he felt. He considered his an honest appraisal because he had seen all the programs, as a coach, a player, and as an NBC commentator.

In 1991, they buried a man from Pikeville with a card from mountain hero John Pelphrey in his casket. They buried an elderly woman with a UK basketball by her side. An autographed picture of the 1948 Wildcats accompanied another fan to the grave. A Hopkinsville widow left the team $42,000.

Simeon Hale, who was in his 90's, rode a bus approximately 200 miles from Pulaski County in rural Southeastern Kentucky to watch UK home games. Although he had a crippled leg, Hale walked from his place in the country to a road where he flagged a bus to Somerset. Then he caught a bus to Lexington He took a nap at the station until time for the game. Hale walked back to the station after the game. He slept on a bench there until three o'clock in the morning; then he rode a back to Somerset, a 24-hour ordeal.

A news distributor, Steve Rardin, attended 626 consecutive UK basketball games. A policeman changed the time of his wedding because it conflicted with a UK game. A New Yorker called for play-by-play accounts. A doctor gave up a lucrative practice in Western Kentucky and moved to Lexington in order to be close to the Wildcats.

Kyle Macy was a two-time All-America guard . He captained the 1980 Wildcats. Macy said UK was the only major college team with a tremendous following all over the state.

*When I was at Purdue, the state of Indiana was about evenly divided in its loyalty among Purdue, Indiana, and Notre Dame. Where else could a player get 100 to 200 letters a week from fans? Where else could a player have babies named after him?...**Kyle Macy***.

Those fans write poems and sings songs about the Wildcats. They bake cakes and cookies; they remember birthdays. Legislators introduce resolutions praising them. Governors and mayors declare days in their honor."

In Kentucky, the idea is not to let life interfere with basketball, That the game holds a higher office in Kentucky's value system than it does in other state is a fundamental fact that I accept on faith and certify after a year of close watching
… **Lonnie Wheeler, 1998.**

*Kentucky is bigger than the Yankees or the Cowboys. No other program is as loved and supported like Kentucky basketball...***Eddie Sutton...1986**

Sutton said it was not until after they had 11,000 fans at a midnight practice, packed houses at scrimmages, and 14,000 fans at a morning shooting practice in Louisville, that he realized the impact of the UK program.

Steve Rardin moved from Newport, to Lexington in 1946.

When he could not get a ticket to a UK game in Alumni Gym, he borrowed a student pass from a young man who worked for him. He purchased a little hat, and passed himself off as a student. He was 34 years of age at the time.

Rardin's attendance streak began after the Wildcats lost to Wisconsin on New Year's Eve in 1968, when he stayed home to attend a wedding. Ten years later, he spent more than $2,000 to take his daughter Amy with him to Anchorage for the Great Alaskan Shootout. The streak ended when Steve became ill during a UK-Indiana game in Indianapolis in 1999.

His traveling companion on many of those trips was Bob Wiggins, a retired employee of the state Department of Transportation. Bob sought a string of his own, which ended at 316 when he had a heart attack while packing for a trip with the team to Alaska in 1997. He immediately started another attendance streak.

Bob Wiggins

Dr. V. A. Jackson drove from Clinton to Lexington on the Saturday of a UK game. He remained for the Monday night game, and then drove back to Clinton. After Doc and his wife Marie eventually moved to Lexington, he paid his own way on the team plane, and for his lodging and meals. Joe B. Hall named Jackson team physician.

Gene Large, a Pineville native, is president of Class Productions of Nashville. He describes himself as probably the biggest Big Blue fan in Tennessee.

When Large visited the Hall home in March of 1981, he suggested a country music album featuring the UK coach. The result also featured songs by such non-country notables as A. B. Chandler, Al McGuire, Cawood Ledford, and Joe B's wife Katherine. The album included the three coaches singing "Elvira." Hall and McGuire teamed up on "The Gambler", Hall and Ledford sang, *On the Road*

Again. Joe B. and Katherine harmonized on *We Love Each Other So*.

"Happy" Chandler was a former Kentucky senator and gover-nor. He also served as baseball commissioner. He once coached the UK women's basketball team. It was a treat to hear him sing "My Old Kentucky Home" prior to a UK game.

Chandler drove nails in the Alumni Gym floor to commemorate record UK long shots. In 1967, Oscar Combs left the weekly pub-lishing business at Hazard in Perry County. He launched the Cat's Pause, a weekly that covers only UK sports. The venture was such a success that other schools adopted similar publications.

For every Steve Rardin, whose Kentucky Fried Chicken look was a favorite of every cameraman, there is a quiet Kentuckian profoundly attached to Kentucky basketball as the elderly cancer patient who received a pair of tickets behind the Wildcat bench and

just before he died wrote back to say his life was now complete, for every Tomb-stone Johnny, who gained a little fame when he drove 775 miles from Iowa to watch games in Rupp Arena, there is an anonymous Kentucky lover like the grandmother in Falmouth who had an icebox full of notebooks with the box score of every UK game for 45 years.
Lonnie Wheeler, *"Blue Yonder,*

Movie actress Ashley Judd is a na-tive of Ashland. She is a UK graduate, a Phi Kappa Delta nominee. Ashley has been a most visible fan at UK bas-ketball games Television seeks her out. Ashley once wrote a Sports Illustrated article about her devotion to UK bas-ketball.

A Matter of Pride*: People often ask me to try to explain why Kentuck-*

ians are so nutty about UK basketball. My guess is that it is because the commonwealth is so diverse, from the mountains to the east, where my family hails; to the central bluegrass, where we have the proud tradition of raising the world's best thoroughbreds; to the farmlands of the west. Basketball is one thing that unites us, something for which we can all be proud. An airline pilot once told my Nana that when he flies over Kentucky at night, he could tell when UK is playing because the roads are empty.

I have had so many wonderful memories over the years, but I will leave you with my most recent. It was March 7 and I was sick with bronchitis, but I made it to Rupp for Senior Day. During the first timeout of the second half, the UK cheerleaders spell out KEN-TUCKY, and a person from the crowd is asked to come out to make the Y. That day cheerleader Jason Keogh hoisted me onto his shoulder and carried me -- and the blue-painted cast on my left foot -- to midcourt. Before I was even introduced, I was given a standing ovation. It was the most extraordinary feeling. Back on Broadway, at that very moment, my play was closing without me, but I was getting the best curtain call of my life at Rupp from the people who mean so much to me: the people of Kentucky ...**Ashley Judd**.

"I'd just as soon freeze to death." --Actress Ashley Judd relating a story of being offered a University North Carolina--Chapel Hill jacket on a chilly movie set.--Lexington Herald- Leader, August 15, 1996.

Jerry Hale was a 12-year-old fan from Albany, Ind., in March, 1966. His father took him to a UK basketball game in Memorial Coliseum. At the end of the game, the Committee of 101 rolled out a large cake commemorating the university's record 1,000th. victory. Rupp invited everybody to come down and get a piece of history. Jerry wrapped a piece of the cake in a napkin. He carried it in his lap all the way to New Albany. He told his father he would eat the cake when he signed a scholarship to play basketball at the University of Kentucky.

Five years later, Jerry was a star player with Floyd Central High in New Albany. He accepted an offer of a scholarship from UK and immediately rescued the cake from the freezer.   J e r r y decided not to eat the cake until his UK team won an NCAAA championship.

The Cats went to the Final Four in San Diego in 1975, Jerry's senior year. His parents packed the cake in dry ice. They took it to California. Kentucky lost the championship, 92-85, to UCLA. By then, the cake was inedible in more ways than one.

Wally Clark and his folding chair of two decades ago started a trend that now has a virtual army of tent-dwellers wrapped around the Coliseum in order to get choice tickets for Midnight Madness. John Calipari and his UK players have delivered pizza's to the campers. The event itself has attracted national TV exposure.

Calipari hopefully started another tradition when he toured the state with the 2012 NCAA trophy. He was accompanied at times by the UK president, Joe B. Hall, Herky Rupp, and some others, including players.. Stops were made at Pikeville, Hazard, Frankfort, Elizabethtown, Owensboro, Paducah, Lexington and Louisville. Crowds everywhere admired the trophy.

"Son, what have you been doing lately?"

"Mom, I've written a book about Kentucky Football."

"Football! What about Basketball?"…Alpha Bowe Rice to son Russell, Wittensville, Ky., 1975.

Chapter XV
Turn Your Radio On

When the word "Kentucky" is spoken, it often evokes thoughts
of a bouncing basketball. The University of Kentucky epitomizes the
best of the sport–eight national championships and the most victories on record. With that success comes national exposure, which
includes nearly every game televised. The exposure each Wildcat
receives is not just as a college basketball player at the University of
Kentucky, but the best college basketball has to offer.. **Joe B. Hall,
Kentucky basketball coach (1973-85).**

Before radio game broadcasts, there was the teletype. When
Kentucky played Georgia in the 1921 championship game of the
SIAA Tournament in Atlanta, UK students and fans gathered at Lexington's Phoenix Hotel, where a telegraph operator stood by to receive news of the game.

In the early 1930s, WLAP aired Lexington's first sports radio program. The format featured interviews with the Kentucky football coach and coaches of the upcoming opponents.

The Graves-Cox Co., Lexington's leading men's clothing store at the time, sponsored the program. Paul Nickell, a salesman, convinced his friend, Adolph Rupp, the youthful Wildcat basketball coach, to serve as the interviewer.

"The program became so popular that people would stop dinner to hear Adolph," Nickell said. "He became known as the Will Rogers of Kentucky radio."

In lieu of pay, Nickell outfitted Rupp in the company's most expensive brown suit and matching accessories: brown hat, brown shirt, brown shoes, brown socks, and a brown tie.

"It was during my second year at Freeport that I bought me a fine-looking blue suit to replace that old brown thing that I had been wearing all the time I had been there. When we lost the game that night, with me wearing that new suit, I said, hey, this blue won't get it done. From then on I wore nothing but brown to my teams' games..." **Adolph Rupp, BBM.**

In 1935, WLAP broadcast several simulated accounts of out-of-town games from its studios in Lexington. Sportswriter Ed Ashford re-created the play-by-play from wire reports. An engineer provided sound effects. The state high school tournament also was broadcast for the first time that year. Rupp and

Cawood's Corner

Happy Chandler assisted Ashford on the microphone.

On March 7, 1935, WLAP aired the first live broadcast of a Kentucky basketball game. It was the season finale against Xavier in Alumni Gym. Kentucky won the game, 46-29.

J. B. Faulconer, a retired major general, became the first "Voice of the Wildcats". He joined WLAP after serving as senior manager of the Wildcat basketball team in 1939. Faulconer broadcast for the first time in 1940, doing football and not basketball. After returning from the army in 1946, he became the station's sports director. He worked the UK basketball and football games.

"We formed the Ashland Oil Network, which sometimes had as many as 40 stations," Faulconer recalled. "I started this business of having recordings before the game and after the game, both for Rupp and Bear Bryant. They mailed them to all the other stations."

During the postwar years, Lexington stations WLAP, WVLK, WLEX and WBKY and Louisville station WHAS carried the UK games. Claude Sullivan, a native of Winchester, became a legend at WVLK. He died of throat cancer in 1967.

Phil Sutterfield reached a large audience through WHAS (50,000 watts) and its network affiliates. He conducted Bear Bryant's popular radio shows.

In 1953, newly established WLEX-TV hired Cawood Ledford, of Harlan, as a sports commentator. On Sept. 10, Ledford worked his first UK game. It was a football loss to Texas A&M. By the sixth game, the station promoted him to play-by-play announcer. Three years later, Ledford joined the sports team at WHAS.

After Claude Sullivan's death, his wife Alyce kept the network together for one year before UK sold the broadcast rights. Ledford left WHAS that year (1968) and joined with Host to form Cawood Ledford Productions.

The G. H. Johnston Agency of New York City entered the high bid. They retained Ledford as play-by-play announcer. Jim Host & Associates entered the high bid in 1974. Host has been a major figure in UK sports broadcasts since that time. He is a member of the

UK Athletic Hall of Fame.

Cawood's style and professionalism endeared him to many sports fans. He retired as one of the most popular sports figures in the state. A section of the Memorial Coliseum floor bears the name "Cawood's Corner".

Ralph Hacker replaced his broadcast partner Ledford. Hacker and Cawood Ledford became known as one of the nation's premier collegiate broadcasting teams for their work with Kentucky football and basketball for 20 years. Hacker was the "voice" of the basketball Wildcats for nine years. He did the play-by-play for Kentucky football for five seasons.

Remembering The Runts: *Rupp began the 1965 -66 season with an unlikely collection of smallish players who would become, perhaps, the most loved team in the history of Kentucky basketball...* **Cawood Ledford, 1966.**

Remembering Cawood: *Cawood was the ultimate in genteel class. He exuded a quiet confidence, but always remembered who he was, where he came from, and who he worked for...* **Jim Host, CEO, Host Communications, 2001.**

Remembering Cawood: *When I was 23 years old and just starting out in the business, I used to sit around with the old-timers at P. J. Clarke's in New York and we'd discuss the top five pro players of all time, top five college players of all time. Inevitably, we'd get around to the best announcers ever and it would always come down to two--Marty Glickman and Cawood Ledford. So, I knew the name Cawood Ledford long before I came to Kentucky. He lived up to all my expectations, not only as an announcer but as a person.* **Rick Pitino, 1992.**

Remembering Cawood: *I was saddened upon hearing of the passing of legendary broadcaster Cawood Ledford. He was one of the real giants in the sport of college basketball. He was so unique and so special. His voice was synonymous with Kentucky basketball. When you think about the pieces that made up the tradition of the Wildcats' program, Cawood Ledford was an important one.*

*People all over the state would stop what they were doing to listen to his broadcasts. His style sold Kentucky basketball. He had a special passion for college hoops and that passion was demonstrated by the way he described the game. You could feel that emotion as you listened to him...***Dick Vitale, 2001.**

Remembering the Audience*: I've always felt that in broadcasting your total allegiance is to the person twisting the dial and giving you the courtesy of listening to you. Sports are the greatest drama in the world because no one knows what's going to happen. And it's your job to paint a word picture...* **Cawood Ledford, 2001.**

Cawood meant as much to fans of Kentucky football and basketball as anyone ever has, **Tubby Smith, UK basketball coach (1998-2007).**

*First of all, Cawood is one of the finest men I've ever known. In his own dignified way, he found ways to educate me in areas that I needed it. There are some people who have the ability to help others without being pushy or offensive, and Cawood had that kind of tact...***Bill Curry, UK football coach (1990-96).**

Remembering Cawood: Cawood and I were island-hopping Marines during WWII. We never discussed those days...*Russell Rice.**

Fans Remember Cawood: *My fondest memories of UK basketball involve my family. My love for UK came from my father. Growing up, I shared many special times with my dad, as we listened to Cawood Ledford and kept score at home. I have passed that love on to my sons. We have many special memories of watching UK on TV, as well as attending numerous games at Rupp Arena and at two NCAA Final Fours. I know my father would be so thrilled to see his son and two grandsons carrying on the family tradition. The love for UK basketball is truly a family tradition passed on from generation to generation...* **Kevin Collins, Mason, Ohio.**

I guess my best memories are too many to describe so, I would simply say Cawood Ledford was my fondest memory as a young boy growing up in Hazard, Ky. I would listen on my transistor radio and dream of someday being a Wildcat and hearing that wonderful man calling my name. That didn't happen, but I still dream of being a Wildcat every time it gets time for the snow to fly even though I'm 49 years old. That little

Cawood Ledford and Ralph Hacker.

boy comes out in me, I guess, Cawood, I know you are watching and listening and the snow is getting ready to fly again as you would say and our Wildcats are starting their journey for another champion-ship and until the flowers bloom in the spring I know you will enjoy another great season. Tell coach Rupp hello for all Wildcat fans. Go Big Blue... **Vaughn Hall, Newport, Ky.**

Basketball in Kentucky gives the populace something to put on a pedestal. In Kentucky, basketball players are our royalty. Cawood Ledford, in addition to near-flawless with his call of the game, he was to UK fans, key to the mythical kingdom... **Pat Forde, Courier-Journal.**

Cawood Says Goodbye: Fittingly, his finale was arguably the greatest game in college basketball history, the classic Duke-Kentucky East Region Final in Philadelphia. After one of the most popular teams in UK history lost the heartbreaking 103-102 overtime thriller, Ledford signed off to countless fans with words he borrowed from legendary UK coach Adolph Rupp upon his own retirement: *"For those of you who have gone down the glory road with me, my eternal thanks. This is Cawood Ledford saying goodbye, God bless, and goodnight everybody."*

The University of Kentucky basketball team's first television appearance occurred in the 1951 NCAA eastern finals when their wins over St. John's and Illinois were televised nationally from Madison Square Garden.

The old *Tonight Show* aired portions of a UK game with Loyola in Chicago Stadium on Feb. 15. 1957, as part of a salute to Coach Rupp. NBC's *"Game of the Week"* series in 1958/59 featured UK wins over St. Louis, LSU, and Tennessee. An ABC-TV series in 1961 aired UK's win over Georgia Tech in Memorial Coliseum.

During that era, a young law school graduate named Eddie Einhorn founded TVS Television Network. It became the leading syndicate of sports programs in the 1970s, which helped give rise to the popularity of college basketball on television.

When Einhorn televised UK's 1962 game with Georgia Tech in Atlanta, he urged UK fans to send in donations, even if just for a dollar, to help pay for the transmission. Since those "pioneer" days, the Wildcats have become regulars on coast-to-coast telecasts. In addition to the SEC series, ESPN, Fox, and other networks, the University created its own TV network, which airs on a delayed basis games not televised otherwise.

During the 2002/2003 season, all the UK games were televised either live or delayed. The Wildcats appeared on national television in 21 of their 36 games. That included 10 times on ESPN and 11 times on CBS. Fox Sports South and/or JP Sports regionally televised 11 games.

Chapter XVI
Appalachian Section

The Appalachian Region Commission lists the following 54 counties as comprising the Appalachian Region of Kentucky: Adair, Bath, Bell, Boyd, Breathitt, Carter, Casey, Clark, Clay, Clinton, Cumberland, Edmonson, Elliott, Estill, Fleming, Floyd, Garrard, Green, Greenup, Harlan, Hart, Jackson, Johnson, Knott, Knox, Laurel, Lawrence, Lee, Leslie, Letcher, Lewis, Lincoln, McCreary, Madison, Magoffin, Martin, Menifee, Metcalfe, Monroe, Montgomery, Morgan, Nicholas, Owsley, Perry, Pike, Powell, Pulaski, Robertson, Rockcastle, Rowan, Russell, Wayne, Whitley, and Wolfe. Boys from those counties who played basketball at the University of Kentucky were as follows:

Bath County (Owingsville)

Dan Swartz 12/25/31–4/15/1997, Fr., (1952). Swartz scored 881 points in his senior year (1950-51) at Owingsville, more than any other high school player. That gave him a three-year total of 2,088 points. Knee problems three games into the season spoiled his chances of breaking Wah Wah Jones' national scoring record.

Swartz played seven games as a freshman at UK before transferring to Morehead State. He played one season as a member of the Boston Celtics team that defeated the Los Angeles Lakers in the 1963 NBA Finals.

Swartz was the Bath County sheriff during the late 1970s and early1980s. He later served as a field representative for U.S. Rep. Scotty Baesler.

Bell County (Pineville)

Max Glickman, 11/9/1897–5/10/1921, 1L, (1918). Glickman appeared in nine UK basketball games in 1918. He transferred to Columbia and was a soldier when he died in May 1921. He was 23 years of age.

Bobby Slusher, Lone Jack 11/18/1938, 1L, (1959). In 1957, Slusher scored 83 points–32 field goals, 19 free throws–as Lone Jack defeated Pineville. He made All-Conference, All-District, All-Regional, and third-team All-America (Parade Magazine). He was second-leading scorer for the East in the annual East-West game.

Slusher scored 165 points and grabbed 117 rebounds, with a high game of 23 points, as a UK sophomore. He transferred to Cincinnati.

Larry Pursiful, Four Mile, 3L, (1960, 61, 62). Pursiful was an All-State guard who scored 750 points in his final high school year. He averaged 19.1 points in nine UK freshman games. Pursiful ranked third in scoring in 1961 with 375 points. They named him to the All-UKIT team. He scored 497 points his senior year, finishing second to sophomore Cotton Nash. Pursiful also dished out 70 assists. He hit 80.4 percent of his free throws, which ranks eighth on UK's career list. He also made the 1962 All-Regional team and the All-SEC team.

Pursiful played briefly with the Phillips 76ers of the old National Industrial League. He currently is a minister of outreach for the Westport Baptist Church in Louisville.

Remembering Rupp: *Coach Rupp expected you to perform to perfection. I knew that coming in. I had no problem with that...* **Larry Pursiful, 2000**.

Remembering Pursiful. *Every time the boy shoots the ball, I think it is going into the basket. My problem is trying to get him to shoot more...***Adolph Rupp 1962**.

Robert Mayhall, Middlesboro, JV, (1974), Mayhall was a 6-8, 220 lb. center who led Middlesboro High to two district titles and a regional championship. He made All-District, All-Regional, and All-SEHC MVP. Mayhall quit the UK team after a limited appearance as a member of the junior varsity.

Ashland (Boyd County)

George Zerfoss NA–8/28/50, 2L, (1916, 18), starred in basketball and football at Ashland High. After earning a basketball letter at UK in 1916, he served in the military during World War II. Zerfoss returned to a starting role at forward on the 1918 UK basketball team. He was an end on the 1919 UK football team that finished 9-8-1. George's brothers Karl and Tom also played basketball for the Wildcats.

Karl Zerfoss, 8/31/1893–11/30/1984, 3L, (1913, 15, 16), earned three letters each in football and basketball and one in track at UK. He served as captain of the 1916 Wildcat basketball team. He was a retired professor of psychology at George Williams College.

Tom Zerfoss, 6/15/1895–8/5/1988, (1984, 1L, (1914). After playing one year of basketball at UK, Zerfoss played both basketball and football at Vanderbilt. He was a first lieutenant in France during World War I. Zerfoss received his medical degree at the Vanderbilt School of Medicine in June 1922. He was Vanderbilt's athletic director from 1940-1944.

Frank P. Phipps, 4/15/1905–9/16/1079, 1L, (1927), starred in basketball and football at Ashland High. He received one letter in basketball and three in football at UK. He started all 16 games and scored 55 points for the 1927 basketball Wildcats. Phipps was K-Man of the Year in 1967. He was a retired director of law enforcement with the state Fish and Wildlife Resources. Phipps also worked with the Public Information Department.

Remembering Basil: *I was a senior when the university hired Basil Hayden as our basketball coach. Most of the good players from the 1926 team had graduated. We opened with five football players starting and one (me) as first sub. Cincinnati beat us 48-10. We won only three games, beating Vanderbilt once and Centre twice. I scored 10 points against Vanderbilt and 11 against Centre, which was unusual in those days of low-scoring games. We were all glad to see that season (3-13) end. I read later where Basil said Rupp was* *famous for winning and he was famous for losing...***Frank Phipps, Paintsville, 1974).**

Ellis Johnson, 8/8/1910-8/5/1990, 3L, (1931, 32, 33), led Ashland's unbeaten 1928 basketball team to the championship of the Kentucky and National high school tournaments. They won 44 straight games before losing to Portsmouth, Ohio. Johnson was the quarterback of three undefeated Tomcat football teams that won or shared the state championship. He was the first UK athlete to letter in four sports–baseball, basketball, football and track. Johnson led the Wildcats to their first national championships under Rupp.

Johnson was All-Southern Conference, All-SEC, and All-SEC Tournament. He became Rupp's second All-American in 1933. Johnson was a charter member of the Kentucky Sports Hall of Fame. He was the first person inducted into the Ashland Sports Hall of Fame. Johnson played baseball in the minor leagues; a football injury forced him to give up the sport.

Remembering Rupp: *Asked why we should hire him, Rupp replied that he was the best d----coach there was, and we believed him...***Ellis Johnson, BBM, 1976.**

Joe Frank Rupert, Catlettsburg, 7/24/1912–2/5/1996, 1L, (1933), starred in basketball, football, and track at Catlettsburg High. He earned three letters in football and only appeared in one basketball game at UK. He also ran track, and was a Navy veteran of World War II. Rupert retired in 1984 as chairman of the board of Rupert-Hager-Crowell Agency in Ashland.

Bert "Man O' War" Johnson, 2/18/12–8/10/1993, Sq., (1935), was an outstanding athlete at Ashland High. He played basketball briefly at UK in 1934-35. His freshman football coaches at UK were Adolph Rupp and Brinkley Barnett. Bert was the father of future UK basketball player Phil Johnson. He played professional football for Brooklyn, Chicago, St. Louis, and Philadelphia. Johnson was a Brown & Williamson Tobacco Co. employee.

Ed Tierney, 10/16/1912–5/29/1980. 29 1L, (1935), was a member of the 1935 UK team that lost a controversial decision to NYU,

23-22, in the school's first appearance in Madison Square Garden.

Earl "Brother" Adkins, 8/13/1933, 3L, (1955, 57, 58), earned All-State honors in basketball while setting the school's all-time career scoring record at Ashland High. He was Kentucky's "Mr. Basketball" following an outstanding performance in the North-South Classic at Murray in 1953. Adkins also earned honorable-mention All-State honors in football at Ashland.

An injury kept Adkins out of action at UK during his sophomore season. He lettered in basketball the following two years. Adkins was a member of UK's "Fiddlin Five." He taught and coached in Union County.

Remembering Earl: *In November of 2008, the University of Kentucky and Seattle played an exhibition basketball game to commemorate the 50th anniversary of the 1958 championship game. Players from both teams congregated in Lexington for a reunion. Some of the players received watches for having won a national title. Others got a medallion. They questioned why they had no championship ring to represent their crowning sports achievement.*

*Earl Adkins arranged for purchase of the rings through former Wildcat guard Mike Casey, who was a sales representative for the Balfour company. ...***Vern Hatton.**

Remembering Earl: *I will never forget one night at Vanderbilt. Our starters were in foul trouble and Rupp put Earl in the game. He got 23 points the second half. Coach Rupp said it was probably the best substitution he ever made.* **Harry Lancaster, 1979.**

Larry Conley, 1/22/44, 3L, (1964, 65, 66), led Ashland to the 1961 KHSAA championship and to the final game in 1962. He made All-Tournament both years. Conley was a first-team Parade All-American his senior season. He joined a UK freshman team that included Tom Kron, a guard from Owensboro by way of Tell City, Ind., and Mickey Gibson of Hazard.

Conley was the first player to lead UK in assists three straight years. His 3.2 assists per game ranks ninth on the UK all-time list. Conley also lettered in baseball at UK. He made the Academic All-

America team in 1966.

Larry was a son of former Ashland coach George Conley.

He worked for the General Electric Credit Corp. in Atlanta. Larry became a television basketball broadcaster.

Remembering Rupp: *When we were on the road, most people would reach for the sports pages. Coach Rupp would reach for the Wall Street Journal.*

*On the first day of practice my freshman year, I was weighing in at a scrawny 168 pounds. Coach Rupp strolled over to the scales and said, "Conley, you had a pretty good high school career. Who's the better coach, me, or that feller who coached you up at Ashland?" I made the mistake of hesitating before giving my answer, and Rupp just shook his head in amazement and muttered, "Damn, son, you've got a lot to learn."...***Larry Conley, 2002.**

Remembering Larry: *There has never been a smarter player than Larry Conley. He played basketball all his life. His daddy, George, was a fine high school coach who lived and died basketball. Larry wasn't strong. He was frail, but he was a fine basketball player. He was a good shooter and despite his lack of size was a good rebounder. He was a great passer and had great anticipation both on offense and defense. Larry Conley was the type of kid you would want for a son..***Harry Lancaster, 1979.**

Remembering Texas Western (UTEP 72, UK 65): *Larry Conley came down with the flu between Iowa City and Lexington and wasn't able to practice. He was a very sick young man that night in Maryland when we lined up to play Duke. We ranked number one and Duke was number two. It was a real tough game, but we finally pulled it out 83-79 to move into the finals the next night against Texas Western. We worked with Conley much of the night and he seemed improved, but still weak when we got to the gym to play the next evening. Then came the jolt of the whole tournament. We were ready to go out on the floor when we discovered Pat Riley had a badly infected toe. He hadn't told us and the trainer hadn't said a word about it to us. Larry was sick, Pat was hurting; Texas Western* *had a good team. They beat us 72-65. It was a bitter pill to swallow...Harry Lancaster, 1979.*

John T. Craig, 5/7/1914–8/29/1969, Sq., (1914), starred in football, baseball, basketball and track for the Ashland Tomcats during the early 1930s. He was named to the 1933 and 1934 Kentucky All-Star basketball squads and to the 1933 All-State football roster. Craig played basketball at UK in 1914. He served with the US Army Air Corps during WW II. He operated a charter fishing vessel in Cape Canaveral, FL.

Clint Wheeler, 1L, (1971), was All-State at Ashland High, where he scored 1,300 points and averaged 17 rebounds a game. He scored 31 points in 27 games during his three varsity years at UK. The Wildcats were SEC champions each of those years. His brother Bill played football at UK. Clint is a pharmaceutical sales representative.

Benny Spears, Sq., (1968), gained second-team All-State honors on an Ashland team that lost to Male in the quarterfinals of the 1966 State Tournament. He averaged 4.3 points as a UK freshman, with a high game of 15 versus the Tennessee freshmen. Spears played one game as a sophomore at UK.

Breathitt County (Jackson)

Bob Stamper, Sq., (1945), was a native of Grayson who played basketball at Jackson High. He played freshman ball at UK in 1944 and was a member of the 1945 team. Stamper was a self-employed dental lab technician in Lexington.

Casey County (Liberty)

Don Branson, Yosemite, 6/18/1882–2/19/1970, (2L, 1905–1906). Branson played on UK's first official basketball team. He also lettered in football and track. He was a Major in the U.S. Army and served for 27 years. He served in the Philippine Constabulary from 1907 to 1915 and was a member of the Philippine Club. He was an instructor in ROTC at OSU and while there won the Hearst Trophy with the University Rifle Team. He was Director of Civilian Defense for Franklin County, 1942-1944. He was an honorary member of both the Scabbard and Blade and the Pershing Military Fraternity.

Nathaniel Buis, 12/22/1924–3/2/2000, 1L, (1944), played basketball three years at Liberty High and two years at Lindsay Wilson Junior College. He played a reserve role at UK in 1943 and 1944, scoring 31 points in 12 games. Buis was a chemical engineering major.

Clark County (Winchester)

Charles Alberts, 2L, (1925, 26), was a reserve on a Wildcat basketball team that was13-8 in 1925. They defeated Centre 39-10 for the state championship.

Henry Carlisle Besuden, 9/12/1904-12/31/1985, 1L, (1926). After graduating from the old Clark County High School in 1923, Besuden attended the University of Kentucky, majoring in agriculture. He played center on UK's basketball team during the 1925-26 season. In 1965, Besuden became one of 30 athletes at that time to receive the Centennial Athletic Medallion.

Remembering Besuden--President Reagan sent a telegram to Besuden when he was honored in 1983. "Through the years, you have played an important part in developing the agricultural resources of your area," the telegram said. "Your accomplishments in this field have improved the economic climate of your state and strengthened the farming system of your fellow citizens.

Gayle Mohney, 6/3/1906-7/25/1980, 1L, (1926). Born in Somerset, Mohney later moved to Winchester. He was leading scorer (11.1 ppg) on the 1926 UK basketball team. Mohney scored 200 points in two years as a Wildcat. He also was a star quarterback on the UK football team. One of his proudest moments came in 1925 when he kicked a field goal that beat Tennessee, 23-20.

Linville Puckett, 7/27/33, 1L, (1954), played five years of high school ball with the Clark County five in Winchester. He participated in four Sweet 16 tournaments and led the Cardinals to the state championship in 1951. He was an All-State selection three straight years. Puckett remains ranked in the top five in many State Tournament records. He scored 47 points in a Sweet 16 game.

Puckett was a starting guard on UK's undefeated 1954 basketball team. He scored 123 points in 24 games. Puckett scored 136 points in 14 games as a junior before transferring to Kentucky Wesleyan.

After a second loss to Georgia Tech midway of the 1954-55 season, the UK players objected to a Rupp ruling that they remain in Lexington during the semester break. He threatened to take away their tickets for an upcoming game with DePaul if they did not report to practice. During the turmoil, Puckett quit the team. He retired in December 2003 from the Department of Transportation in Frankfort.

Remembering UK: *I enjoy participating in basketball as much as anybody in the world does. However, basketball in Kentucky is not regarded as a game, but as a matter of life or death, with resemblance of going to war*...**Linville Puckett, 1955.**

Remembering Rupp: *My leaving wasn't Rupp's idea. It wasn't a problem with Adolph and me as much as with the team. When I left, he took my No. 3 from the rafters; I don't think he should have done that*...**Linville Puckett, 1955.**

Lindle Castle, Sq., (1950). After starring in Winchester, Castle scored 123 points for an 8.8 average as a UK freshman.

Tom Harper, 1L, (1964), was an All-State player who averaged 25.7 points in his senior year at Clark County High. He scored a school-record 919 career points. As a UK freshman, Harper started 17 of 18 games and averaged 16.7 points with a high game of 32 versus Tennessee. He saw limited action during the remainder of his UK career.

Harper is a realtor in Richmond, KY.

Clay County (Manchester)

Richie Farmer, 8/25/1969, 4L, (1989, 90, 91, 92). Farmer was the only player in KHSAA history to appear in five Sweet 16 state basketball tournaments. He led Clay County to state runner-up finishes in 1985, '86, and the state championship in 1987. He was the tournament's MVP two years in a row (1986 and 1987). Farmer was Kentucky's "Mr. Basketball" his senior year. He scored 51 points on Alan Houston, a 6-6 high school All-American who later played for Tennessee. Farmer's figures still rank among State tournament leaders in several categories.

Farmer closed his four-year UK career with 898 points, 184 rebounds, and 184 assists. He scored 24 points against Notre Dame in 1992, grabbed seven rebounds vs. Vanderbilt in 1990, and dished out nine assists vs. Louisville in 1989. His six straight free throws in the waning moments gave UK a 100-95 win over LSU in 1990. Farmer led UK in free throw percentage with 84.7% in 1990 and 84.2% in '91. Farmer was a member of UK's 1992 "Untouchables", and of the high school and UK Athletic Halls of Fame. He went into sports marketing and financial planning before becoming Kentucky's Secretary of Agriculture. He was an unsuccessful candidate for lieutenant governor in 2010.

Remembering Rick: *When Coach Pitino got the job, he called me in Manchester to tell me what he expected of me. I read later where he said we talked for 12 minutes and he only understood two minutes of what I said. Well, I only understood about 30 seconds of* *what he said. Manchester and Manhattan just don't speak the same language...***Richie Farmer, 1992.**

Remembering Richie: *Richie's just a country boy at heart. He chews tobacco and loves to go hunting and fishing. He got a shotgun for Christmas, and his New Year's resolution was to learn how to turkey shoot.*

*He once told me, "Coach, you always know where you stand with these people. If they like you, they'll give you the shirt off their backs. If they hate you, they'll kill you."...***Rick Pitino, Full-Court Pressure, 1992.**

Ray Mills, 9/26/33, 3L, (1955, 56, 57), was an All-District, All-Region, and All-State basketball player who helped Clay County to State Tournament appearances in 1952 and 1953. In his junior year, Clay County became the first mountain team to win the title in 31 years. Mills received a broken jaw in a collision with Johnny Cox just before his senior season at UK. Wearing a protective mask, he played in all but seven games that season. Mills scored 262 points and 316 rebounds in 67 games as a Wildcat. He retired as a teacher in Monticello.

Estill County (Irvine)

Guy Strong, 6/15/30, 2L, (1950, 51), was an All-State selection who led Irvine to its only appearance in the Sweet Sixteen in 1948. He also led the baseball team to the State Tournament, and once pitched and won both games of a doubleheader during the regional tournament. Strong was a member of the University of Kentucky's 1951 NCAA championship basketball team. He won two baseball letters before transferring to Eastern Kentucky.

Remembering Rupp: *He was a master psychologist. He was great at knowing what to say and when to say it. After I got into coaching, I had a lot better understanding of why he did some of the things he did.*

You did not challenge Coach Rupp. You didn't do your thing; you did his thing. One of the things that set him apart was that a star player had to learn his system of play. He didn't adapt to the star player... **Guy Strong, 1965.**

Fleming County (Flemingsburg)

Crittenden Blair, Ewing, 8/21/1908–5/6/1994, 1L, (1934). Dr. Blair earned a varsity letter on the UK basketball team that finished the 1934 season, 16-0, and suffered an upset loss to Florida, 38-32, in the SEC tournament. During World War II, he served with the Army in England, France, and Germany as commander of the 536th Quartermaster group. He retired as a colonel in the Army Reserves.

Dr. Blair conducted his practice in dentistry in Flemingsburg for 27 years. He was instrumental in bringing the Randall Textron Manufacturing Company and the U.S. Shoe Corporation to Flemingsburg. He served as chairman of the Fleming County Board of Education for 22 years.

William Clay Evans, 3/8/34–8/7/2000, Sq., (1954), played in seven games at UK in 1954 before he transferred to Morehead. He was a teacher, basketball coach and school administrator in the Fleming County school system. He retired as a retired agency manager for State Farm Insurance.

Floyd County (Prestonsburg)

William Sturgill 7/31/24, 2L, (1945, 46), won county, district and regional honors for two consecutive years at Prestonsburg High School. He played varsity basketball at Berea College before transferring to UK. Sturgill was sixth-leading scorer on the 1945-46 Wildcat team that was 22-4, winning the SEC regular and tournament championships. He and his brother Barkley were teammates the following year as UK finished 28-2. The Wildcats won the NIT and repeated as SEC overall champions. Sturgill thrived as an east

Kentucky businessman and coal operator. He has served UK in many capacities, including UK board chairman. The Sturgill Development Building is part of his legacy.

Barkley Sturgill, 7/14/1928, 1L, (1946), was a sophomore on the 1946 UK team that also featured his brother Bill. Barkley practiced law for more than 50 years in Prestonsburg. He practiced before the U.S. Court of Appeals, Sixth Circuit and the U.S. District Court, Eastern District of Kentucky. Barkley served as the county attorney for Floyd County. He also was chair of the Kentucky Public Service Commission. Sturgill sat as a member of the Big Sandy Community and Technical College Board of Directors, the Eastern Kentucky Economic Development Commission, the Kentucky Crime Commission and the Big Sandy Area Development District Board of Directors.

Lowell Hughes, NA 2L, (1958, 59), rewrote a majority of his brother Delmar's high school records at Prestonsburg. He was football All-State two years and basketball All-State one year. Lowell earned three letters as a quarterback and two in basketball at UK. He was a member of the 1958 "Fiddlin' Five" team (23-6) that won the NCAA championship; UK finished 24-3 the following year. Lowell served many years as an attorney in Ashland. He served two terms in the Kentucky State Senate. Lowell retired to Ocala, Fla.

Remembering Rupp: *We were ahead by 25 points or so at halftime. As the second half started, we immediately increased the lead to put the game all the way out of reach. I had been running as the second or third substitute but because the games never seemed to be in doubt, had not been getting much playing time. With about 16 or 17 minutes remaining in the second half, the K-Men's section of the Coliseum, which was composed basically of our football players, began chanting, "We want Hughes." They kept this up for an extended period.*

Coach Rupp began substituting and every time he would substitute the chant would go up again, "We want Hughes." After every substitute was in the game with the exception of myself, only about a minute and a half remained. Coach Rupp said, "Hughes, you can go in now. You be sure and tell your oblong football players that I coach this team and that they cost you about fifteen minutes of playing time tonight."

*Coach Rupp even took this matter up with Coach Collier for the assurance that the coach's football players would no longer attempt to contribute to coaching the basketball team...***Lowell Hughes, BBM.**

Larry Hall, Martin NA, Fr., (1966), was an All-State guard who led Martin to the 1965 State Tournament. He hit 52 percent of his shots, averaged 22 ppg, and grabbed 15 rebounds a game. Hall left UK after his freshman year.

Bob Tallent, 4/26/1946, Langley, 1L, (1966), scored 891 points in 22 games for a 40.5 ppg average at Maytown High, good for second in the state. His high point as a senior was 51 points. Tallent compiled a four-year total of 2,337 points. He was All-State and third-team All-America. He was class valedictorian and a straight-A student.

Tallent served as captain of UK's 1965 freshman team. He averaged only 3.0 points in 18 games his sophomore year. He scored 13 game-saving points in an 89-73 win over Texas Tech in Lubbock. That UK team, known as "Rupp's Runts", finished 32-2 after losing to Texas Western in the NCAA championship game.

The following year, Rupp dismissed Tallent from the team following a dispute after a loss to Tennessee.

Remembering Tallent: *When Red is having a hot night as he did in that second half against Texas Tech, you could put a lid on the basket and he'd still score. His statistics, which were spotty because he played so much in relief, hid the fact last year that this boy is one of the finest shooters the hills have ever produced. ..Adolph Rupp.*

Tallent Played one superb season (1969) at George Washington after transferring from Kentucky. He set single season marks for scoring average (28.9), field goals (284), field goals attempted (677), and consecutive free throws (41). Tallent later coached the

Colonials for seven seasons. He is a member of the GW Athletic Hall of Fame. GW named Bob and his brothers Mike and Pat among 23 men to its All-Century team.

Remembering Rupp: *We could have had a very good season in 1967. We lost five or six close games. I'm a coach now, and I know when things start going wrong you want to blame the players. Adolph tried to find someone to blame. He tried to use me after I was injured. I finally lost my temper after something happened and said a few things, and it was all over.*

It wasn't that I was a bad player. It all started with that injury. I was the second leading scorer up to then. He always got after me for losing the ball, but I said I handled it 80 percent of the time. He said when you have to take criticism and can't, go sit on the bench.

I would love to have a team that could handle the ball like his teams. I may disagree with his handling of players, but his system was great. His game plans were great. We tried to copy that at George Washington.

Kids change and as the years go on it gets a little harder. I would just about do anything my coaches said, but now the kids ask why? You have to come up with reasons. Rupp treated everyone the same. He had no pets. He was just as hard on Riley and Dampier as on the rest of us.

*He put so much pressure on you in practice, if you didn't take it, you weren't tough enough to play for him. That's not a bad philosophy, if you've got the players. Besides, Adolph's players were normally from Kentucky and Indiana. There was no internal friction. They didn't have black athletes. Now, you have inter-city youths, black kids from the country, Jewish kids, and all mixtures. It takes a lot more today to keep harmony….****Bob Tallent, 1975.****

Remembering Rupp: *Someone else was impressed, too. Coach Rupp stopped the scrimmage, walked out to the free throw circle, gathered the team around him and said, "Son, I've been coaching* *this game for over 30 years, and that's the best exhibition of shooting I've ever seen."* Then, he got on the first string for not figuring out how to stop Bob from getting the shot....**Glenn Goble. "Sea of Blue."**

Pete Grigsby, Martin, NA (1954). Grigsby was an All-State guard who scored 2,543 points during five seasons (one as an eighth grader) at Martin High School. He was a reserve on Rupp's undefeated 1953-54 UK basketball team. Grigsby also played baseball at UK. He finished his college career at Kentucky Wesleyan, where he also lettered 2 years in baseball.

Grigsby coached high school basketball and averaged more than 20 wins a season. He also served as superintendent of Floyd County Schools,

Remembering Rupp: *As a substitute on the bench during UK's 71-59 win in St. Louis in December 1953, I witnessed UK assistant Harry Lancaster slug Pat Hickey, son of Billiken coach Ed Hickey, for firing a timer's gun too close to his leg. Officials soon restored order. Lou Tsioropoulos fouled out. The fans started getting on him, shouting some nasty stuff. Lou gave them a one-finger salute. Women with high-heeled shoes came down behind our bench and started kicking us in the back and hitting us with their umbrellas. We hadn't done a thing, we weren't even playing, and yet we were getting whipped. I was never so glad for a game to end.*

In the locker room after the game, Coach Rupp instructed us to not even take showers and to just put our street clothes in our duffle bags, put overcoats on over warm-ups, and hustle out to some waiting taxicabs he had just called to the arena. I don't know if he was worried the fans were going to storm our locker room, but we did as he said.

I remember squeezing in beside the driver in the front of a taxi. Coach Rupp was in the back on the passenger side, and as we got about halfway back to the hotel, the taxi driver started talking about what a dirty team Kentucky was. I didn't know what was going to

*happen, but then Coach Rupp started agreeing with everything the guy was saying. Coach said, "You're right, those Kentucky boys are mean as rattlesnakes. They shouldn't be allowed to play college basketball". I'm sure the guy never had an inkling he was carrying some of those dirty Kentucky players and the coach that St. Louis fans loved to hate....*Pete Grigsby to Denny Trease. 2002.

Jimmy Rose, High Hat (1963), averaged 22.6 points and 16 rebounds as a 6-2 All-State guard/forward at Wheelwright High School, where he held all the school's records. He was on a UK freshman team that finished 14-3 in 1962-63. Rose quit the team prior to his sophomore season.

Greenup County (Greenup)

Mike Scott, South Shore, 1/14/1967, 3L, (1987, 88, 89), averaged 20.9 points and 11.9 rebounds a game in leading Greenup County High to the State Tournament. He scored 38 points against eventual champion Hopkinsville in a first-round game. Scott earned All-State honors and was a member of the Kentucky All-Star team. He previously attended Wake Forest where he averaged 9.0 points and 6.0 rebounds a game. Scott entered UK as a sophomore in mid-December. He was not eligible to play until Jan. 17, 1987. He averaged 0.4 points and 0.6 rebounds a game. Scott started five of 32 games in 1989, scoring 47 points and 36 rebounds.

Harlan County (Harlan)

Wallace "Wah Wah" Jones, 7/4/26, 4L, (1946, 47 48, 49), established a new national scoring record of 2,398 points in three years at Harlan High. He was an All-State and All-Conference choice in both football and basketball. Jones was All-Conference in both sports Jones was UK's last great multiple sports star--football, basketball, and baseball. He played on two national championship basketball teams, and on the 1948 U.S. Olympic team, that won the

Gold Medal in London. He was All-SEC in basketball each of his four years at UK, All-SEC as a football end in 1946, and an All-America basketball player in 1949. Jones scored 1,151 points during his four years at UK and was a star baseball pitcher in 1947 and 1948. He also holds the unique distinction of being an All-Star under both legends Adolph Rupp (basketball) and Bear Bryant (football) when both coached at Kentucky. He is the only player to have his number retired in both football and basketball at Kentucky.

Jones played three years, scoring 452 points, for the Indianapolis Olympians, in the NBA. He returned to Lexington and served a term as sheriff of Fayette County before entering private business. Jones was one of the first persons inducted into the Kentucky Hall of Fame and the UK Athletic Hall of Fame.

Remembering Rupp: *We were playing Alabama down at that old gym, Foster Auditorium, that they had in Tuscaloosa. There was a balcony above the playing floor. The fans threw coins down on the floor when things didn't please them. And they had a stuffed owl up there. When they'd shoot the gun to end the half or the game, somebody would throw that bird on the floor, as it had just been shot.*

Before the game, Adolph told us, "Now, I don't want to see a damned one of you paying any attention to that crowd. When they throw that money on the floor, you ignore it." We were playing and then a decision went against Alabama that the crowd didn't like, and here came the money piling down in the floor, most of it pennies and nickels and dimes.

Bernie Shively was our athletic director then and basketball teams didn't have as much money to operate on as they do now. Anyway, here came all these coins. A big half-dollar rolled right by Shively, who was sitting at the end of our bench. It was too much for him and he just reached out, picked it up, and put it in his pocket. This was after Coach Rupp had warned all the players to ignore it. Adolph just looked down at the end of the bench and said, "Well, Shive, I see they've met your price."....**Wah Jones, 1974.**

Remembering Wah Wah: *The fans packed Boston Gardens for* *our game with Holy Cross, and they were wild. It was a brutal game. Cliff Barker and Bob Cousy got in a fight. Wah Wah Jones fouled out with four or five minutes left in the game. Wah sat next to me on the bench and he had barely taken his seat when a fan right behind our bench really started to get on him. He kept daring Wah to turn around until it was more than Jones could stand. Just as he turned, the fan threw a wet, wadded cigarette pack hard into Wah's face. Wah was strong as a bull. He turned, grabbed that fan by the tie and shirtfront, and landed a hard right hand to the man's jaw. Jones knocked him clean out of his clothes. The man was lying on the floor and Wah was standing there holding the man's tie and shirtfront in his left hand. The man's friend was trying to hit me but I beat him to the punch. I knocked him down and went after him. He kicked me while he was on the floor leaving his footprints on the stomach portion of my white shirt…***Harry Lancaster, 1979.***

Humzey Yessin, NA, (Mgr. 4L, 1946, 47, 48, 49). Harlan High won the state championship in Yessin's junior year and advanced to the quarterfinals his senior year. He was a student manager with Wildcat teams that won two NCAA championships and an Olympics Gold Medal, among many other honors.

Yessin coached baseball and basketball at Georgetown College. He became a Class A PGA golf pro and the director of golf for the Kentucky Department of Parks. He also developed the courses at Juniper Hill in Frankfort, Tates Creek (which is now a country club), and Greenbrier, an all while at Georgetown College and then worked in State Government as a golfing expert.

Remembering Rupp: *His practices were always rough. During a scrimmage, a wild elbow from Bill Spivey hit Roger Layne in the mouth and knocked him to the floor. Layne got up and spit something out on the floor. Rupp asked, "What in the world are those?" I told him I thought those were teeth from Roger's mouth." Rupp asked Layne if he was all right and he replied, "Hell yes. Let's play some ball." Rupp turned to Harry Lancaster and said, "Now, that's what I'm looking for-a fellow that will lose three teeth and still say let's* *get back in the game." ...Humzey **Yessin, BBM.***

Yessin, Rudy (1944): Yessin was a teammate of Wah Jones on Harlan's 1942 state champions. He earned a letter as a freshman at UK in 1944 before joining the Army in World War-II. Rudy played basketball in the Army Air Force as a member of the Randolph Field, Texas, team. He returned to UK in 1946, concentrating on earning a law degree. Yessin is a practicing attorney residing in Frankfort, Ky.

Richard "Dicky" Parsons, Yancey, 4L, (1959, 60, 61) played quarterback on the football team, ran the 880 in track, hit .450 his final season in baseball and was starting at guard on the basketball team at Harlan High. He was a second team All-State selection who scored 1,277 points in his high school career.

Parsons was an All-SEC shortstop, treasurer of the K Club, and an inductee of national men's leadership society, Omicron Delta Kappa; which recognized him as the "Outstanding Student of the College of Education." He was recipient of the Chandler Trophy, given annually to UK's outstanding basketball player. Parsons served as captain in two varsity sports-basketball and baseball. He holds more school baseball records than any other player. He was an All-SEC shortstop in 1959 and 1961, All-NCAA District, 1960, '61, and All-America 1961. He hit .400 his senior year.

Parsons was an assistant football coach at Glasgow High School two years and baseball and basketball coach at Boyle County High School from 1963 to 1968. While working on his Master's Degree at the University in 1968-69, he scouted, recruited, and helped with the Wildcat freshman team. He later accepted a part-time assistant-ship in basketball in addition to his baseball job. When named junior varsity basketball coach and No. 1 varsity assistant, Parsons gave up his job as baseball coach. He was an assistant on Joe B. Hall's UK staff before joining the University's fund-raising program.

Remembering Starkville (1959): *We were playing in Starkville when Bailey Howell, Babe McCarthy, and all the cowbells were there. I will never forget an experience. The coaches tried to prepare* *us for what to expect, but there was no way they could prepare us for that. I can remember staying on campus the night before the game and some of the students beating on dishpans all night long, trying to keep us awake. They did a good job of it.*

We went out to the old basketball arena about five o'clock, and it was full. We did not take the floor until we saw them take the floor because we did not want to be subjected to all those boos and cowbells. When they went out, we went out; some students would boo, some would cheer, and eventually it would turn to jeers. When they left the playing floor, we threw our basketballs down and just followed them into the locker room and again you would have some booing and some cheering.

*You just could not hear during a time out. Coach Rupp would yell into each individual player's ear the type of instructions he wanted. It was the loudest place I ever played in. The conference ruled that you did not have to shoot free throws as long as they were ringing those cowbells. Cox was at the line once and he did not shoot; we kept waiting for the crowd to be quiet. Finally, McCarthy went to the mike and told the students, "Please be quiet. They're going to miss, anyway."…***Dick Parsons, BBM**

Remembering Yancey: *Our little gym looked more like a barn than anything else did. It had many cracks, no heat, although at one time there was a potbellied stove. It was so cold in winter that we played in sweatshirts. We would play before school, at noon, and after school. We would go home, eat, and come back at night. There were some naked lights, so we would just take two wires and cross them and play until about 9 or 9:30…***Dick Parsons, 1975.**

Remembering Tradition: *I will never forget at the end of that second year (1959-60) how terrible we thought the season was because we had lost seven games. There is so much tradition, so much pride in basketball at UK that I will never forget how we felt a little embarrassed and ashamed of ourselves…***Dick Parsons, 1975.**

Johnson County (Paintsville)

Remembering Paintsville: In the fall of 1941, my grandmother died. I had to attend the funeral in Paintsville, and I received Coach Rupp's permission to do so. A few days after my return, during practice, Coach Rupp blew his whistle and called the squad into a circle for a talk. We received the usual lambasting, "My God, boys, we're just not going to continue playing like this. We are not playing girls' rules. This is WAR!" Then he singled me out, "And another thing, boys, we're not going to have any more of this grandmother dying business." ...**Vince Splane, 1975.**

Carroll Burchett, Fuget, 12/11/1937, 3L, (1960, 61, 62), was a 6-4 second team All-State performer at Flat Gap High. He enrolled at UK in mid-term of 1958, and averaged 10.6 points and 9.1 rebounds in 12 games as a freshman. Rupp held him out the following season. Burchett made the SEC All-Sophomore team in 1960. He finished his UK career with a total of 578 points and 489 rebounds in 72 games. Burchett retired as Commissioner of the Kentucky Department of Rehabilitation.

Remembering Burchett: *I called Carroll Burchett "Ozark Ike." He had a great heart, but not all of the ability in the world. He looked like he was all arms and legs flying in different directions simultaneously...***Harry Lancaster, 1979**.

Alvin Ratliff, Williamsport, 2/4/47-9/16/2011, Fr., (1967), averaged 19 points a game and earned All-State honors as a senior at Meade Memorial High. He performed well in the Kentucky-Indiana series and the East-West All-Star game. Ratliff left UK after his freshman season and entered the Army.

Ratliff later enjoyed success as a coach, winning more than 400 games. He led Johnson Central's girls to a pair of 15th Region championships and later won a 16th Region All 'A' Classic championship at Bath County.

John Pelphrey, 7/18/1968, 4L, (1989, 90, 91, 92), was a three-time All-State basketball player from Johnson County. While a player at Kentucky from 1988-1992, Pelphrey led the Wildcats to the SEC Tournament Championship and an NCAA Tournament appearance, including the epic battle with Duke in the 1992 Elite Eight.

Pelphrey was a two-time captain while at Kentucky and in 1989, he was UK's Student Athlete of the Year. Pelphrey started 90 of 114 games, and averaged 11 points per game at UK. In1992, a relatively unheralded Kentucky team coached by Rick Pitino, in its first year after coming off NCAA probation, lost to Duke in the Élite Eight. This game is often considered one of the greatest in college basketball history. It ended with Chris Laettner. The four seniors, as undisputed team leaders who showed their loyalty to UK during some of the program's darkest hours, would forever be known by Wildcats fans as "The Unforgettables" (A name given to them by Coach Pitino). Pelphrey is one of only 29 former Kentucky players to have his jersey retired (#34). He is a member of the KHSAA and UK Athletic halls of fame.

Pelphrey coached the University of Arkansas to a victory over UK in 2010, one of only three losses by the Wildcats that year. Prior to coaching the Razorbacks, he served as head basketball coach for South Alabama. Pelphrey also served as an assistant coach under Eddie Sutton at Oklahoma State and Billy Donovan at Marshall and Florida. He returned to Florida as an assistant coach in 2011-12.

Todd Tackett, 9/22/1979, 2L, (1999, 00), averaged 14.3 ppg as a sophomore on Paintsville's 1996 state championship team. He was first-team All-State as a junior and senior, and honorable mention All-America by Street & Smith and Parade magazines. Tackett holds school records for career assists (601) and most points in a single game (56 vs. Pike County Central). He was a Kentucky All-Star and MVP of the Kentucky Derby Classic. Tackett earned two letters in a reserve role at UK. He missed his sophomore year with a knee problem.

Landon Slone, 1/14/1990, 1L, (2009), was All-State and All-Regional at Paintsville High. He averaged 25.1 points and 7.2 rebounds as a senior. Honors included Region 15 Player of the Year and 2008 Appalachian Player of the Year. He was First Team All-Mountains, and Lexington Catholic All-Tournament. Slone was a walk-on player who transferred to Pikeville.

Knott County (Hindman)

Ernest Sparkman, 8/20/1925–1/15/2010. Sq., (1945), played high school basketball at Carr Creek under legendary coach Morton Combs. He played for UK in 1944-45 on a team that included future All-Americans Alex Groza and Jack Parkinson. The Wildcats were SEC season and tournament champions, finishing with a 22-4 record after losing to Ohio State, 45-37, in the NCAA tournament. Sparkman also played for the United States Air Force. He was president of the Kentucky Broadcaster's Association in 1975 and his voice was one of the most recognized in east Kentucky, echoing across the mountains for six decades. In the 1950s, Sparkman started WSGS, the first FM station in eastern Kentucky and the most powerful at 100,000 watts. He died in January 2010, at the age of 84.

Remembering Rupp Sparkman, you see that center circle. I want you to go over there and s---. Then you can go back to Carr Creek and tell them at least you did something in Madison Square Garden...**Rupp in N. Y. for 1944 NIT**.

E.A. Couch, 2/1/1937–2/29/2012, Sq., (1957, 58), scored 17 points in a 72-68 Carr Creek win over Henderson in the championship game of the 1956 State Tournament. He was an All-Tournament team selection. Couch was a member of UK's *"Fiddlin' Five"* squad that won the 1958 NCAA championship. A four year starter for the Carr Creek Indians, Couch was high-point man his sophomore, junior, and senior years. He averaged 24 points per game his senior year, and for four years led his team in rebounds. Couch was captain of the 1956 Carr Creek High School State Championship Basketball Team. He, Corky Withrow and Kelly Coleman were chosen on the American All-South Team in 1956.

Carr Creek closed its doors in 1974, a victim of consolidation. The school sent five teams to the state tournament, winning the championship over Henderson, 72-68, in 1956. Their most memorable game was a 68-67 win over Wayland and the great Kelly Coleman in the 1956 semi-finals that year. Coleman scored 50 points in that game, but it was a one-hander from the head of the circle by Freddie Maggard with four seconds left that won the game for Carr Creek.

Remembering Rupp: I ended up with a family, and that was great, but getting married ended my career. Coach Rupp did not like married players**...E.A. Couch...1980.**

Bobby Shepherd, Fr., (1957). Shepherd transferred to Carr Creek from Kingdom Come. He scored 17 points in Carr Creek's 72-68 win over Henderson in the 1956 State Tournament, which tied him for second-high honors with teammate E. A. Couch. Shepherd made All-Tournament. He left UK after his freshman year.

Knox County (Barbourville)

Terry Lee Mills, 8/15/1948, 3L, (1969, 70, 71), scored 1,622 points and 279 rebounds in a three-year career at Knox Central High. .He scored 43 points and had 24 rebounds in two State Tournament games his junior year, and 32 points against state champion Shelby County his senior year. Mills played in the East-West and Kentucky-Indiana all-star games. He was All-America, All-State and All-State Tournament his senior year. He was All-District, All-Regional and

All-Conference three years.

At the University of Kentucky, Mills played on three Southeastern Conference championship teams and an Associated Press national championship team. He scored 424 points and 117 rebounds in 63 games at UK.

Mills pursued an insurance career with Massachusetts Mutual in Lexington.

Laurel County (London)

Arthur E. Bastin, East Bernstadt, 4/29/1898–3[9/1957, 1L, (1918), attended high school in Lexington. He played in 12 UK games (9-2-1*) and finished with 48 points, second highest on the team. Bastin owned and operated the Elkhorn Coal Company at Kona. Ky.

The unique tie game–UK 21, Wesleyan 21–occurred on Feb. 9, 1918, on a scorer's error that went undiscovered until after the teams left the Wesleyan gym.

G. J. Smith, 6/13/1953, (1973, 74, 75), was All-State at Laurel County and Hazel Green high schools. He won four letters in basketball and five in baseball. He was the surprise player of the 1970-71 UK freshman team, averaging 14.6 points and 1.3 rebounds with a high game of 24 points against Xavier. He was a valuable sixth man on UK's drive to the Final Four, where they lost the NCAA championship game to UCLA. G. J. is athletics director and baseball coach at South Laurel High School.

Remembering G. J. *"G. J was one of the most called for and cheered players In UK history"*...**Joe B. Hall, 1975**.

Paul Andrews, London, 3/21/1965, 4L (1984, 85, 86, 87). As an All-State senior at Laurel Co. High, Andrews averaged 21.3 ppg. and 5.9 rpg. He hit 52.1 percent from the field and 76.1 percent from the free-throw line. His spectacular half-court shot enabled Laurel County to defeat North Hardin, 53-51, in the championship game of the 1982 state tournament. Andrews was All-District three times, and All-Region twice. He started both Kentucky-Indiana All-Star games. Andrews scored 46 points, grabbed 72 rebounds, and dished out 54 assists in 86 games at UK. He and James Blackmon were captains in 1987.

Andrews is CEO of Ten Broeck Hospital in Jacksonville, Fla.

Lee County (Beattyville)

Hubert Blakey, Sq., (1920). Blakey transferred to UK from Centre College during his senior year. He was second-leading scorer (7.0 ppg) to Basil Hayden (10.8).

Larry Stamper, 3L, (1971, 72, 73). Stamper was a prep All-America and an All-State forward at Lee County High, where he averaged 30 ppg and 29 rebounds as a senior. He scored 437 points and 458 rebounds at UK.

Jeff Ginnan, Sq., (1989). Ginnan was a six-eight center who played in four games for UK after transferring from Transylvania.

Letcher County (Whitesburg)

Sam Potter, Kona, 3/17/1914, 1L, (1934), received worldwide prominence in 1931 when Ripley's Believe It or Not featured him as the nation's leading football scorer after he tallied 234 points in nine games for Whitesburg's unbeaten football team. He was a reserve on the 1934 UK basketball team that finished the regular season undefeated 16-0 and lost to Florida in the conference tournament. (See Coaches).

Milt Ticco, Jenkins, 9/22/1922-1/26/2002, 3L, (1941, 42, 43). After starring in multiple sports at Jenkins High, Ticco continued his career in basketball and football at UK. He earned three letters in basketball, scoring 465 points in 63 games. He was third-team All-America in 1943. After serving in the U.S. Army during World War II, Ticco played basketball for the American Basketball League. He played baseball for both the Brooklyn Dodgers and the Cincinnati Reds. Ticco retired from a career in sales.

Remembering Ticco. *When I was in the war in Germany in 1945, a former UK player, Milt Ticco, wrote Coach Rupp and said, "Dear Coach, I have been playing with a boy who I think could help the UK basketball program." Ticco gave him my name, age, accomplishments, etc., and then said, "P.S. My basketball shoes are worn out; could you please send me another pair?"*

*Rupp wrote Ticco a very gracious and kind letter and stated that he would like to have me write to him when I got out of the Army and possibly visit UK to look at the facilities and campus. He ended up with a P.S. to Ticco, "Milt, don't you realize there has been a war going on? As a result, it has created a severe rubber shortage and therefore I am unable to send you the shoes. However, I am interested in you sending me the boy." ...***Dale Barnstable, 1975.**

Remembering Rupp. Ticco was high-point man with nine points in a 43-41 loss to Ohio State in Columbus, but he missed a shot under the basket near the end of the game, causing Rupp to sarcastically suggest that Ohio State award him a varsity letter.

Lewis County (Tollesboro)

James C. Mathewson, Vanceburg, 2/2/1920-10/4/2009, 1L, (1942), played both basketball (1942) and baseball at University of Kentucky. He graduated with an A.B. in education and went on to receive a masters in business from Xavier University in 1960. Mathewson served with the Navy in the Pacific until 1946 and then re-entered the service in 1950 to serve as a lieutenant commander in the Korean Conflict. When he returned from active duty he was stationed in St. Louis, Mo., where he served until his discharge in 1954. James coached basketball in his hometown of Vanceburg, and from 1946 until 1950 at Lewis County High School. He also taught and coached at Arlington High School in Columbus, Ohio, as well as ninth grade football until he re-entered the Navy in 1950.

Chris Harrison 7/26/1971, 4L, (1992, 93, 94, 95), averaged

29.4 points, 7.2 rebounds and 4.8 assists per contest during his senior year at Tollesboro. He scored 73 points in a high school game. He was twice first-team All-State, Naismith Player of the Year in Kentucky Academic All-State, and first in his senior class with a perfect 4.0 GPA.

As a substitute guard at UK, he scored 162 points with a high game of 16 against LSU in 1995. That total included four three-point goals. Harrison is a pharmaceutical salesman in Northern Kentucky.

Remembering Big Comeback. (UK 99, LSU 94): LSU was leading UK by 31 points with 15 minutes to go in Baton Rouge in February 1994 in Baton Rouge. At that point, coach called a time-out and just glared at us. He said you guys are going to pay for this tomorrow in practice. Then he told me to go in the game, and I remember Travis Ford saying to me, "You're going to light it up tonight." I hit my first shot, and the next one, and all of a sudden everybody seemed to get in on the act. We started rattling threes the way they had in the first half. Walter (McCarty) hit a three-pointer to give us the lead, 96-95, with 19 seconds to play. While LSU failed to score, we hit four free throws for one of the most remarkable comebacks in college basketball.

Looking back on it now, if LSU had not taken another shot all night and just started milking the clock after going up by 31, we probably couldn't have scored enough to catch them. I think that's the night their coach started considering retirement." …**Chris Harrison to Denny Trease, 2005.**

Madison County (Richmond)

James Park, 11/10/1891–12/17/1970), 1L, (1914), was a three-sport star at Normal High School in Richmond. Before entering UK, he played baseball with the Richmond team in the Blue Grass

League and later played with the Lexington team in the Ohio State League. While at UK, Park was All-Kentucky quarterback, played center on the basketball team and pitcher on the baseball team. He won four varsity letters in football, three in basketball, and three in baseball. Several of his football records at UK still stand. Park served as captain of the 1914 UK football team.

In his senior year at UK, Park served as an assistant football coach and next as head basketball coach, guiding the basketball Wildcats to an 8-6 record in 1916. He pitched three years for the old St. Louis Browns, and also played for Columbus and Kansas City. Park graduated cum laude from the UK Law School in June 1920. He scored the highest grade of those taking the state bar exam. Park taught one year in the UK College of Law. Park served with the Army Air Corps during World War II. Then he enjoyed a long and successful career as a lawyer. He died in 1970 at age 78.

George Gumbert, 9/15/1894–1/14/1954, 2L, (1914, 15, 16). Dr. Gumbert was a native of London, Ky., who played sports at Caldwell High School in Richmond. He lettered in both basketball and football at the University of Kentucky. Gumbert was a starting guard on the 1916 UK basketball team. He left UK after mid-year exams, (later getting his masters there) to take a teaching position in Marion. He served as an ensign in the Navy during World War I. After the war, he was in charge of visual education at Eastern Kentucky and between 1920 and 1940 was professor of agriculture there. Before coming to Richmond, he was a teacher and athletic coach at schools at Harlan and Marion. His son, George M. Gumbert, Jr., an orthopedic surgeon, served many years as a UK football team doctor.

Alonzo Nelson, 1L, (1945), was an All-State performer with Madison High's 1944 state tournament semi-finalists. He participated in 14 UK games in '44.Nelson retired as an employee development specialist at the Blue Grass Army Depot in Richmond.

Hugh Coy, 7/19/1934, 1L, (1954), was a second team All-State selection at Madison High in Richmond. He earned a letter playing on UK's undefeated 1954 team. Coy also was a pitcher on the UK baseball team. He played four years for the St. Louis Cardinals organization. Coy retired as a pharmaceutical representative living in Fruitland Park, Fla.

Remembering Rupp. *When I was a freshman, all we did was practice, as we were under suspension that year. We were scrimmaging Memphis State and beating them but not as much as we should have been doing. They were real scrappy and that gave Hagan and Lou a hard time on the boards. Coach Rupp had some cattlemen from Chicago visiting him that day, and he invited them out to watch us practice. Well, our style of play did not improve much, and Coach Rupp blew his whistle, turned to the visitors, and said, "You fellows from Chicago have heard of our great All-American Cliff Hagan. Cliff, come over here where they can see you. I'm sure they couldn't tell which one you were by the way you were playing." Cliff took a bow....*__Hugh Coy, 1974.__

Billy Evans, Berea, 9/13/1932, 3L, (1957, 58, 59). An outstanding amateur tennis player, Evans is better known for his basketball achievements. He was a starting guard on Kentucky's unbeaten 1953-54 team and captain of the next season's 23-3 team. Evans led UK in free throw shooting with 77.8% in 1954 and 74.3% in '58. His biggest honor was serving as captain of the 1956 U.S. Olympic team that won the gold medal in Melbourne, Australia. He also was a member of the 1958 U.S. team that won the gold in the Pan-American games. Evans retired as an executive with Kentucky Fried Chicken.

Remembering Evans: *I think Billy was one of the most underrated players at Kentucky. He was overshadowed by "The "Big Three," (Cliff Hagan Frank Ramsey, and Lou Tsioropoulos). Evans was a very valuable man. He was highly intelligent in running the offense and was an outstanding player on defense. We always assigned Billy to one of the other team's top guns and while Evans may score only 7 or 8 points, he would hold a man averaging maybe 25 points to 7 or 8....* **Harry Lancaster, 1979.**

Don Mills Berea, 3L, (58, 59, 60), was a 6-7 center/forward who played three years at Berea, scoring 1,988 points and picking up All-State honors in 1955 and '56 along with honorable mention All-America. As a UK yearling, he posted a 27.2 scoring average. He hit 11 of 11 free throws vs. West Virginia in 1958 and led the team in field goal percentage with 82.7 percent in '59. He was second-team All-SEC in 1960. Mills' big moment came in UK's win over Seattle in the championship game of the 1958 NCAA tournament. Trailing for much of the game, UK grabbed its first lead with 6:08 left when Mills hit a hook shot to give the Wildcats a 61-60 lead. Moments later, Cox hit a jump shot to make it 63-60 and UK never trailed again. Mills scored nine crucial points in that game. He worked with State Farm Insurance in Richmond.

Marquis Estill, 9/15/1981, 3L, (2001, 02, 03), was the 1999 Gatorade Player of the Year in Kentucky and a finalist for Mr. Basketball honors. He averaged 20.5 points and 11.3 rebounds in his senior year at Madison Central High. In leading Central to a berth in the Sweet Sixteen, he made All-District, All-Regional and All-State teams. Estill earned numerous honors including King of the Bluegrass and the Kentucky Holiday Classic.

He scored 936 points and 472 rebounds during his three seasons with UK. Estill ranks seventh in career blocks with 1.430 per game. His 43 blocks (1.3 per game) tied Tayshaun Prince for team high blocks in 2000. Estill led UK with 64 (1.8 bpg) the following year. He had six blocks vs. Mississippi State in2002.

Estil was second-team All-SEC, All-SEC tournament and All-NCAA Regional in 2003. He played professional basketball in Italy.

Magoffin County (Salyersville)

Abraham Lincoln Collinsworth, 2/12/1935. 3L, (1956, 57, 58), averaged 28 points and a record total of 2,652 points over a four-year span at Salyersville High. He lettered three years at UK and was a member of the 1958 "Fiddlin' Five" NCAA champion Wildcats. He is a retired Titusville school official living in Orlando, Fl. His son Cris is a television sportscaster who played college football for the University of Florida. Cris played eight seasons in the National Football League.

Remembering Rupp: *Lincoln Collinsworth told me that Rupp and I might have trouble getting along. Rupp wanted everything that was worthwhile to be his happening. He didn't want anybody to outshine him. ...***Kelly Coleman, 1998.**

Martin County (Inez)

R. C. Preston, 3/9/1890–2/16/1929, 4L, (1911, 12, 13, 14), was the first Martin County boy to play for UK. He was a starting guard on the 1912 undefeated UK team that claimed the Southern championship with a 9-0 record. Preston led the team in scoring his junior and senior years. He had a high game of 22 points in a 42-16 win over Marietta in 1913.

Billy Ray Cassady, 2/11/1935–11/26/1997, 3L, (1956, 57, 58). A 6-2, left-handed shooting guard, Cassady garnered All-State and All-Tournament honors in leading Inez to the 1954 KHSAA championship. He was a second-team All-America after a sparkling exhibition in the North-South game. Cassady received the Star of Stars award following the Kentucky-Indiana game in Louisville. He also was an outstanding baseball player.

Cassady was a reserve on UK's 1958 NCAA champions. Four players on that UK team-- Earl Adkins, of Ashland; Lincoln Collinsworth, of Salyersville; John Cox, of Hazard, and Cassady–were from east Kentucky. All but Collinsworth were All-State in high school. Cassady retired from the Wolf Creek Coal Co.

Remembering Rupp: *"I claim credit for changing Rupp's method of coaching free-throw shooters. He made everybody shoot the bloomer (underhand) shot. I was the worst foul shooter on the team. One day in my sophomore year, I started shooting one-hand-*

*ed. Adolph and Harry were sitting on the sidelines. I got up to 56 straight and everybody gathered around trying to cause me to miss. I missed the 119th shot"...***Billy Ray Cassady, 1980.**

(During the 1953-54 and 1954-55 seasons, Rupp required two-handed underhand shots from the free-throw line. Then, in the 1955-56 season, he made it a rule that anyone with an average of 60 percent or better could shoot one-handed. He noted that Cassady, shooting one-handed, made 95.2 percent of his foul shots).

Adolph told the other guys to shoot them one-handed. Everybody switched but Hatton and Cox, who continued to shoot the underhand shot. We became a better foul-shooting team, hitting 64.9 percent of our free throws in 1955/56. We improved that mark to 69.8 in 1956/57 and 73.8 the following year. I hit 82.3 percent during my varsity career. I had 18 straight going in my sophomore year and George Conley called a technical on the opposing team. Conley asked Rupp whom he wanted to shoot the free throw. Rupp told him to put me on the line because I hadn't missed all year. When I missed the shot, Rupp called me over to the sideline and said, "Son, you're going to have to practice tomorrow."....**Billy Ray Cassady, BBM.**

Remembering Cassady: *Rupp's practice sessions did not end until someone made 10 straight free throws. Cassady would always get us out early. He could make 50 or 75 straight at a given time. It was unbelievable...***Vern Hatton, 1980.**

*I saw him make 100 straight. He just stood there, shooting left-handed; however, he never got the opportunity to play. You know how Coach Rupp was...***Earl Adkins, 1978.**

Tim Stephens, 6/15/1958, 2L, (1977, 78), was a 6-3 guard/forward who lettered four years in basketball at McCreary County High. He was twice All-State and a four-time All-District and All-Regional performer. Stephens averaged 23.4 points and 15.8 rebounds in his prep career. His single game highs were 54 points and 26 rebounds. He scored 18 points in the Derby Classic and played in the Kentucky-Indiana game. Stephens joined a Central Kentucky group that toured Spain and Russia. He won tournament MVP honors in Spain.

Stephens was a member of UK's 1978 NCAA champions. He played three years at UK before transferring to Cumberland. He became a high school coach and teacher in McCreary County.

Howard Kinne, Stearns, 2/19/1896–9/29/1918, 2L, (1915-17), played four sports–basketball, baseball, football and tennis–before leaving school in the spring of 1917 (Junior year) to enter military officers training camp.

He was killed when his airplane was shot down behind the German lines September 29, 1918.

Kinne won fame at the University largely through his splendid athletic record. He won the hotly-contested UK win (18-14) over the University of Louisville, almost without assistance, in 1915, and to him was given the credit for the defeat of Purdue University 7-0 when he recovered the ball on a fumble by one of his opponents and carried it across the line, making the only touchdown of the game.

Metcalfe County (Edmonson)

J.P. Blevins, 5/8/1979, 4L, (1999, 00, 01, 02), started playing varsity basketball in the seventh grade and started at point guard in the eighth grade. He scored 2,994 career points at Metcalfe County. Blevins made first-team All-State twice while leading the Hornets to a 97-73 record during six seasons winning five 16th District titles and five Class A regional crowns. He made the All-District team five consecutive years, the All-Region team four times, the All-Class A Regional Tournament team five times and the Class-A All-State Tournament team three times. Blevins scored a career-high 51 points against Clinton County. He averaged 23.7 ppg, 6.6 rpg and 3.6 apt as a junior, and 26.2 ppg, 5.6 rpg and 4.2 apt as a senior. He was a Kentucky All-Star who participated in the Derby Classic.

Blevins was UK's top three-point and free-throw shooter in 2000. He was team co-captain in 2001-2002. Blevins earned Academic All-Southeastern Conference honors for three consecutive years. He was a member of the UK Athletic Director's Honor Roll for five consecutive semesters, graduating magna cum laude in Communications. He joined the Kentucky Recreation and Parks Department.

Montgomery County (Mt. Sterling)

Joe Coons, 1882–7/26/1909, 1903, 04, 1L, (05). After starring in high school at Mt. Sterling, Coons was on the starting five of UK's first basketball team in 1903. He was one of the students who met with Walter Mustaine in the fall of that year and formed the team. Coons captained the team in 1905. He also earned two letters in football at UK. Coons died of tuberculosis in 1909 at the age of 27.

Charles T. Heinrich, 1/5/15–7/17/2000 (1935), was a member of the 1935 UK team that lost to NYU, 23-22, in UK's first appearance in Madison Square Garden. The Wildcats lost one other game that year, at Michigan State 32-26. They were 19-2 and SEC co-champions.

Walter Johnson, d. 7/30/45, (1944), was an All-star guard on a Mt. Sterling team that lost to St. Xavier, 33-27, in the semi-finals of the 1943 state tournament. He earned a UK letter with the 1944 Wildcats who won 19 of 21 games and were SEC regular season and tournament champions. They lost to St. John's, 48-45, and defeated Oklahoma A&M, 45-29, in the consolation game of the 1944 NIT. For his part in molding a championship contender Rupp became the 10th coach elected to the Athletic Foundation College Basketball Hall of Fame. Johnson was a gunner's mate aboard the cruiser Indianapolis, which carried Atom-Bomb supplies. After taking part in many of the major campaigns in the Pacific, including Iwo Jima, Guam, the Philippines and Okinawa, he was missing when a Japanese submarine sank his ship. In September, the navy reported Seaman Johnson as killed in action.

Rupp took a group of freshmen players just out of high school, and directed them to 19 victories in 20 games this year .It was one of the outstanding achievements of the 1944 basketball season.... Coach of the Year Committee, 1944.

Charles "Chili" Ishmael, 6/21/1942, 2L, (1963-64), was a 6-5 guard who came to UK on a football scholarship after earning second team All-State selections in both basketball and football along with most valuable player designations at Mt. Sterling High. He gave up football after averaging 12.9 points on the Kitten basketball team with a high game of 22 vs. Lindsey Wilson J.C. Ishmael played in 25 of UK's 27 games in1964, averaging 5.5points a game. The Wildcats were Sugar Bowl and SEC champions his senior year. Ishmael retired from coaching at Montgomery County High School.

Remembering Rupp: *Traveling with Coach Rupp we had lots of rituals that we never thought much about. We were at Auburn in '64 and had just begun to eat in a crowded restaurant. We were quiet, polite-almost formal--that's just the way it always was.*

*Coach Rupp did not eat with us but sat with Lancaster and Shively close by. I can imagine he was pleased with the dignified appearance we made. When all of us had eaten, we stood up in unison, placed our chairs, and filed out. In this particular case as we walked past the cash register, each of us picked up a toothpick. Now usually, we would go on outside, but this time we just milled around the magazine rack in the motel lobby, casually picking our teeth. Coach Rupp hadn't taken his eyes off us. This breach of etiquette was too much for him. At any rate, he came storming out into the lobby hollering about our bad manners and telling us we were not to pick our teeth in public. He got everyone's attention. The scene he caused seemed more impolite than our picking our teeth-but nevertheless, we got the point...***Charles Ishmael, 1975.**

Perry (Hazard)

Charles S. Combs, Happy, 11/11/1914-10/28/2007, 1L, (1938). When Combs was 12, his family sent him to Berea to receive his education. While at U.K., Combs earned two letters in basketball. He also played baseball and ran track. Combs was a teacher, principal, administrator, and coach for 43 years in Daviess County. He served as the director of pupil personnel for the Daviess school system until retiring.

William Owen "Racehorse" Davis, 1/17/1911, 2/25/1981, 2L, (1933, 34), played basketball on Hazard's 1932 state championship team. He also played football for the Bulldogs. Davis was third leading scorer on the 1933 UK basketball team, which was 21-3 and repeated as conference champion. He was second-leading scorer on the 1934 team that finished the season 16-0, but lost to Florida in the opening game of the SEC Tournament. He was All-SEC (Second Team) and All-SEC Tournament in '33 and All-America (Converse 3rd.), All-SEC and All-SEC Tournament in '34. Davis left school due to the illness of his mother. He and his brother Roscoe ran a hardware store in Hazard, for the better part of four decades.

John A. McIntosh Jr., 10/26/1913-2/23/2012, (1937). After leaving Hazard High School, McIntosh played sparingly three years for Rupp at UK, failing to earn a letter. He was a former company pilot and engineer for Irvin Industries. McIntosh died in 1984 at the Veterans Administration Medical Center in Lexington after a long illness.

Carl Luther "Hoot" Combs, 11/11/14–10/28/2007, 1L, (1940), was all-tournament on a Hazard High team that went to the semifinals of the 1937 Kentucky State Basketball Tournament. He was a starting guard in seven of the 16 UK games he played in 1940, averaging 3.9 ppg with high games of nine against Alabama and Tennessee. He appeared in 12 games in 1941, when he made honorable mention All-SEC. He earned three letters as a running back and defensive back.

Combs served as a second lieutenant with the 1st Armored Division in North Africa and Italy in World War II. He earned the Purple Heart, Combat Infantryman Badge, and EAME Ribbon with four battle stars. He ultimately retired as a major.

Combs worked briefly as a part-time sports information director at UK. He earned a law degree at UK in 1950. Combs served as a scout for Rupp and was a graduate assistant to then football coach Paul Bryant.

He spent almost two decades in private law practice until he became legal adviser to the Lexington police department in the 1970s. He was also the first president of the Homebuilders Association of Lexington.

During the '60s and early '70s, Combs was a sportscaster and a public address announcer. For several years, he called Keeneland's feature race of the day for WBLG-1300. He was the first sports announcer for WBLG-TV, which became WTVQ-TV. He also was a sportscaster and a public address announcer for UK sports and the state high school basketball tournament.

Remembering Rupp: *During the 1939-40 season, we headed north to Marquette, a team then regarded as the best team in the country. By the time we got to Cincinnati just about everybody was ailing. We left one guard in the bus there and another one at Chicago. They were Lee Huber and Carl Staker as I recall. By game time we had only two able-bodied guards left, Mickey Rouse and I. In the dressing room, Adolph was very relaxed. He told us to just go out and have some fun. He told me I would be guarding a fellow who had already been All-American twice and this was his senior year. We tied into Marquette pretty good; at half time, we were only a point or two behind. Adolph came charging into the dressing room and said, "By God, don't forget this is a Kentucky team and I am the .... coach. What I said to you before the game is out. We are going to beat these bas.... there will be no more t*t&! fun this trip." We beat them, 51-45, and went on to win the SEC title. He never told us again to just have some fun."* **Hoot Combs...1975**

Chester Duff, Dorfork, DOD 5/7/2000. Sq., (1945), played a reserve forward on the 1944-45 Wildcat team that finished 22-4 and defeated Tufts 66-56 in the NIT consolation game.

Garland Townes, NA, 1L. (1950). A slick, six-foot, 180–pound guard, Townes was great on defense and equally good in the fast-breaking offensive drives. However, he played sparingly on two championship UK squads that were loaded with talented players. Townes was a retired business and radio personality in Hazard.

Remembering Garland: *One afternoon right in front of Adolph, Garland Townes, and Bob Brannum really got into it. Townes was smaller and quicker and it was just bap, bap, bap, and Brannum came out of there with blood streaming down his cheek from a cut over his eye. The trainer was patching him up when Adolph walked down the sideline and nodded for me to join him. When I got over there he asked, "What happened?" I said "if you want to know, Townes just knocked the hell out of Brannum!" A slight smile came across Adolph's face as he said, "He did?" He walked on back down to the other end and we started scrimmaging again with Brannum still getting patched up....***Harry Lancaster...1979.**

Johnny Cox, 11/1/1936, 3L. (1957, 58, 59), closed his high school career with a thirty-point performance in a 74-66 victory over Adair for the 1955 KHSAA championship.

He is one of only five players in Kentucky history to make the first team All-SEC three times. The list includes Dan Issel, Kenny Walker, Kevin Grevey and Kyle Macy.

Cox ranks in UK's top 20 in: career points, career rebounds, career free throw attempts, career free throws made, career field goals attempted & field goals made. He made All-America and All-NCAA Regional teams. Cox entered the insurance business in Hazard.

Remembering Cox: Even if that boy doesn't get a single point, he'll be mighty handy as a rebounder. He has a heart as big as the moon and he has plenty desire. The way that boy loves basketball, I am sure he can help us."... **Rupp to Billy Thompson, 1957.**

Remembering Johnny: *The KHSAA declared Cox ineligible for competition his junior year at Hazard after he transferred from*

*Fleming-Neon. Johnny spent much of his time in the gym during that year of banishment. He would ask me for the key to the gym so he could practice at night. When it got dark, Johnny would wrap himself up in football jerseys to keep warm and spend the night. In the morning, he would go home, take a bath, and eat breakfast, then come back to school...***Goebel Ritter, 1960.**

Remembering Rupp: *"Sidney, I want you to meet Johnny Cox of Hazard, Kentucky. He's working over on that side of the court. He is a pretty good basketball player. He just won the national championship for us last year. But he won't have a chance to do it again this year unless you let him feel the ball once in a while."...***Rupp to Sidney Cohen, 1959.**

*Cox was a great leader. When we were in trouble, we just got the ball in to him. I will never forget those hook shots and the jumpers he would take...***Dick Parsons, 1974.**

Johnny Cox was one of our great ones to me. He didn't have great speed. He didn't have much strength. He was such a skinny kid. But Johnny was a great shooter and a harder competitor never lived. He gave our opponents such a hard time with his great shooting he took a tremendous physical beating. They banged him around game after game after game, but he was tougher than hell. He took such beatings that Adolph and I were screaming our heads off from the bench, but Johnny never showed any anger. He had just picked himself up off the floor and put another one or two in the basket... **Harry Lancaster, 1979.**

*They called him (Cox) the Kentucky Long Rifle. He had a long, one-handed shot that was deadly. He had to be deadly because when he was practicing in Hazard, in the hollows, if he missed, the ball would roll 500 or 600 yards down in the hollow, and he would have to go chase it. So he wanted to make sure he hit that shot...***Vern Hatton, 2003**

Mickey Gibson, 12/2/1942, 1L, (1967), was a 6-foot-2 All-State forward from Hazard who once scored 51 points in a game. He also was a pitcher-first baseman in baseball and a high jumper.

After Gibson averaged 23.1 points and 12.7 rebounds as a UK freshman, Rupp called him "a left-handed Johnny Cox who is as good as anyone I've seen at this stage."

An ankle injury limited Gibson's playing time to 17 games his sophomore year as the Cats prepared for the Mideast Regional at Minneapolis. Gibson quit the team after a confrontation with trainer Joe Brown.

Gibson transferred to the University of North Carolina at Asheville. Gibson was Honorable Mention, NAIA All-America.

Pike (Pikeville)

Walter Hatcher, 6/28, 1916–10/11/1994, Sq., (1937). Dr. Hatcher was a reserve on the 1937 UK team that won both the SEC regular season and tournament titles. Dr. Hatcher received his dental degree from the University of Louisville Dental School. He practiced dentistry in Pikeville for 43 years, until his retirement in the mid-80s. He was a former president of First National Bank of Pikeville. Dr. Hatcher was in the Battle of the Bulge during World War II and received a Bronze Star. He also had interests in the coal business in Pikeville. He donated the land that became the Pike County Airport, which bears his name, Hatcher Field.

Gordon L. George, Betsy Layne (1933), was a reserve on the UK team which finished 21-3 and was SEC champions. That 1933 team featured future All-Americans Aggie Sale, Ellis Johnson and French DeMoisey. George was in the coal industry in Kentucky and West Virginia.

John William Trivette, 2/10/1917–1/3/1993, Sq., (1938), played basketball and baseball for Pikeville College Academy from 1932-1935. He played for Rupp at UK, failing to earn a letter. Trivette gained recognition for his outstanding work as basketball coach at Pikeville High for 16 years. John Bill invented the full court press. His 1956 team, which lost to Hazard in the State Tournament, never played a home game during the season because the Big Sandy River overflowed its banks and flooded the entire town, including the gymnasium. Trivette's Pikeville teams won 427 games and lost 126. During his career, Trivette led his teams to seven regional championships and 14 district titles. The Louisville Courier-Journal named Trivette coach of the year in 1957, when his team finished third in the state tournament after being ranked No. 1 much of the season.

Zeb Blankenship, Elkhorn City NA, 2/23/2012. (1946), starred at Elkhorn City before committing to the Wildcats near the end of World War II. He scored two points in six games.

Woodrow Preston, NA, Sq., (1952). Preston played on Pikeville's 1949 team that advanced to the quarterfinals of the State Tournament, played in the North-South Classic. He appeared in two games during UK's 1952 SEC Championship season.

John Lee Butcher, 9/12/1925-1/4/2009. Sq., (1955) Butcher was one of the state's highest scorers in 1954, earning All-Conference honors in basketball and All-State in football .at Pikeville. Butcher received the "Star of Stars" award for the Kentucky-Indiana game in Indianapolis. He served as quarterback of the UK freshman football team in '54. Butcher transferred to Pikeville College after one year at UK.

Dan Hall, Betsy Layne 9/26/1954, 1L, (1975), was a 6-10, 220 lb. All-State center who led Betsy Layne to a 100-35 record during a four-year career. He averaged 25.ppg and 14 rebounds as a senior. He scored 41 points against Bracken County in 1974. Hall scored 2,642 career points, a 19.6 average. He was four-time All-District, All-Regional, and twice All-State. He played on the Kentucky All-Stars vs. The Russian National Junior Team and the Kentucky East-West All-Star game.

After playing in all freshman games and nine games as a sophomore at UK, He transferred to Marshall in mid-semester of his sophomore year.

Remembering Danny: *Hall was a part of an historic UK recruiting class that included Rick Robey, Jack Givens, James Lee, and Mike Phillips. The 1974 class made it to the championship* *game in 1975, won the NIT in 1976, reached the elite eight in 1977 and won the national title in 1978. Robey was the third overall pick in the NBA draft while Givens was drafted 16th. Hall quit because of outside influences......***Thomas Boyd, 1976.**

Todd May, Virgie (1983). 7/5/1964, led Virgie to a 33-3 record in 1982 and to the semifinals of the Kentucky State Tournament, where the Eagles lost to eventual champion Laurel County. He earned MVP honors his sophomore season. He earned MVP his sophomore year by scoring 82 points and grabbing 46 rebounds in three games. A three-time all-starter and Kentucky's "Mr. Basketball," he made several prep All-America teams, and he played in the Kentucky-Indiana All-Star Series. May scored 14 points and grabbed 10 rebounds for UK before transferring to Wake Forest.

Powell (Stanton)

Harold M. Hurst, 9/28/1933–/26/2009, 2L, (1954, 55). A native of Ezel, Hurst was a member of the Powell County Pirates Basketball Team where he excelled as an athlete. He was a member of UK's undefeated team (25-0) in 1954. He returned to Powell County and taught Vocational Agriculture from 1956-1971. During his tenure he worked with students of agriculture, and they received many state and national FFA awards.

Pulaski (Somerset)

Brinkley Barnett, 12/25/1889–7/24/1977, 2L, (1911, 12, 13). Barnett played high school basketball in Somerset. The team always practiced outdoors and played games in a small gym, "where the ceiling was so low we sometimes banked the ball off it." At UK, Barnett scored 151 points and was leading scorer on UK's 1912 team (19-0). He was team captain the following year. Barnett served in the Marine Corps in France during World War I. He was a professor of engineering and an assistant professor of electrical engineering at UK.

Remembering How It Was. *I was only 5-9 and weighed 130* *pounds when I played. As the designated shooter, I shot all the foul shots. They did not allow dribbling. You could pass the ball one time and shoot. We played in football pants, with the padding taken out. We had to buy our own shoes. I wasn't any star at all. W. C. Harrison was the best center in the South. He had a reach of about half a mile on the jump and generally did what he pleased with his opponents...* **Brinkley Barnett, 1973.**

Remembering the All-Winning Season: *The whole season bears the impress of the magical hand of Coach (E.R.) Sweetland. To him, if to any man, the credit for this most successful season must be given. He filled the boys with confidence, trained and instructed them, as only he can, and, as is his invariable custom, turned out a championship team...*The Kentuckian, 1912.

Lloyd B. Ramsey, 5/29/1918, 2L, (1941, 42). A native of Somerset, Ramsey attended University High in Lexington. He played basketball two years at UK scoring 93 points in 39 games. The Wildcats were SEC season and tournament champions his senior year.

During his army career, Ramsey served in World War II, Korea and Vietnam. He worked with many world leaders, including Winston Churchill and several Presidents of the United States. As Aide-de-Camp to British Field Marshal Harold Alexander and then as a front line battlefield commander, his memoirs are filled with vivid first-hand accounts and descriptions.

From June 1969 to March 1970, he was Commanding General of the America 1 Division of Vietnam. Two junior officers on his staff later became well known to all Americans, Major Colin Powell and Lt. Col. Norman Schwarzkopf. Ramsey's combat career ended in the crash of his command helicopter deep in enemy territory. He is a doctor in Nashville.

William Tuttle, 1/30/1892–4/4/1981, 4L, (1912, 13, 14, 15), was a freshman member of UK's 1912 undefeated basketball team (9-0). The Wildcats were 33-10 during his four years at UK. Tuttle was captain of the 1914 team and coach of the 1917 team. He earned three letters as a football end, played baseball, and was an assistant football coach at UK in 1915 and 1916. He moved to Hawaii with his wife in 1920 as an employee of the California Packing Co. on Oahu. They moved in 1932 to Maui, where he became manager of the newly formed Maui Pineapple Co. Tuttle was chairman of the Maui County Police Commission for 20 years .

Dickie Prater, 1/23/1931, (1950) left UK after his freshman year.

Reginald "Reggie" Hanson 9/8/1968, 3L, (1989, 90, 91), averaged 23.1 points and 10 rebounds in leading Pulaski High School to a 32-4 record and the 1987 KHSAA championship. He was MVP after scoring 92 points and pulling down 39 rebounds in four tourney games. Hanson shot a career school record 62 percent from the floor and 87 percent from the free throw line. He set other school records, including points (1,681), field goals (633), rebounds (903), and steals (368). He was All-District and All-Region three times and All-State his junior and senior years. Hanson played in the Derby Classic and the Kentucky-Indiana series. He also played for Coach Eddie Sutton's South squad in the 1987 U. S. Olympic Festival in Chapel Hill, N. C.

Hanson guided the 1991 Wildcats (22-6) to the best record (14-4) in the Southeastern Conference, although UK was not eligible for the league title. As team captains, Hanson and John Pelphrey led the Cats in scoring, averaging 14.4 ppg. He tallied 16.4 ppg in 1990. Hanson led the team in field goals made (1990), rebounding (1990, '91), blocks (1990, '91), and steals (1989, '90).

His dedication to the program led Pitino to rename the team's sacrifice award -- the Reggie Hanson Sacrifice Award. He also was All-SEC as both a junior and senior and earned numerous team awards including MVP and the Leadership Award his last two seasons.

Hanson made first-team All-SEC and was a team captain his senior year. He played briefly with Boston and spent seven seasons in Japan, serving as both a player and a coach. He also played one season (1991-92) with the Louisville Shooters of the Global League.

Hanson served seven seasons as an assistant coach at UK before accepting a similar post at South Florida, in 2007.

Remembering Senior Day: *I realized how important it was to them. I had seen that last year when Reggie Hanson had come out to center court, accompanied by his young nephew, who had a sign pinned to his back that said, "I love my Uncle Reggie." Reggie and his nephew both cried. . .* **Rick Pitino, 1992.**

Whitley (Williamsburg)

Marion Cluggish, Corbin 6-8, 9/10/1917, 3L, (1938, 39, 40), was a 6-foot-8, 235 lb. center, a towering person in his era. He was a member of the Corbin team that won the state basketball championship in 1936. With the center jump still in effect, it was almost a certainty that Corbin would control the ball after each basket. Cluggish played two seasons at Williamsburg and one at Catlettsburg before transferring to Corbin.

Cluggish scored 301points in 63 games as a Wildcat. They were SEC regular season and tournament champions his final two years. He was a World War II veteran who played one year with the New York Knicks. He was a retired coach and educator living in Florida.

Remembering Marion Cluggish: *I think he was the first individual player to dominate the tournament. There was no way to stop him. They could control the ball and then lob it in to him under the basket. The smaller players couldn't get it away from him....* **John McGill, 1985.**

More about Cluggish. *It was Marion Cluggish, the Goliath, who took the dominating part in one of the most spectacular drives to a state championship that the battle-hallowed U.K. gymnasium has ever witnessed, and as he proved himself impervious to the missiles fired from the slingshots in the hands of every little David who opposed him, he won the hearts of the crowd and the admiration of his enemies. The mammoth one strolled out of the gymnasium the most popular player who has taken part in the annual tournament* *in years...* **Neville Dunn, 1936.**

More Cluggish. *Before the game started, we always dribbled the ball the length of the floor, and Cluggish would stuff it through the hoop. Adolph said such showmanship would win over a critical crowd. We were playing LIU in Madison Square Garden. So when we dribbled down the floor, J. Rice passed the ball off to Clugg to stuff. Clugg was nervous and missed the basket and we got the thunder beat out of us (52-34).*

Adolph warned Clugg, "We'll be playing (St. Joseph's) in a new place in Philadelphia, son, and it'll be a critical crowd. Now, by gravy, Walker's going to dribble down the floor and give you a good pass before the game. I want you to jam your arm through that basket, or I'm going to ship your tail back to Corbin." Clugg made the basket. We won, 41-30.... **Fred "Cab" Curtis, BBM.**

(1940). Stan Cluggish was a World War II veteran and a member of the Corbin team that won the state basketball championship in 1936. Stan and brother Marion both made the All-Tournament team. They played one season, (1939-40) together at UK.

Paul Adkins 8/28/1899–3/10/1962, 2L, (1921, 22). Dr. Adkins attended Cumberland College two years and earned a letter before joining the Wildcats n 1920-21. He was the center on the 1921 UK team that defeated Georgia, 20-19, for the first basketball championship of the South. They named him to the All-Tournament team. Adkins led UK in scoring the following year and made the All-Southern team. He was also a state collegiate tennis champion and a baseball player.

Dr. Adkins was a graduate of Cumberland College, UK and the University of Louisville Medical School. He was a past president of the Bell County Medical Society and chairman of the county Democratic committee.

Remembering Dr. Adkins: *Paul was a consistent performer whose forte was scoring goals from different and difficult angles. Sam Ridgeway (1920-21) was the backbone of our team. He was a big fellow and quick as a cat, a good jumper with enough weight to* *push around. I always told him he and Paul made me an All-American...***Basil Hayden 1975.**

Jerry Lee Bird, Corbin, 2/2/1935, 3L, (1954, 55, 56), was an All-State selection for two seasons at Corbin High. He led the Red Hounds to a third-place finish in the 1950 State Basketball Tournament. Bird was a star of the North-South cage classic at Murray in 1952. Bird's teammates at Corbin included Frank Selvy, who went on to make headlines at Furman University, when he scored 100 points against Newberry.

Bird scored 713 points and grabbed 589 rebounds during his three varsity seasons at UK, when the Wildcats won 68 of 76 games played. They included SEC championships in 1954 and 1955 and an undefeated season in 1954. He was All-SEC second team in 1956. Jerry's brothers Calvin, Rodger, and Billy Bird earned football letters at UK.

Jerry spent two years in the Army. He played one year (1959) with the New York Knicks.

Bird worked 10 years with the Phillips Petroleum Co. He retired after 30 years as human resources administrator for the American Greetings Corp. in Corbin.

Remembering Phillips Petroleum: *They sent me to Indianapolis before assigning me a territory to work. At the end of my training, a Phillips manager called me into his office and apologized for the inconvenience, but told me the company was going to send me to Corbin, Kentucky. They couldn't believe I was from Corbin. They thought I was from Lexington...My wife and I bought a home here and we've lived almost 40 years in this house...***Jerry Bird to Gregg Doye, 2005.**

Chapter XVII
Bluegrass Section

The Commonwealth of Kentucky geographically contains five regions: Eastern Coal Field, Bluegrass, Pennyroyal, Western Coal Field, and Jackson Purchase. There is some inter-lapping of counties, especially in the Eastern Section. The Commission also has a different interpretation of those borders, which assigns Lewis, Fleming, Menifee, Rowan, Powell, Estill, Madison, Rockcastle, Pulaski and Wayne counties to its eastern border. That leaves the following counties in the Bluegrass umbrella:

Anderson, Bath, Boone, Bourbon, Boyle, Bracken, Bullitt, Campbell, Carroll , Fayette, Fleming, Franklin, Garrard, Gallatin, Grant, Harrison, Henry, Jefferson, Jessamine, Lincoln, Marion, Mason, Mercer, Montgomery, Nelson, Nicholas, Oldham, Owen, Pendleton, Robertson, Scott, Shelby, Spencer, Washington, and Woodford.

Anderson (Lawrenceburg)

William Waller White, 3L, (1940, 41, 42). Born in Tyrone, White scored 236 points on Wildcat teams that compiled a 51-20 record and were runners-up to Dartmouth, 33-30, in the 1942 NCAA Tournament in New Orleans. He was an Air Corps veteran of the European Theater in WWII. White worked in marketing management for Gulf Oil for 29 years.

Remembering Waller White. *He loved volunteering as "Bingo Bill" at MCH and he also enjoyed being a member of the Ukulele Band at First Baptist Church, Conroe.*

Paul S. McBrayer, 10/12/1909, 3L, (1928, 29, 30), was a star at Kavanaugh High School in Lawrenceburg before going to UK. He played for Coach John Mauer and was team captain and UK's fourth All-American. McBrayer was an assistant coach at Kentucky for nine years under Adolph Rupp before entering the Army during World War II.

McBrayer accepted a job as head basketball coach at Eastern State College when Rupp failed to hire him. McBrayer became the winningest basketball coach in Eastern Kentucky University history. His 219-144 record included two Ohio Valley Conference titles and two trips to the NCAA Tournament.

Former Wildcats who played as freshmen for McBrayer held what was called "the McBrayer Dinner", usually during UK homecoming weekend activities. The 37th reunion was held just prior to his death.

Remembering McBrayer: *He was bitter at the beginning, but he was forgiving and put it behind him He said he wouldn't have had the great bunch of players he had at Eastern, and he wouldn't have been married to the woman who is now his widow. He was a strict disciplinarian and a no-nonsense coach. He was able to get the best out of every player. You were afraid of him in one sense, but you were loyal and close, too....***Roy Allison, Former Eastern Player1951-56.**

Ralph Carlisle, 1/26/15-8/7/1999, 3L, (1935, 36, 37), earned three letters at UK, where he was All-SEC Tournament his junior and senior years. He scored 504 points on Wildcat teams during his three varsity years at UK. (See Coaches).

After his retirement from coaching in 1961, Carlisle began working as a manager for an insurance company, Equitable of Kentucky, where he received several awards for his work. He was eventually promoted to district manager for Equitable Life Assurance Society of New Jersey. (See Coaches)

Remembering Carlisle: *He was a drill sergeant in practice and a father figure off the court. He always pushed his players to be the best players and the best people they could be....* **Bob Mulcahy, a member of Lafayette's 1950 state championship team.**

Jimmy Dan Conner, 3L, (1973, 74, 75). A Parade All-America, Jimmy Dan was Kentucky's "Mr. Basketball" for 1971 after leading Anderson County to the 1984 KHSAA championship. He was All-NCAA Regional at UK, which lost to UCLA in the 1975 NCAA championship game. He scored 1,009 points and grabbed 344 rebounds at UK. Jimmy Dan played one year with the Virginia Squires in the ABA.

Remembering Jimmy Dan: *I first saw Jimmy Dan Conner play for Anderson County in the Central Kentucky Conference Tournament at Danville when he was a 15-year-old sophomore. Even then his coolness and maturity on the court impressed me before anything else. In recruiting him, I best remember the day in his senior year when we went fishing and pulled in a nice string of bass and redeye. On that day I felt that UK had landed Jimmy Dan, too. He was a true Kentucky boy. It would have seemed like heresy if he had gone somewhere else....* **Joe B. Hall, BBM.**

Boone (Burlington)

Milton James "Bud" Cavana, 9/13/59, Sq., (1931). Known well as a swimming instructor, he was for 20 years athletic director and physical education teacher at Newport Junior high school. He earned varsity football letters at UK in 1929, 30 and 31, and was a member of Rupp's first basketball team at UK.

Allen Feldhaus, 7/15/1940, 3L, (1960, 61, 62), played on Wildcat teams that were 62-19, with a best season of 23-3 in 1962. He scored 299 points and got 320 rebounds in 72 games. They were SEC champs in '62, losing to Ohio State in both the 1961 and 1962 regionals. Feldhaus also played baseball before and after UK, and coached high school sports. (See "Kentucky Coaches.)

John R. "Frenchy" DeMoisey, 1913–8/1/1963, 3L, (1932, 33, 34), made All Southeastern Conference in 1933-34 and was named All-America in 1934, the same year he served as captain of the team.

During his basketball career, the Wildcats won 50 games and lost six and, in 1933, were named Southeastern Conference and Helms National champions.

UK Coach Adolph Rupp credited DeMoisey with being the first basketball player to use the one-hand overhead pivot shot. The six-foot, five-inch-tall All America developed the shot in 1932 and first used it in a game between UK and Vanderbilt, according to Rupp.

DeMoisey graduated from the University in 1934 and played baseball with the old American Association for a time. He later served as recreation director for the Kentucky Houses of Reform at Greendale and became superintendent there in 1941, a post he held three years before resigning to manage the Blue Grass farms of the LeBus brothers.

DeMoisey also taught school and coached basketball at Harrodsburg and Grayson high schools and once pitched for the Louisville Colonels. He also was a well-known referee of amateur athletic contests in the Central Kentucky area.

DeMoisey participated in the 1935 political campaign conducted by A. B. "Happy" Chandler and joined his first administration in 1963.

Remembering Frenchy: *He was a big, rugged fellow. I used to ask one of my granddaughters how much she loved me and she'd say, "As big as Frenchy"....***A. B. Chandler, 1963.**

Rupp Remembers Frenchy: *He was a self-made basketball player who worked and worked at it. It was encouraging to see the boy play....***Adolph Rupp, 1963.**

Truitt DeMoisey, 1/9/26–8/2/2005, Sq., (1944), lettered one year at UK. After service in the Marine Corps, he transferred to Ohio State. He was a retired consultant with the Kentucky attorney general. He also was a vice president of the A.B. Happy Chandler Foundation, a past president of the National Association of Hearing Officials and a Marine Corps veteran of World War II.

John Crigler, 5/31/1936, 3L, (1956, 57, 58), was a second-team All-State performer who scored 699 points (27.8 ppg) in his senior year at Hebron High. He was high scorer and MVP in two all-star games. Crigler scored 696 points and got 528 rebounds in three seasons at UK. He was a starter in UK's win over Seattle in the 1958 NCAA championship game. Crigler got 14 points and 14 rebounds that game.

Remembering Rupp: *John Lloyd, 150 years from now there will be no University, no field house. There will have been an atomic war and it all will have been destroyed. But underneath the rubble there will be a monument, which will be inscribed, 'Here lies John Lloyd Crigler, the most stupid basketball player ever at Kentucky, killed by Adolph Rupp', because, boy, if you don't play better, I am going to kill you.*

Remembering Seattle: *(Elgin) Baylor would guard (Ed) Beck, who was averaging only 4.8 ppg. However, Crigler had failed to score the night before so Seattle coach John Castellani switched Baylor to guarding him out on the floor. When Rupp observed that, he told Crigler to drive on Baylor. Crigler drove, got a couple fouls on Baylor, and at the same time scored a couple baskets. Seattle loosened up a bit, but by halftime Baylor had three fouls on him. The rest is history...***Harry Lancaster, BBM**

Bill Smith, 3L, (1956, 57, 58), made All-State honorable mention three straight years at Walton, where he scored 1,805 points in four years. He played on UK's 1958 NCAA championship team. Smith taught and coached in the Owen County school system.

Remembering Champions: *The old men wore matching brown sweaters and slacks, a nod to Coach Rupp who wore a brown suit to each of their games. A half century ago, they had played for Adolph Rupp on the University of Kentucky basketball team that won the 1958 NCAA tournament. In basketball-crazed Kentucky, they had been young heroes back then, handing Rupp his fourth national title, the final jewel in his NCAA crown.*

In the huge arena named for their coach, they formed a wide line that stretched across the midcourt of the playing floor. They were there to be honored at halftime on the golden anniversary of their championship season. No one mentioned that the head coach now sitting on the University's bench had not yet been born in 1958.

When each man's name was called, he stepped forward and waved to the crowd. A television camera zoomed in for a close-up shot, and then a larger than life electronic image of the former player flashed on a giant screen near the roof of the arena. . . **Georgia Green, Owen County News-Herald.**

Bourbon (Paris)

Alvin S. Thompson, Clintonville, 3/17/1897–4/21/1960, (1917), attended the University of Virginia Prep School and the University of Kentucky in 1916 and 1917. He played basketball one year at UK. He was a student at the University when he enlisted in the famed Barrow Unit, a local Medical Corps unit that served overseas in World War I. Thompson was an officer in the Internal Revenue Service office 25 years and formerly a division chief in the Office of the Collector of Internal Revenue.

Basil Hayden, 5/19/1899–1/10/2003, 3L, (1920, 21, 22), was a 5-foot-11 play-making guard who started basketball in the sixth grade in Paris. They played on a cinder floor in an area under the city auditorium. Six padded posts held up the place. They also played in a tobacco warehouse; then they moved into a new YMCA that had a small floor and a nice, tall ceiling. Three men brought the ball down the floor. You always threw it to the man running toward you. At UK, Hayden's responsibility was to get the ball to Bill King or Paul Adkins. He got most of his points by following their shots.

Hayden was UK's leading scorer as a sophomore in 1919-20, with a 10.8 average. He averaged 9.6 points as a junior. He suffered a knee injury high-jumping for the Wildcats before the 1922 basketball season, but still managed to average 5 points per game.

The Wildcats were 28-14 in the three years that Hayden played at UK. Hayden captained the 1921 team that beat Georgia 20-19 in the finals of the Southern Intercollegiate Athletic Association Championship in Atlanta. It was Kentucky's first significant basketball championship, and possibly the first college basketball tournament ever played. During his three varsity years, the Wildcats were 28-14. They outscored their opponents, 1266–902. While at UK, he also played on the tennis team and threw the javelin, setting a school record with a toss of 163 feet and 3 inches.

Hayden worked one summer for Dodge in Detroit. He taught and coached at Clark County High School and later got into the insurance business in Richmond. He left his insurance job to coach at UK for one season–1926-27–in which the Wildcats had an abysmal 3-13 record.

Hayden also taught school, did tax work, and was a bank officer, state bank examiner and hospital administrator. He retired in his 70s from a position with the Kentucky Conference of the Methodist Church. Hayden also worked again for a Richmond insurance firm and later worked for many years at a bank in Paris. He died at age 103.

Remembering 1927: *The players I inherited were pretty green. I started five sophomores (Combs, Owens, Milward, McGinnis, and McBrayer.) All were Kentuckians. They had a lot to learn....* **Basil Hayden, BBM.**

Singing the Blues. *Ray Eklund left me a bunch of scrubs. What we had were players who had played in the YMCA and church leagues mostly. Our starters opening night were all football players. I couldn't get a very good effort out of them all season. It wasn't that bad. No one expected much, so you weren't disappointed. You didn't get too many boos...* **Basil Hayden, BBM.**

Robert Lavin, 8/31/1900-11/1/1972, 3L, (1920, 21, 22). Lavin and Basil Hayden were teammates at Paris High and at UK. Lavin made SIAA All-Tournament in 1921.

Alexander T. "Chuck" Rice, 4/22/1962, 2L, (1923, 24), was a reserve on UK teams that were 16-13. He was a coach and teacher at Frankfort High School between 1927 and 1942 and later was a traffic department employee of Schenley Distillers Inc.

Cecil D. Bell, 10/19/10–11/30/2004, 1L, (1931), graduated from Millersburg Military Institute in 1928. He was Captain of his ROTC Company and Captain of the basketball team, which won the state tournament. At UK, he was a two-year letterman in basketball having played for Adolph Rupp's first teams. He operated the scoreboard at the press table for the University's basketball games for 33 years. Bell was honored by the Georgetown Farm City Committee as a Pioneer Farmer.

Remembering Cecil: *In 1943 his farm was chosen by the University Experiment Station as one of 10 sample farms in Kentucky and as their tobacco enterprise demonstration farms by using the best methods. He was a farmer and breeder of pure-bred registered Angus cattle.*

Walter Hodge, NA – 2/23/2012, 1L, (1937), lettered in 1937, but played sparingly in 1939. He also was a UK football player.

Jim Goodman, 1L, (1938, 39). After starring at Paris High, Goodman played two years on UK teams that were 29-9. They won the SEC Tournament in 1939.

Jim LeMaster, 8/12/1946, 3L, (1966, 67, 68), earned All-State honors at Bourbon County High, where he was a 24-point shooter who scored 1,661 in his career. He was a member of the 1966 "Rupp's Runts" team that was 27-2 after losing to Texas Western in the NCAA championship game.

Gayle Rose, 11/2/32, 3L, (1952, 54, 55), made All-State in his senior year at Paris High. He was Mr. Basketball in Kentucky that year. Rose was also a schoolboy All-American. Rose was a starting guard on UK's undefeated 1954 team. He scored 443 points and 125 rebounds in 75 games.

Remembering Rose: *It was Gayle's dribbling artistry that enabled the Wildcats to control the ball for a vital two minutes and eke out a close victory over DePaul in Chicago Stadium…***Kuhn, UK**

SID, 1954.

Remembering Rupp: *Rose, you look like a Shetland pony in a stud-horse parade. Stop practice everyone and take a shower, I know we are going to have a successful season now. Rose got a rebound...*Gayle Rose, BBM.**

Remembering Rupp: *One· afternoon during the 1955 56 season while the players were going through some warm-up drills Coach Rupp suddenly stopped practice and said in that familiar drawl of his, "Hold everything!" Then as everything got so quiet you could hear a pin drop he turned to Harold Ross, a quiet, easygoing guard from Hickman, Kentucky, who at the time had been whistling while we were going through drills, and said: "Harold, I didn't bring you down here all the way from Hickman to listen to you sing. If you wanted to do that you should have talked to Warren Lutz (U.K. Band Director), and maybe he would have given you a scholarship...*Ken Lehkamp, BBM*

Preston LeMaster, 10/5/1986, 4L, (2003, 04, 05, 06). Preston scored more than 2,000 points at Bourbon County High. He was All-District, All-Region, and All-State. LeMaster played on UK teams that were 90-28. They were SEC East and Tourney champions his first two seasons and were East champions in 2005. His father Jim was a member of Rupp's Runts.

Bracken (Brooksville)

Clyde Cooper; 1010/25--3/15/1995, Sq., (1945), played on the 1943-44 Brooksville team that was undefeated in regular season. He played one semester at UK. Cooper was a mechanic for GE. He coached the YMCA team of Kanakee, Ill., to a national title.

Alvin Cummins, NA, (1947, 48). Cummins transferred to Michigan after appearing in 32 games as a Wildcat. He owns a financial company and is a real estate broker in Lexington.

Campbell (Newport)

Joseph G. Hermann, 4/13/1886–11/26/1965, 1L, (1906). There are no statistics available for Hermann's one year on UK's fourth basketball team, which won five of 14 games played.

Stanley John Ridd, 8/14/1890–1/28/1964, Sq, (1912). Ridd appeared in one game for the Wildcats in 1912. He retired after 43 years as a former personnel director of the American Creosoting Company. Ridd was a chief maintenance mate in the United States Navy during World War I.

Ralph R. Morgan, 6/8/1891–2/20/1984, 3L (1913, 14, 15). During the three years that Morgan played for UK, the Wildcats were 34-10. He was team captain and leading scorer in 1915. Morgan served in WWI as a 2nd Lt. He was an agent for the Northwestern Mutual Life Insurance Co. in Louisville for 40 years. He traced his ancestry back to David Ramsey, a president of the Continental Congress and signer of the Declaration of Independence.

Elmer "Baldy" Gilb, 12/12/1907–10/1/1991, 1L, (1929), was an outstanding three-sport athlete at Newport High. 1925…He was All-Regional in football and played in the 1925 Sweet Sixteen® where Newport lost to eventual state champion Manual in the semifinals… At UK in 1925, he received the "Fros Cup" that went to an outstanding freshman. Gilb played on UK's 1929 team that finished 12-5 after losing to Georgia 26-24 in the Southern Conference Tournament. He was team captain of the UK baseball team his senior year. (See Coaches)

Milton "Bud" Cavana, (DOD) 9/13/1959, Sq. (1931). Cavana played against Georgetown in Rupp's first game. He earned three letters in football at UK. Cavana was a swim instructor who served 20 years as athletic director and physical education instructor at Newport High.

Mark Krebs, 10/10/1986 (2008, 09, 10), was Ninth Region

Player of the Year, two-time All-Tournament selection. He was a walk-on who earned a scholarship at UK. Krebs wrote a book-- Beyond a Dream: A Mother's Courage, A Family's Fight, A Son's Determination-- about his career and about his mother's battle with breast cancer.

A Review: *Mark walks us through his journey at UK, from thrilled walk on to red shirt to scholarship player and the complex emotions that accompanied his career and personal life...***Ashley Judd, Actress.**

Remembering Krebs: *At the University, I found a real team-mate in Mark Krebs. He will remain like a brother to me forever. Mark's book chronicles his family's fight and captures that unforget-table experience under Coach Calipari...* **John Wall, #1 pick in the 2010 NBA draft.**

W. C. Fox, 1887–12/18/1918, 3L (1907, 08, 09), played four sports–baseball, basketball, football and track–at UK. He was chief engineer of the United States Structural company, and one of the most widely known member sof the profession. Fox died at the Miami Valley hospital after a brief illness of pneumonia. Mr. Fox was born and raised in Newport, Ky., and had attained distinction as an engineer before he came to Dayton six years ago.

Howard G. "Dutch" Kreuter, 2/5/33–4/10/78, 2L, (1932, 33). Born in Cincinnati, Kreuter played on Rupp's first team at UK. He resided in Fairfield 15 years and retired from Travis AFB in 1965 as a lieutenant colonel with 23 years of service. He was a former administrator of the La Mariposa. He started two years on Rupp's 1932 and '33 teams that were 36-5. They won the SEC tournament in 1933.

Breckinridge (Irvington)

Michael Parks, 10/30/1970, Sq., (1990). Parks was an all-district selection in high school. His team won their first game in regional playoff. Parks played in 3 games at U.K.

Carroll (Carrollton)

David Miller, 2/27/54, (Sq.) (1974). Miller led Carroll County to the 8th. Region Championship. He averaged 25.7 ppg and 18 rebounds earning All-State honors. Miller appeared in two games as a UK freshman.

Fayette (Lexington)

Ruric Roark, 3/13/1887–5/9/1962, 1L, (1904). A native of Greenville, Roark attended schools in Lexington. He was one of a small group of UK students who started basketball at UK.

Dr. Roark received his Ph.D. at Washington University in 1917. He was chief chemist of U.S. Products Corp. in Chicago.

Richard C. "Dick" Barbee, 5/20/1889–3/12/1950, 3L, (1906, 07, 09). After starring at Lexington Senior High, Barbee reportedly played five seasons with the fledgling UK team. He served as captain of the 1908 basketball squad, and the 1909 football team. He earned three letters each in football and track.

Remembering 1909: *No dribbling was allowed. You had to pass the ball. You could bounce it one time and shoot. We played in football pants, with the adding taken out. We bought our own shoes...***Brinkley Barnett, BBM.**

Joel White Guyn, 4/23/1883–4/14/1953, 1L, (1904), was a leader in a group of football players and students who started basketball at UK in 1903. He coached the UK football team for four seasons, and was a former member of the board of the family Welfare Society.

John S. Crosthwaite, 11/2/87–9/11/1971, 1L, (1910). Born in Versailles, Ky., Crosthwaite resided in Lexington 19 years. He was a retired engineer for General Electric. He was a graduate of the University of Kentucky and a member of the K-Man's association, the Veterans' association 78th division, and was a Kentucky colonel. He also served with the U.S. Army in World War I.

Shelby Shanklin, 6/6/1888–3/31/67, 3L, (1907, 08, 10). There are no stats available for Shanklin's three varsity years. He had lived in Florida since 1937 where he was a Florida flower grower..

William Rodes, 10/9/1887–10/18/1950, 2L, (1909, 10). Rodes received his early education in Lexington schools and later attended the University of Kentucky, where he was a varsity standout in basketball, football and track. Rodes held a master's degree from the University. He operated a farm near Clintonville.

Paul Anderson. 1/13/1898–11/9/1983, Sq., (1917). Anderson played on a 1917 UK team that played an abbreviated wartime schedule, winning four of six games.

Remembering Anderson: *In a formal ceremony witnessed by French civilians in 1944, Army Capt. Frederick Paul Anderson, of Versailles, was recently awarded the Bronze Star "for meritorious achievement in military operations". In order to acquire information on harbor, beach and railway facilities of the St. Malo vicinity while the area was still occupied by the enemy, Captain Anderson subjected himself to sniper, machine gun and artillery fire and entered heavily mined areas without benefit of mine detectors.*

Captain Anderson was a director of highway pavement research in civilian life.

William "Doc" Rodes, 10/7/1894–1/28/1946, 1L, (1917). After he was graduated from Lexington high school, Rodes played on the U.K. freshman football and basketball teams in 1914 and was varsity quarterback on the 1915 and 1916 teams. Described by University officials as one of the greatest football players who ever performed in a Wildcat uniform, he was chosen as All-Southern quarterback in 1916. Besides basketball and football, Rodes played baseball at the University. In `1917, he served as a second lieutenant with the American forces overseas. After returning to Lexington, he coached the University freshman football team and in 1923 served as assistant coach under Jack Winn. Later he became a member of the University's athletic council and served until 1938. Rodes and O.B. Murphy operated the Union Transfer and Storage Company.

William R. Campbell, 8/19/1897–11/6/1922), Sq., (1917, 18), was a reserve at UK. He scored 67 points.

Arthur Lee Bastin, 4/29/1898–3/9/1957, 1L, (1918). Bastin was born in East Bernstadt and educated in Lexington public schools. He was second-leading scorer on the 1918 Wildcat team that finished 9-2-1. The unique tie game (21-21) with Wesleyan resulted from a scorer's error that went unnoticed until after the teams had departed. Bastin was the owner and operator of the Elkhorn Coal Co. at Kona, KY.

James R. McFarland, 8/10/1904, 3L, (1924, 25, 26), attended Lexington High School, now known as Henry Clay High School. He was a member of the Blue Devils basketball team that won the national high school championship in 1922. McFarland was leading scorer and team captain in 1925. He scored 405 points on UK teams that were 40-14. Also during the 1920s, McFarland was the Lexington singles tennis champ for several years and a doubles champ, teaming with O.G. Steele.

Doug Flynn, 4/8 1951, Fr., (1970), played football, baseball and basketball at Bryan Station High School. UK presented him its Basketball Freshman Leadership Award in 1970. Flynn played second base . with five Major League teams. He was a member of Cincinnati's 1975 and 1976 World Series championship teams. Flynn won a Golden Glove with the Mets. He is a correspondent banking officer with Central Bank in Lexington

Cameron Mills, 2/10/75, 4L, (1995, 96, 97, 98), signed with UK after a stellar career at Lexington Dunbar. Honors included 11th Region All-Tournament and Sweet 16 MVP. Mills played on Kentucky basketball teams that were in three straight *NCAA title*

games in the 1990s. He ended his career as UK's all-time leader in three-point accuracy, hitting 47.4 percent from 1995-98. Mills is head of Cameron Mills Ministries.

Remembering First UK Game. *The first UK game I saw in person came on Dec. 12, 1987. It was my 12th birthday. My father Terry took me to the Kentucky-Louisville game in Rupp Arena as a present. Forward Cedric Jenkins won the game 76-75 with a tip-in seconds before the final horn. After Cedric's tip, Rupp Arena just erupted. I never forgot how loud that was....***Cameron Mills.**

Remembering Cameron. *Cameron is a young man who is very dedicated and had a strong desire to become a Kentucky basketball player and that speaks highly as he turned down a number of places to come here...***Rick Pitino, 1994-95 UK Media Guide.**

*Cameron you are the fattest (expletive) ballplayer I have ever seen. I cannot have you on this team if you are going to look like this...***Rick Pitino, 1995.**

*After losing 30 pounds over the next three weeks, Mills recalled saying to himself, "I don't know if I can take four years of this man". After Mills scored 13 points in a heartbreaking loss to Arizona, Pitino said, "I cannot believe what you have accomplished for us, Cameron. I think back to your freshman year when you showed up a fat 211 pounds. You've got a lot to be proud of, son." Mills went from hating Coach Pitino to thinking he was the "most incredible person on earth."....***Denny Trease, 1999.**

Will Emmet Milward, 1/1/1904–10/19/1972, Sq., (1924, 25, 26), graduated in 1922 from Lexington High School. He played center on UK teams that were 26-11 during his two varsity years. Milward was second-leading scorer in 1924 and No. 3 scorer in 1925.

In 1932 he married Miss Rebecca Hart Shelby, of Danville. She was a great-granddaughter of Kentucky's first governor, Isaac Shelby.

Milward was a managing partner of the W.R. Milward Mortuaries and a distinguished business and community leader. He entered funeral service with his father in 1926.

George Burgess Carey, 12/2/1961, 2L, (1925, 26), was captain of the old Lexington Senior High School team, the school's first team to win a national basketball championship. He was UK's second All-American in 1921. Carey also served as captain of the UK team. During his two varsity years the Wildcats were 28-11. They won one tournament championship, and lost in the second game of another.

Remembering Burgess: *His path to UK was paved with bruises; taken and given; and with hurrahs and accolades. As team captain and defensive bulwark, he led the 1922 Lexington Senior High School team to state and national championships, collecting many honors along the way...***BBM, 1976.**

Remembering Burgess: *The first time I saw Burgess he had a patch over one eye. That was during my first year at UK. No, I don't know where he got it, and I didn't ask. I remember he loved the free-for-all rough type of game. When he stood in front of the basket, nobody could budge him.* **Mrs. Burgess Carey, 1974.**

*He was just the best there was in his time. Of course, people today probably can't understand how a man can make All-American honors without scoring a lot of points, but that was his role. His job was to stop the other team from scoring, and he did it well...***George Buchheit, UK coach, 1920-24, 1971 interview**

Len Miller, 1/21/1907–5/1/1945, (1927), played on the 1924 Lexington High School basketball team that went to the national tournament. He gained recognition at the University of Kentucky as one of the best quarterbacks in the South. Miller was unable to play much after 1927 because of a knee injury. In 1929 he was added to the coaching staff. He remained at the University for that season only, but returned as an assistant grid mentor in 1932-33. Miller was head of the physical education department at Morehead State Teachers College. He had been acting coach of all athletics at Morehead in the absence of Ellis Johnson, another former U.K. athlete then in the Naval Reserve.

Stanley "Spooks" Milward, 7/25/1907–3/2/1982, 3L, (1929), played basketball at the old Lexington Senior High School and earned several awards while on that team. He played .at UK from 1928 to 1930 under the late John Mauer, who preceded Adolph Rupp as head coach. He later was inducted into the Kentucky Lions' High School Basketball Hall of Fame. Milward was a retired Army major and a former employee of the General Adjustment Bureau of Memphis, where he worked for 35 years.

Lawrence L. (Big) McGinnis, 5/8/1907–2/5/1987, 3L, (1928, 29, 30), earned basketball letters at UK in 1928, 1929 and 1930 and football (1930). He was a guard and team captain in 1929. His brother, W. Louis McGinnis, played basketball with him for a time at UK.

McGinnis taught at three high schools. He coached basketball, football and baseball at Owensboro High School. He retired from Owensboro High School in 1975 as assistant principal and athletic director.

Remembering Lawrence: *He was a very fine player– very loyal to his coach and his team. . He was not a great scorer. We played different basketball in those days from the one-on-one you see today. It was a team effort...***Paul McBrayer, BBM.**

Louis "Little" McGinnis, 2/12/1910–8/23/2003 3L, (1929, 30, 31). With 347 points, McGinnis was among UK's leading scorers each of his three varsity years. He was All-Southern Conference in 1931. He retired as a mortician in Lexington.

Remembering Tulane: *The spectators sat at the out-of-bounds. If you went out, they would not help you back; they would throw you back. The game was so rough that coach Mauer sent in his 'wrecking crew' and that's how it ended, like a football game...***Louis McGinnis BBM.**

Remembering Notre Dame: *in January, 1929, we played Notre Dame for UK's first game ever with the Irish. We traveled by train to South Bend, riding a sleeper all night. We got there in time for practice. They played their home games on a temporary floor in the* *field house. There was a small crowd in attendance. They thought we would be a pushover .Out-of-bounds were not common then, but we had practiced hard on them. We worked two plays to perfection, getting crip shots at the end of each. We beat them 19-16. It would be 14 years before UK beat them again....*.**Louis McGinnis, BBM.**

Charles Jacob Bronston, 9/20/1909–6/5/2006 2L, (1930, 31), was born in Richmond but he grew up in Lexington.. He was on Coach Rupp's first basketball team. Bronston delivered ice from a horse drawn wagon. By high school he was working for Greyhound Lines, Inc., where he remained until his retirement in 1970.

Arthur Price Shanklin, 11/4/1899–8/20/1968, 1L, (1918), appeared in 12 games for UK in 1918. He was vice president and general sales manager of Carrier Corp., Syracuse, N. Y.

Clarence Foster Helm, 8/19/1904–8/21/1973 (1925, 27), won four basketball letters at UK. He played on teams with a record of 54-27. Helms was a Leaf supervisor of the R.J. Reynolds Tobacco Company.

Henry Clay Simpson, 5/27/1896–12/18/1986, Sq., (1919), played basketball at the old Lexington High School. He played football and basketball at the University of Kentucky. Simpson was a great-great-grandson of statesman Henry Clay. He was a first lieutenant in the Army during World War I. A retired farmer, he was instrumental in developing Lexington's Chevy Chase area, which once was part of his great-great-grandfather's farm.

Maurice Jackson, 6/19/11–8/11/1995, Sq., (1931, 32, 33), was born in Franklin County but lived in Lexington for 80 years. He was a member of the first football and basketball teams fielded by Lexington's Henry Clay High School, from which he graduated in 1930. He also was on the first University of Kentucky basketball team coached by the legendary Adolph Rupp, and a member of the 1933 team that won all its regular season games, but lost to Florida in the SEC tournament.

He worked for the Veterans Administration. He also coached basketball and baseball at the old University High School and Clark

County.

Jackson's term as sheriff came after he had worked for 12 years as a local deputy sheriff. He defended his office against charges of nepotism in 1973 -- his wife, Elizabeth Montague Jackson, who died in 1987, and several other relatives worked in the sheriff's office during his term.

A Sheriff Remembers: *If hiring my grandmother could make us the number one office in the state, I would do it...***Maurice Jackson.**

James B. Kittrell, 10/1/1904–05/15/1966 Sq., (1926), attended Lexington public schools. He appeared in one basketball game for UK during the 1926 season. Kittrell was a captain in the Army during World War II. He was associated with the U.S. Rubber Co. before becoming a partner with his father in Kittrell Motors.

William Douglas Kleiser, 1/28/1909–2/28/1988, 1L, (1930-31-32), starred at Henry Clay High School before becoming was a member of Rupp's first basketball team at UK. He was a former owner and operator of Lexington Granite Co. He earlier was the agriculture agent in Greenup and Owen counties. During World War II he was a Lieutenant Colonel in the Army.

Hiram Hays Owens, 11/2/1907–7/24/1972, 3L, (1928, 29, 30), was born in Bryantsville. He was a reserve on two UK basketball teams. He also lettered in football and track. Owens was a Prudential Insurance Co. salesman before a 25-year career in the U.S. Army and after retirement was employed with the Duesterberg Drug Store.

Carey A. Spicer, 4/23/1909–12/5/1996. 3L, (1939, 30, 31), was one of the top football and basketball players at the old Lexington High School. He made the All-State team in basketball, was president of his senior class and received several other honors. Spicer was the first two-time basketball All-American at UK, and the first All-American player under legendary coach Adolph Rupp. In 1964 he became the second former UK player to be elected into the Helms Basketball Hall of Fame.

Spicer coached basketball for several years at Georgetown College.

He was a captain in the Army during World War II. After the war he joined Spalding Sporting Goods Co., selling primarily equipment for a sport he was not particularly good at--golf. Spicer retired from Spalding.

Allan "Doc" Lavin, Athens, 11/22/1911–1/14/1974, Sq., (1931). A native of Paris, Lavin saw action in Rupp's first game as UK coach in 1931.He later served thoroughbred racing in many capacities.

Remembering Rupp: *My impression and association of His Holiness-The Baron? I will be ever grateful to him because of a short time around him I have gotten many miles of publicity from coast to coast and of one comment which was picked up by AP and UPI. I was often asked what kind of a player I was, and I said I was a situation player. When I was put in a game we were too far in front for the opposition to catch us or too far behind for us to ever catch up.*

I spent much time out of Kentucky the past 40 years, and the mention of Kentucky and basketball or the fact that you are a Kentucky Colonel will immediately create an interested audience. A current Kentucky Colonel card is just about as valuable as a Bank Americard–if you are about four states distance from the Commonwealth.

When Rupp arrived at Lexington, he had lost the figure he had when he was performing for Phog Allen at Kansas. In several of his ball handling operations for the benefit of us rookies it showed that he had not been taking his daily dozen push-ups during the previous few years. He got his points over well just the same.

Rupp as I knew him had a touch of "Patton" in him, and when he arrived at UK he was presented with one All-American (Carey Spicer), and two (Ellis Johnson and Darrell Darby) who played on the Ashland High School National Championship team –plus "Aggie" Sale, another gifted sophomore who was a high school All-American if there ever was one.

I don't think that any coach ever walked into a greater wealth of talent. Rupp knew what to do with the material when he did get it, which helped make him great. I know several players who thought he was a great guy while I knew several who hated him with a passion. This is perhaps natural on all teams when everybody can't be in the starting five...**Doc Lavin, BBM.**

Ralph G. Kercheval, 12/1/1911–10/6/2010, 1L, (1933). Born in Salt Lick, Kercheval graduated from Lexington's Henry Clay High School and earned a degree in animal husbandry from UK, where he played basketball, track and football. He was inducted into the Henry Clay High School Hall of Fame, the UK Athletics Hall of Fame and the Kentucky Athletic Hall of Fame. Kercheval worked part-time on the C.V. Whitney farm during the offseason. His friends from the horse industry remember him fondly. Kercheval was general manager at Sagamore Farm in Maryland, where he bred Native Dancer.

Remembering Ralph: *Ralph Kercheval was one of the greatest gentlemen I've ever met. I will always miss his great dancing. I love his wife very much. I loved them both*...**Mary Lou Whitney.**

Robert M. Tice, 6/16-1916-6/16-1960, Sq., (1937), was a teacher and coach at Athens High. He later worked for the Lexington Recreation Department. He was supervisor at the Ft. Lauderdale Recreation Department at the time of death.

Tom Moseley, 1L, (1944), was an All-State performer on Lexington Lafayette's 1942 state championship team. He played in the Kentucky-Indiana All-Star game. He was a reserve on UK's 1944 team.

William H. Spicer, 3/19/1929–5/8/1995, Sq., (1952). Spicer played in five games for UK and was executive vice president of the La Grange Federal Savings and Loan Association. He was a lieutenant in the Navy in World War II, commanding an infantry landing craft in the Pacific.

Walden Edward Lander, 11/22/1911–1/19/1974, 1L, (1943), was a Lexington native who played basketball at Picadome and Lafayette high schools. He went on to letter in basketball at the University of Kentucky in 1942 and 1943 and was a member of UK's baseball and tennis teams. He received a bachelor's degree from UK and later a master's degree from EKU. He served in the Army during World War II and received a Bronze Star with Oak Leaf Cluster. Lander retired as principal at Lexington Junior in the early 1980s after about 14 years in that position. He previously had been a teacher there. Lander was a freshman basketball coach at Eastern Kentucky University under legendary coach Paul McBrayer. He also taught and coached high school basketball in Utah.

Dick Derrickson, (Fr. 1945), played at Lafayette High. His UK tenure was cut short by induction into military service. He is a retired postal employee living in Lexington.

Ed Allin, (1L 1945), was a graduate of Henry Clay High who played two years at UK, lettering in 1945. He retired as a coach and school administrator.

Jim Howe, (Sq. 1945), played high school ball at Highlands in Ft. Thomas. He saw action in five games for the 1945 Wildcats. Howe served as an administrator for a Cincinnati company.

William Rouse, 8/4/1932-3/22/2007, 1L, (1954), was a 1950 graduate of the old University High School in Lexington. He received a degree in business administration from UK in 1954 and later was a pilot in the U.S. Air Force. He played basketball at UK in 1952 and 1954. Rouse was former chairman and chief executive officer of First Security National Bank & Trust Co. He devoted much of his time to various organizations in the years after he returned home from the military.

Vernon Hatton, 1/19/1936, 3L, (1956, 57, 58), was a two-time All-State player at Lexington Lafayette High. He scored 1,059 points during a three-year schoolboy career. He was selected on Chuck Taylor's All-America team. Hatton won MVP honors in all the all-star games that he participated.

Hatton was a starting guard on UK's 1958 Fiddlin' Five team. He led all UK scorers with 30 points in the championship win over Seattle. Hatton was All-America, All-Final Four, All-NCAA Regional and All-SEC. He scored 1,153 points at UK. His game-winning buckets in two wins over Temple cemented Hatton's reputation as one of UK's greatest clutch performers. With one second left in the first of three overtimes left in Lexington , Hatton took an in-bounds from Crigler and hit a 47-foot shot that tied the game. Hatton scored six points in the final overtime to help put the Owls away. Hatton is a well-known auctioneer in Lexington.

Remembering Hatton: *It doesn't matter what Vernon Hatton accomplished as a Kentucky basketball player; his name has become a part of the Wildcat mystique for just one shot in his career...**Cawood Ledford, 1995.***

Remembering Hatton: *If I were a gambling man and wanted to send my money to Las Vegas, I'd send it with Vern Hatton...**Adolph Rupp, BBM.***

Phil Johnson, 3L, (1956, 58, 59), scored 527 points (25.1 ppg) at U-High. He scored 208 points and 281 rebounds for UK. Johnson was a member of Rupp's 1958 championship team.

Billy Ray Lickert, 3L, (59, 60, 61), was a Kentucky "Mr. Basketball" and a Scholastic Magazine All-American at Lexington Lafayette High.

At UK, he was a three-time, first-team All-SEC selection, including a second-team All-America selection by the Helms Foundation in 1961. Lickert ranks 48th on Kentucky's all-time scoring list, with 1,076 points. He was named to the 1961 NCAA All-Region Team.

Lickert led UK in scoring during the 1959-60 and 1960-61 seasons, averaging 14.4 points per game in his junior year and 16.0 in his senior campaign. He finished his career with a 14.7 scoring average. He was also UK's leader in field-goal percentage in 1959-60 (.401) and 1960-61 (.420).

Herky Rupp, (1L, 1961). After lettering at University High in Lexington, Herky lettered for his father, Adolph Rupp, in 1961. After coaching Shelby County to a state tournament berth, he entered the banking and farming business.

Remembering the Father: *Every year daddy would buy up a* *big block of tickets to the Shrine Circus, take them over to the pre-dominantly black neighborhood on Prall Street, and hand them out himself because he knew that was the only way most of those kids would ever get to see the circus...***Herky Rupp to Denny Trease, 2002.**

Scotty Baesler, 7/9/1941, 2L, (1962, 63). An All-State second-team choice, Baesler scored 2,137 points in three years at Bryan Station High. Baesler was captain of the 1963 Wildcats. In his final two seasons at UK, Baesler averaged 10.3 ppg and three assists, while averaging 83 percent from the foul line.

After graduating from the UK Law School, Baesler served as mayor of Lexington from 1982-93, and as a congressman from Kentucky's 6th District from 1993-1999.

Mort Fraley, Fr., (1967), led the Lexington Catholic Knights in scoring with a 22.6 average, rebounding at 18 per game as the team advanced to the State Tournament. His 585 points as a senior gave him 1,800 points. Fraley played freshman basketball at UK.

Thad Jaracz, 15/1946, 3L, (1966, 67, 68). After starring at Lafayette High in Lexington, Jaracz was an H.M. All-America at UK in '66. He registered 982 points, 626 rebounds at UK. Jaracaz was a starting center on "Rupp's Runts."

Remembering Thad: *Thad was a pleasant surprise. He was a big kid who was not fat exactly, but he had too much weight and was kind of lazy. I kept telling Harry to sign him. Harry did not think he could play. I told Harry that kid sure makes a couple of moves. I believe we could teach him how to play basketball...* **Adolph Rupp, BBM.**

Jack Givens, 9/21/1956, 4L, (1975, 76, 77, 78). A prep All-America, Givens was twice All-State. He was Kentucky's "Mr. Basketball" in 1978. Givens led Bryan Station to a 76-17 record. He scored a school record 1,777 points (18.7 ppg).

Givens led UK scorers each of his three varsity years at UK. His 2,038 points rank third among UK scorers. He scored 41 points in UK's 94-88 win over Duke in the 1978 NCAA championship game.

Givens was unanimous All-America. He was All-SEC, All-NCAA Final Four, Regional MOP, and National Player of the year. He did TV broadcasting in Orlando.

James Lee, 1/17/1956, 4L, (1975, 76, 77, 78). Noted for his tremendous dunks, Lee was prep All-America and twice All-State at Henry Clay High. He led the Blue Devils to a 65-21 record. Lee set school scoring records in points (1,671) and rebounds (1,194). His high game was 42 points vs. Fairview. Henry Clay won two conference and a regional under his watch.

Lee scored 906 career points, 589 rebounds, and 128 assists on UK teams that were 72-19 in his varsity years. They won two conference championships, an NIT and an NCAA. They lost to UCLA in the 1975 final, but came back three years later to defeat Duke for the national championship.

Kirk Chiles, 1/8/1949, Sq, (1972). A graduate of Henry Clay High, Chiles saw brief action at UK in '72. He became a team manager. Chiles was head basketball coach at Henry Clay High.

Dirk Minniefield, 11/17/61, 4L, (1980, 81, 82, 83), was the fourth Lexington Lafayette player to earn Mr. Basketball honors. He led Lafayette to the 1979 Kentucky state championship. He was a two-time prep All-American and a three-time All-State choice. Minniefield averaged 18.1 points 6.0 assists, and hit 56.3 percent from the field.

At UK, Minniefield scored 1,069 points, 646 assists, 331 rebounds, and 156 steals. His assists average of 5.3 is still a UK record. The Wildcats were 96-28 during his varsity years. They were SEC champs or co-champs each of his four years and advanced to the Midwest Regional in1983. Minniefield was MVP of the 1982 SEC tournament.

Minniefield is a retired professional basketball player who is currently an Employee Assistance Professional for the NBA, managing drug aftercare programs for the league's players.

Melvin H. Turpin, 12/28/1960–7/8/2010, 4L, (1981, 82, 83, 84). As a senior at Bryan Station, Turpin averaged 24 points and 15 rebounds a game.

Before entering UK, Turpin spent a year at Fork Union Military Academy, a prep school in Virginia, working on his skills on the court and in the classroom. He also served as the school band's drum major.

Turpin ranks 16th in UK history with 1,509 career points. He averaged 15.2 points per game as a senior, when he was the team's leading scorer.

Turpin's career shooting percentage of .591 is third-best in UK history. Turpin was named a Helms Foundation All-American in 1983.

Their senior team, which included Jim Master, Kenny Walker and Dicky Beal, made the NCAA Final Four. Turpin was a consensus second-team All-American that season. In 123 college games, he averaged 12.3 points and 5.9 rebounds. As a junior, he turned in one of the most remarkable performances in UK basketball history. He scored 42 points in a 65-63 loss at Tennessee on Jan. 31, 1983.

After six seasons with the Cleveland Cavaliers, the Utah Jazz, CAI Zaragoza and the Washington Bullets, he retired.

In 1988–89, prior to his last season altogether, Turpin played in Spain with CAI Zaragoza, later being exchanged to the Jazz for José Ortiz.

Remembering Mel Turpin: *A guy that was always in a good, happy frame of mind., Everybody loved Melvin Turpin that knew him, and the ones that didn't know him don't know what they missed...* **Joe B. Hall, 2010.**

Mourning Turpin: We are deeply saddened by the passing of Melvin Turpin. Our h*earts and prayers are with his family and friends as they mourn their loss. The University of Kentucky and the Big Blue Nation will forever remember Melvin and all his contributions to our basketball program...* **UK athletic director Mitch Barnhart. 2012.**

Leroy Byrd, 1/11/1963, 3L, (1984, 85, 86), was a former Bryan Station star who transferred from UNLV to UK, where he lettered three years. He was a member of UK's 1984 Final Four team, and of two SEC championship teams.

Matt Heissenbuttel, 9/24/1981, 1L, (2003), led Lexington Catholic to the 2,000 KHSAA championship game. He played sparingly at UK.

Doug Flynn, 4/8 1951, .Fr., (1970), played football, baseball and basketball at Bryan Station High School. UK presented him its Basketball Freshman Leadership Award in 1970. Flynn played second base . with five Major League teams. He was a member of Cincinnati's 1975 and 1976 World Series championship teams. Flynn won a Golden Glove with the Mets. He is a correspondent banking officer with Central Bank in Lexington.

Franklin (Frankfort)

Herndon J. Evans, 12/22/1895–2/26/1976, Sq., (1920). A native of Morehead and 1914 graduate of Frankfort High School, Evans played on the 1920 UK basketball team that finished 18-7. Basil Hayden, UK's first All-American (1921), was a teammate.

Evans was owner and editor of the Pineville Sun for 30 years before joining The Lexington Herald as editor in 1956. He retired as Herald editor in 1967. The following year, he joined the F.L. Dupree & Co. Inc., an investment bond firm here, as director of public relations.

Evans served as publicity chairman for the late Sen. Alben W. Barkley in 1954 and for former Sen. Earle Clements in 1950. He also was publicity chairman in the unsuccessful bid of Bert Combs for the Democratic gubernatorial nomination in 1950. Combs was later elected governor and it was reported that Evans was in line for a cabinet post, but declined to accept it.

Active in conservation projects, Evans' work resulted in four lakes being built in Bell County. From 1935 to 1950 he served as

U.S. commissioner at Pineville. The lodge at Pine Mountain State Park is named in his honor.

Coleman E. Marshall, 7/25/1906 Sq.), (1927), was a graduate and played sparingly. He used his business degree to teach typing and bookkeeping during night school.

Grant (Covington)

Otto George Schwant, 11/23/1894–11/25/1965 Sq., (1916), played in one game each of two basketball seasons at UK. He was a retired general manager of the Hutchinson Coal Co., and president of the First Federal Building and Loan Association in Logan, W. Va. He also was consulting engineer for several coal companies.

Carl M. Riefkin, 1/26/1924–5/16/1977, 2L, (1923, 24), was leading scorer (133 pts.) on the 1923 UK team that was 3-13. He also lettered in football and track, and he was a champion diver and swimmer at UK.

Riefkin started off as a director of purchasing at the former Andrew's Steel Mill, in Newport. He retired in 1969 as vice president and general manager of sales for Interlake Steel.

Dave Lawrence, Corinth, 3/18/1912–1/10/2000, 3L, (1933, 34, 35) starred at Corinth High School in 1930 when they were named state champions by a score of 22-20 over Kavanaugh. He was a high school All-American. Recruited by the University of Kentucky's new coach, Adolph Rupp, Lawrence played forward and was named All-American in 1935. He scored 347 points in three varsity seasons and was second-leading scorer and co-captain in 1935, when the Wildcats were 19-2 (11-0 SEC).

Lawrence served as Dean of Men before being named Dean of Students at the University of Louisville in 1963. He was a Navy veteran of World War II.

Remembering Dave Lawrence: *Birkett Pribble and I drove up to Corinth to see Dave. He was working on putting a ditch in the ground under a railroad track. He was down in the mud digging* *around. We talked to him and asked him to come to UK. There were some fences on the campus that needed painting. That sounded better to him than fooling around with that dynamite, which gave him headaches, and digging in the mud...***Adolph Rupp, BBM.**

Sam Gates, 5/10/1923–10/14/1993, Sq., (1935, 36), played basketball in high school and on UK teams that were 15-8 and17-5, winning the SEC Tournament in '36. He used his business degree to teach typing and bookkeeping during night classes at Holmes High School to save enough money to start his own business – Gates Home Appliances on Madison Avenue in Covington.

"We opened the store after World War II and sold all kinds of appliances and toys and Lionel trains," said his wife, Helen Frisch Gates of Edgewood. "We were one of the first to sell televisions."

Harrison (Cynthiana)

Karle Hermann Rohs, 10/25/1902–5/28/1942, 1L, (1923, 25), played basketball at Cynthiana high school. He played two years as a reserve on UK basketball teams coached in 1923 by George Buchheit, and 1925 by C. O. Applegran. He was also a member of the University football squad and later attended Harvard.

Lt. Rohs was called into active service on February 16, 1925 He was in charge of the giant Post Exchange at Fort Knox. Rohs later managed the base's six movies..

William Douglas Kleiser, 1/28/1909–2/28/1988, 1L, (1930-31-32), starred at Henry Clay High School. He was a member of Rupp's first basketball team at UK. Kleiser was the former owner and operator of Lexington Granite Co. He earlier was the agriculture agent in Greenup and Owen counties. During World War II he was a lieutenant colonel in the Army.

George T. Skinner, 1[13/1913–2/19/1983), Sq., (1933), played in four games, garnering four points in three varsity years at UK. He also played football and ran track. After serving in the military, Skinner was an attorney for U.S. Steel.

Joe B. Hall, 11/30/28, Sq., (1947, 48) starred in basketball and football at Cynthiana High. He played one year of varsity basketball at Kentucky before transferring to the University of the South (Sewanee). Hall toured with the Harlem Globetrotters and later returned to Kentucky to complete his undergraduate studies. Hall graduated from Kentucky in 1955. (See "Coaches")

Remembering the Feeling: *"I'll never forget the moment when I went out for my first game in Alumni Gym," Hall said. "The band played 'On, On, UK,' and I thought I'd throw my first layup over the basket. I wonder if players today have the same sensation that I had.*

To really feel like that you've got to have grown up in Kentucky and to have followed the team. I'll never forget how fortunate I was to have that opportunity, to be chosen among the many thousands of kids like me who had grown up idolizing Kentucky athletics, both basketball and football."

Coleman E. Marshall, 7/25/1906–7/29/1980 (Sq.), (1927). A native of Frankfort, Marshall played sparingly for the Wildcats in 1927.

Jack Tucker, 9/13/1911–1/5/1997, 3L. (1933, 34, 35), played on UK teams that were 56-6. They were undefeated (30-0) in regular-season SEC play, but were upset by Florida 38-32 in the 1934 conference tournament. Tucker was a farmer, a retired training supervisor for the Department of Agriculture, Tobacco Division, and a former principal and basketball coach in Butler.

Remembering Rupp: *During the 1933-34 season--my first year as a regular varsity player-we were playing the University of Cincin¬nati in old Alumni Gym and, as the game progressed, I was fouled and went to the free throw line and missed both of them. A little later on I was fouled again for two shots, and I knew I had better make these because Coach Rupp was breathing down my neck. I stepped up and got the ball and behold! I missed these too.*

Although we beat Cincinnati-and after the game Coach Rupp told us we played a nice game-I was still very uncomfortable about missing those four free throws. This was on Saturday night. The fol-

lowing Monday we reported to practice and, as usual, Coach Rupp had us sit down around the center circle while he reviewed the Cincinnati game with us.

After the review he told us to start running some drills. I took my place and he yelled, "Tucker, come here and get that chair and place it on the foul line and you sit there the rest of the afternoon and look at that goal"... which I did...with much embarrassment while the other players came by and made remarks to me which did not help matters. My foul shooting percentage the rest of the season was quite good... **Jack Tucker, BBM.**

Henry (Campbellsburg)

Kenneth Haynes England, 4/14/45 2L, (1941, 42), scored 154 points on UK teams that were 36-14. They were SEC regular season and tournament champs. England was a starting guard on UK's Final Four team in 1942.

During the war England commanded the 10th Mountain Division, the only ski troop in America. In 1944 he led the division in taking Mt. Belvedere from the Nazis, for which he won the Bronze Star. In the final campaign in Italy he died of wounds received while crossing a mine field on April 14, 1945. Besides the Bronze Star he was awarded the Silver Star. They named an athletic field in Italy after him.

Jefferson (Louisville)

Van Buren Ropke, 4/19/1906–2/26/1975, 1L, (1927), played basketball and football at Manual High in Louisville and in 13 games for the Wildcats in 1927. He was a supervisor in the shipping and receiving department of the U.S. Plywood Division-Champion International warehouse until his retirement in 1971.

Russell Ellington, 7/14/1912–4/24/1986, 2L, (1935, 36), lettered in basketball and football at Manual High in Louisville. He played in 32 basketball games at UK. They were 19-2 overall and11-0 in the SEC in 1935. He was a former car salesman for Glenn Buick and Fred Bryant Motors in Lexington, and at one time ran Ellington House, an antiques business, on Henry Clay Boulevard. He served in the Navy during WWII.

Remembering Ellington: *Duke was a fine, fine athlete. I guess basketball was probably his number one game...* **Elmer Gilb, 1974.**

Ray F. Ellis, 1/13/1905–1/23/1992, Sq., (1926). A native of La-Grange, Ellis earned one letter in basketball and three in football at UK. He coached college football in Georgia and was an original member of the Tampa Sports Authority. Ellis moved to the Tampa Bay area from La Grange. He spent more than 30 years with WE-DU-TV, Channel 3, as assistant general manager.

Edwin C. Knadler, 10/19/1907–11/29/1977, 1L, (1927), played freshman football, baseball and basketball and was a member of the UK varsity football and basketball squads. He was second-leading scorer on the 1927 UK team.

Joseph "Red" Hagan, 3L, (1936, 37, 38), played both basketball and football at Male and St. Xavier Highs Schools in Louisville, continuing both sports at UK. He was second-leading scorer in basketball as a sophomore and junior and leading scorer as a senior, totaling 502 points in three years. He was All-SEC and All-SEC Tournament in 1938. Hagan also was football team captain in 1937. He retired as a Louisville auto dealer and banker.

Remembering Rupp: *After UK defeated Alabama in 1936, Hagan ran to the locker room with the game ball. Rupp demanded the ball. Hagan handed it to him with a little more force than Rupp thought necessary. He had athletic director Chet Wynne suspend Hagan. When the Wildcats prepared to leave for a game in South Bend, Hagan accompanied team mates Ellington and Goforth to the station.*

"What are you doing here?" Rupp asked. "Well, as long as you are here, you might as well make the trip because it will be the last one you make anyway."

When UK fell behind Notre Dame by 14 points in the first half, Rupp pilled a piece of paper from his pocket. He waved it at Hagan, who was seated at the end of the bench.

"I just got a telegram," Rupp said. "Your suspension has been lifted. You can go in now."

Hagan scored six field goals, but UK lost the game, 41-20. **BBM.**

Carl E. Althaus, 1L, (1943), earned letters in five sports at Manual High School. He played football on a 1938 National Championship team. Althaus played one year of college basketball at UK. After serving as a bomber pilot in WWII, he returned to work in his father's business, Althaus Plumbing.

Remembering Althaus: *Carl always talked about his mom's cooking– soup, stuffed cabbage, and Sunday morning "kuchenÓ (German coffee cake) and how hard his dad worked. The family attended Market Street Methodist Church, where his mom taught Sunday school. His mom loved to hear people talk about the Bible and she would invite preachers and young students for dinner, which on one occasion included young Billy Graham.*

James W. Goforth, d. 6/22/1944, 3L, (35, 36, 37), played on UK teams that were 51-13, winning two SEC championships. Marine Lt. Goforth was killed by machine gun fire on Saipan during WWII after leading his company for several days after his captain was wounded. His decorations included the Bronze Star, the Presidential Citation and the Silver Star.

Bruce O. Bartee, 11/3/1897–12/5/1968, Sq., (1918, 19), was a Jessamine County native who served as a squad member on the 1919 UK team that was 16-8. An engineering graduate of UK, he served as a field artillery captain in WWI.

Leonard G. Tracy, 3/3/1905–3/13/1967, Sq., (1925). A native of Winchester, Tracy was a member of the old Lexington Senior High School basketball team that won the national championship in 1922. He won letters in football, basketball and track at the University of Kentucky. Tracy was a public relations employee of Hialeah

Race Course. He was a former sportswriter for The Lexington Herald and The Lexington Leader. He also had been a staff member of the Thoroughbred Record and operated a horse van business.

Paul Jenkins, 11/8/1905–2/27/1985, 3L. (1926, 27, 28), played on Manual's 1923 state championship team He was a quarterback of the UK football team and captain for two years of the basketball team. He was All-Southern in 1926 and UK's leading scorer in 1927.

Jenkins was a retired athletic director at Northeast High School and a football coach at St. Petersburg High School from 1949 to 1954.

Until his retirement in 1972 Jenkins had served as the head of sports at Northeast since the school opened in 1954. He also taught journalism and was the advisor for the school newspaper and yearbook.

Irvine F. Jeffries, 9/10/1905–6/8/1982, 1L, (1928). Jeffries' athletic career began at Manual High School in the early 1920s where he starred in football, basketball and baseball. In 1944, he coached football, basketball and baseball at the old Flaget High School. He was leading scorer (11.5) on the 1928 UK team that finished 12-6 after losing to Ole Miss 32-24 in the his SIAA championship game. Jeffries' professional baseball career started in the late 1920s. He was an infielder for the Chicago White Sox, the Philadelphia Phillies and the Cincinnati Reds. He retired in 1941.

Jeffries later managed several minor league teams and in 1948 was a scout for the Chicago White Sox.

Remembering Paul's Mother: *Mrs. Jenkins attended her first state tournament in 1923. She had a long attendance streak that included only one miss, when a broken ankle kept her home in 1929, she correctly predicted that Midway would win the championship in 1937, Sharpe in1938, Brooksville in 1939, and Hazel Green in 1940.*

Lee Huber, 2/16/1919–9/22/2005, 3L, (1939, 40, 41), was an All-State performer, who led St. Xavier to the semifinals of the 1937 KHSAA Tournament. He also was an excellent tennis player. Huber averaged 5.4 points a game his junior year and 5.9 his senior year at UK. He scored a total of 312 points in 64 games and was named All-

America, first team Southeastern Conference, and All-SEC Tournament in the 1940-41 season. He was UK's 10th All-American. After one year with the Akron (Ohio) Goodyear Wingfoots.

He served four years in the Navy during World War II. He worked 30 years for various furniture companies, including a period as vice president for the Thomasville furniture company.

Remembering Rupp: *After an important Saturday night win, Adolph presented the game ball to me, a rare occurrence. The following Monday before practice, he called me into his office. He had heard I was out on the Friday night before the game after training hours. Coach gave me a lecture and said I did not deserve the game ball since I broke training rules and he wanted it back. There was quite an explosion when I told him I had sold the ball to one of the fraternities. I never received another game ball...* **Lee Huber, BBM.**

Remembering Dan Tehan: *I regarded Dan Tehan as a fine referee. He told me the following tale: In the last few seconds of a game with Vanderbilt, Kentucky was leading by 25 points. Dan gave Vandy the ball out of bounds before Kentucky was set defensively. Vanderbilt immediately scored a basket. Adolph came charging out like a mad bull. Dan pointed to the scoreboard and told Adolph he was ahead by 25 points. Adolph replied that without Dan's bonehead call, it would have been 27...* **Lee Huber, BBM.**

A true Kentucky Wildcat, former athlete Lee G. Huber was laid in his coffin wearing a University of Kentucky tie with his casket covered by a UK blanket.

Frank Etscorn, 2/23/1921–11/21/1986, Sq., (1941, 42). Born in Valley Station, Etscorn was a member of two UK basketball teams. He also swam.

Ralph Beard, 12/2/27–11/29/2007, 4L, (1945, 46, 47, 48, 49), was the first four-sport letterman in Male High School history (football, basketball, baseball and track). He was two-time All-State and star of Male's 1945 state basketball champions. Beard also starred on Male's 1943 state baseball champions and was the state champion in the 880 yard run on Male's 1945 team.

A speedy, 5-foot-10 guard, Beard was one of Rupp's famed "Fabulous Five", along with Alex Groza, Wallace "Wah Wah" Jones, Cliff Barker and Kenny Rollins. The Wildcats finished 36-3 in 1948, beating Baylor 77-59 for the national title. The following summer, Rupp and the five starters teamed with the AAU champion Phillips Oilers to win the Olympic gold medal in London, then won another NCAA championship. From 1946 -- when Beard and Jones joined Adolph Rupp's varsity team as freshmen -- through 1949, Kentucky played in the finals of a national tournament four straight years. The Cats won the NIT in 1946, finished second in '47, then won back-to-back NCAA crowns in 1948 and '49.

Beard finished with 1,517 points, currently 14th on Kentucky's scoring list. He was the school's first four-time All-SEC selection and three-time All-American. Before the start of the 1952 season, Beard and Groza were among several players involved in a point-shaving scandal that rocked college basketball. They received suspended sentences, but were banned for life from the NBA. Beard admitted to taking $700 from gamblers while at Kentucky, but said he never shaved points.

Beard was later assistant general manager at Gould's Pharmaceuticals in Louisville.

Remembering the Scandal: *The scandal is never mentioned by people unless I bring it up. But the scandal was really a blip on the screen for Kentucky basketball. You just can't kill something that big...* **Ralph Beard. 2003 interview.**

Remembering Beard: *Ralph was the best guard I ever saw. "I'd do anything in the world for him. He was just a regular guy. We all got along, had a lot of good times together...* **Wah Jones**

Ralph would be an All-American in today's game. His style of play was timeless. He was so aggressive and quick, a tenacious defender. He would make any adjustments offensively it took to make himself better... **Joe B. Hall**

Ralph was without question one of the greatest to ever wear the Kentucky uniform... **Kentucky athletic director Mitch Barnhart**

Lucian "Skippy" Whitaker, 8/9/1930, 3L, (1950, 51, 52), was from Louisville by way of Sarasota, Fla. He scored 522 points at UK. "Skippy" was a member of UK's 1951 NCAA champion Wildcats.

Phil "Cookie" Grawemeyer, 1935–3/20/2008, 3L, (1954, 55, 56), played basketball and baseball at Louisville's DuPont Manual High School. He was a member of the Manual Hall of Fame. He played in the North-South All-Star game.

Grawemeyer was UK's third-leading scorer in the 1954-55 season, averaging 13 points a game. He was the fifth-leading scorer in the 1955-56 season, with an average of 8.4 points. The undefeated 1953-54 UK team did not go to the NCAA tournament that year. An NCAA rule banning post-graduate players from the tournament meant top UK players Cliff Hagan, Frank Ramsey and Lou Tsioropoulos could not play. UK Coach Adolph Rupp decided that the rest of the Wildcats would not play in the tournament. The UK team defeated LaSalle in the UK Invitational Tournament that season. La-Salle went on to win the NCAA tournament.

Grawemeyer also was a pitcher on the UK baseball team.

He was a member of the UK Hall of Fame, and his No. 44 basketball jersey is retired. Grawemeyer worked for the state highway department and was a real estate developer.

1955 NCAA Bid: We were kids. We wanted to go ahead and play. It would have been nice to go, but I'm sure without those guys (Hagan, Ramsey and Tsioropoulos), we wouldn't have gone very far...Phil Grawemeyer...2008 Interview.

Rupp Replies: *I had hoped you would not vote to and not to put this record, undefeated team in jeopardy. If we can't play with our full team, we won't allow a bunch of turds to mar the record established in large measure by our three seniors. We are not going to Kansas City...***Adolph Rupp, BBM, 1976.**

Jim McDonald, 2/17/1940, 3L, (1960, 61, 62), played high school ball at St. Xavier High in Louisville. During his varsity years at UK, the Wildcats went 60-19, won an SEC championship and played in two NCAA Tournaments. He scored 152 points and grabbed 159 rebounds.

Named Chief Executive Officer of three different companies, McDonald earned both a bachelor and masters in electrical engineering from Kentucky. Following a 21-year career with IBM, he made huge contributions to the rapid growth of video, data and voice technologies. From 1984 to 1991, McDonald served as president and CEO of Prime Computer, and in the same capacity for Gould, Inc., where he led the successful restructuring of both organizations. Since 1993, McDonald has led Scientific Atlanta as it has continued to provide a comprehensive array of products, systems and services for the cable and broadcasting industry. In 1999, he received the National Cable Television Association's Vanguard Award, which recognizes outstanding achievements by leaders of the cable industry.

McDonald, himself, holds patents in image processing and communications, and is a member of several advisory councils, including three for his alma mater. In 2007, he received a lifetime achievement award from the Juvenile Diabetes Research Foundation.

Ted Deeken, 9/10/41, 3L, (1962 63, 64), scored 20 points in Flaget's 65-56 win over Monticello in the championship game of the 1960 KHSAA tourney, making All-State in the process. He starred in the Kentucky-Indiana series and the East-West game. He also was a cross-country runner and baseball pitcher in high school.

Deeken was All-SEC at UK in 1964, when he was second in scoring (18.5) to fellow co-captain Cotton Nash (24.0). Deeken scored 757 points and pulled down 488 rebounds at UK. He scored 34 against Auburn in 1964.

John Brewer, Anchorage, 3L, (1956, 57, 58). A former Louisville Eastern High star, Brewer earned three letters at UK. He was a member of the 1958 "Fiddlin' Five" team that defeated Baylor for the 1958 NCAA championship. Later, he was a senior VP with the Motal Exchange in St. Louis.

Tom Payne, 11/19/1950, 1L, (1971). Payne didn't play organized basketball until his sophomore season at Shawnee High

School, where he was All-America and All-State. He averaged 22 points and 15 rebounds and was a league MVP with a Lexington AAU team. By his senior season, he was one of the most coveted players in the nation, with Kentucky and UCLA recruiting him. On June 9, 1969 the high-school All-American signed with Kentucky; he was not only the tallest player (7-foot-1) ever to play at the school, he was also legendary coach Adolph Rupp's first-ever African-American player. Payne scored 473 points and got 283 rebounds at UK his sophomore year; then he turned pro.

Derek Anderson, 7/19/1974, 2L. (1996, 97). After starring at Doss High in Louisville, Anderson played two years at Ohio State before transferring to UK. He was a vital part of the Wildcat drive to the 1996 NCAA championship. He missed his second year at UK with a torn anterior cruciate ligament. Anderson scored 674 points and 199 rebounds in 55 games at UK. He was All-NCAA Regional.

Scott Padgett, 4/19/1976, 4L, (1995, 97, 98, 99), scored 19.0 ppg, 12.6 RPG, and 5.0 APG as a senior at St. Xavier. He finished his career in the school's top ten in rebounding, scoring, assists, and three pointers. An All-State selection, Padgett was team captain his senior year. AT UK, Padgett scored 1,252 points. He had 651 rebounds, 238 assists, 147 steals and 68 blocked shots. Padgett was All-Final Four with UK's 1998 NCAA champions. He won the Wooden Award and several All-SEC honors. He is an assistant coach at Manhattan College.

Winston Bennett, 2/9/1965, 4L, (1984, 85, 86, 88), was named Kentucky's "Mr. Basketball" at Louisville Male High School for the State of Kentucky in 1983. He also earned Parade Magazine All-American and McDonald's All-America honors, sharing MVP honors with Dwayne Washington. As a freshman in 1983–84, Bennett appeared in 34 games for UK, averaging 6.5 points in 19 minutes per game as the Wildcats reached the Final Four, losing to Georgetown, 53-40.

The following season, he averaged 7.2 points in nearly 20 minutes per game to help UK to the West Regional Semi-Finals. In

1985–86, his junior season, Bennett was named to the All-NCAA Regional Team and the SEC All-Conference Team after averaging 12.7 points and 7 rebounds per game. Playing under first-year coach Eddie Sutton, Bennett shot better than 50 percent from the field and helped lead the Wildcats to a 32-4 record.

After red-shirting in 1986–87 to rehab a serious knee injury, Bennett served as team captain and averaged 15.2 points and 7.8 rebounds per game the following season, again earning All-SEC honors. The Wildcats won their 37th SEC title with a 27–6 record. In May 2007, Bennett was named the head men's basketball coach at Mid-Continent University, an NAIA school in Mayfield, Kentucky.

Kerry Benson, 3/25/1989, (Sq. 2008). An All-District selection at Pleasure Ridge High, Benson averaged 15.5 and 8.1 rebounds, 3.2 steals. He played in the Kentucky-Ohio All-Star Game.

Matt Scherbenske, 10/14/1987, 1L, (2008), played basketball at Lexington Christian and Oak Hill Academy. Shot 47 per cent from the three-point line in leading Oak Hill to a 40-1 record. He transferred to UK from Oral Roberts and saw brief action at UK in 2008.

Rajon Rondo, 2/22/1986, 2L, (2005, 06). During his junior year at Eastern High School, Rondo averaged 27.9 points, 10.0 rebounds and 7.5 assists. He was named the 7th Region Player of the Year. He transferred to Virginia's Oak Hill Academy for his senior year where he averaged 21.0 (ppg), (3.0 rpg) and 12.0 assists per game. He finished the 2003–04 season with a 38–0 record. In his senior year at Oak Hill, Rondo broke Jeff McInnis's single-season school record of 303 assists, while averaging a double-double. There, he included two efforts of 27 assists and a single-game school record of 31, merely four away from the all-time national record He also had a 55-point game. Only Calvin Duncan with 61 surpassed that total at Oak Hil. Rondo was named to the McDonald's All-American Team in 2004. He scored a total of 14 points, 4 assists and 4 rebounds in the all-star game. He also participated in the 2004 Jordan Capital Classic game, logging 12 points, 5 assists and 4 steals. He ended his career as Oak Hill Academy's all-time assists leader in a single season with 494 assists, surpassing Jeff McInnis.

Rondo led Kentucky to several wins including clutch-shot victories against the University of Louisville, South Carolina and Central Florida. He was named to the SEC All-Freshmen Team. Rondo set a UK record for most steals in single-season, with a total of 87 steals in his freshman year.

In his sophomore year he had a career high 12 assists against Ole Miss, despite playing just 23 minutes, and 25 points against Louisville. Rondo also set another UK record for most rebounds in a game by a guard, with 19 rebounds in an early season loss to Iowa He was not known for being a shooter, however, going 18–66 from three with a 57.1% FT average. He averaged 11.2 points, 6.1 rebounds, 4.9 assists and 2.1 steals per game in his sophomore year. Rondo was also named to the 2005 USA Men's Under-21 World Championship Team, which traveled to Argentina for the FIBA World Championships. He averaged 11.0 ppg and 4.5 apg in the eight-game tournament, garnering much attention from NBA scouts. The USA U-21 team won a gold medal at the Global Games held in Texas in late July.

Remembering Rondo: *I see some Bob Cousy in him. There are more similarities than you might think...***Frank Ramsey, 2012.**

Jessamine (Nicholasville)

Thomson R. Bryant, 1/8/1885–6/25/198?, 3L, (1905, 06, 07), played center on the UK basketball team from 1904 to 1906 and managed the school's football team. He came to Lexington from Nicholasville in 1903 and was among the group of students that started basketball at the college. Bryant was employed as an assistant in the husbandry department of the Agricultural Experiment Station. In 1910 he was appointed to organize and teach the first course in elementary bacteriology at UK. This was in addition to his work as assistant director.

In 1965, Bryant was one of 81 recipients of the Distinguished

Alumni Centennial Awards given by UK. He was the only recipient to have served under every president of the University.

Remembering The Beginning-- *I remember helping buy the ball. It was one of those you inflated with a foot pump and then laced it. If something had happened to it, we couldn't have played…* **Tommy Bryant, BBM.**

Remembering Mustaine: *He was a prince of a fellow. He had a wonderful team of tumblers and he taught a class in swinging Indian clubs, but he didn't know or care much about basketball...***Tommy Bryant, BBM.**

Remembering 1905 KU game: *We were as dirty as smut. There was an ugliness that showed its head. We didn't play for a championship but for bloody noses. I remember when those guys from KU came onto the floor wearing football pads while we came out in our jerseys and basketball panties. I am 95, but I've still got a tender ankle that I inherited when J. Franklin Wallace, a 6-foot-4 1/2 tackle stepped on it. He poked me with a left jab, and I came back with a haymaker to the face. They threw both of us out...***Tommy Bryant, BBM.**

Singleton Yeary, 8/8/1925-11/15/2000, Sq., (1945), played center on Lafayette's first State Champion. He saw action in five games at UK in 1945. He was a former president of the Lexington Concrete Co., and a former employee of the Second National Bank.

Kenton (Covington)

Randy Noll, 12/5/1949, 1L, (1970). A prep All-America, scored 1,200 career points, averaging 22 points and 17 rebounds as a senior at Covington Catholic High. He was captain of the All-State team. Noll also lettered in tennis. He transferred to Marshal after his sophomore year at UK.

Lincoln (Stanford)

Evan Settle, Crab Orchard, 10/13/1922–2/2006, 2L, (1933, 34), was an Owen County native who played basketball at Crab Orchard and Owenton high schools. He lettered for Rupp on teams that were 21-3 in 1933 and 16-1 1934.They were undefeated in SEC play both years. Settle also lettered in golf and baseball at UK.

Settle turned down an offer from the Cincinnati Reds to play Class D baseball, opting instead to coach basketball in Shelby County. He coached the Red Devils boys' basketball teams to seven regional titles, and the school's golf and baseball teams to three regional titles each. He served in the Army Air Corps. In addition to coaching, Settle taught algebra and physics at Shelbyville High during his 28-year career.

Remembering Coach Settle: *As a teacher, he was full of wit and he had a certain form of sarcasm that would get you to achieve at your highest level...* **Duanne Puckett, Shelby County schools.**

Mason (Maysville)

James Edward Parker, Jr., 5/6/1898–9/19/1986, 1L, (1919), played on the 1919 UK basketball team that was 16-8. He was a former vice president of First Security National Bank & trust Co.; from 1948 until 1973, he headed the bank's farm and real estate department. Parker also had been a Fayette County agricultural extension agent for about 25 years and had served as an agricultural agent in Bath. He served in the Navy in World War I. His son, J. Ed "Buddy" Parker III, earned UK basketball letters in 1945, 46, 47.

Ben G. Marsh, 10/20/1897–5/2/1954, 1L, (1918). Marsh attended Maysville schools, and lettered three years in basketball at UK. He was county agent at Somerset for several years, later worked as a dairy inspector in Birmingham, Ala. and for a time owned and operated a dairy products plant at Cynthiana. He was a section chief of the agricultural conservation and price support programs for the

US Department of Agriculture, and had worked with the USDA for many years.

Remembering "Gone With The Wind": Marsh was a brother-in-law of the late Margaret Mitchell, (Mrs. John Marsh) and in 1895 he made foreign-language editions of her "Gone With the Wind" and personal mementoes of the author available to the Lexington Public Library for display. The Belle Whatley of Mitchell's novel was Belle Brezing, who operated a noted Lexington brothel. Brezing's final and most elaborate "working house" was located at 59 Megowan Street (now 153 N. Eastern Ave). The brothels in the area were shut down in 1915 under order of the US Army since they were considered a distraction for the soldiers in the area. Belle continued to live there until her death in 1940. Her estate was auctioned off over several days. The house was converted into apartments and in 1973 a fire consumed the upper floor. The remaining architectural details were auctioned off. Bricks salvaged from the home were sold to the public with the inscription: "Brick from the Belle Brezing Home - The most orderly of Dis-orderly Homes".

Still standing, one of her other former houses is on the campus of Transylvania University, and houses a women's locker room.

Harry Denham, 6/17/1918-8/25/2001, 1L (1939), played basketball and football at Maysville High. He played three years at UK, lettering in his junior year. He founded the Denham Medical Clinic in Maysville.

Carl Staker, 9/24/1920–11/11/1991, 3L, (1940, 41, 42), earned three varsity letters for basketball and three for baseball at UK. He scored 225 points in three seasons. Staker was captain of the team that was the school's first to qualify for an NCAA national tournament.

Staker was president of Osborn Engineering Co. in Cleveland from 1972 to 1979. During his 32 years with the company, he worked on the construction of stadiums and office buildings across the country. Projects that he worked on included Milwaukee County Stadium, Robert F. Kennedy Stadium in Washington D.C., chemical plants and major office buildings.

Staker graduated magna cum laude in 1941. He began working for the Goodyear Tire & Rubber Co. in Akron in 1942 and played on the company's team in an industrial basketball league. He served as an officer in an antisubmarine unit in the South Pacific during World War I.

Gerry Calvert, 9/19/1935, 3L, (1955, 56, 57), averaged almost 22 points a game at Maysville High and made the All-State list two consecutive years. He scored 777 points and 299 rebounds on Wildcat teams that were 66-14, SEC champs in 1955, and also SEC and Sugar Bowl champs in 1957, when he served as co-captain. Calvert is an attorney practicing in Lexington.

Ronnie Lyons, 3/7/52, 3L, (1972, 73, 74). Kentucky's "Mr. Basketball", Lyons was the state's leading scorer in 1971 with 1,250 points. His high game was 60 points. He scored a four-year total of 3,398 points. Lyons was honorary captain of the All-State team, and All-America. He hit .748 his senior year and pitched two no-hit games. Lyons scored 786 points and 171 assists in 78 games at UK. He was second-team All-SEC. Lyons is with IBM.

Deron Feldhaus, 12/6/1968, 4L, (1989, 90, 91, 1992), starred at Mason County, where he was coached by his father, former Wildcat Allen Feldhaus. Deron scored 1,231 points and 540 rebounds in 124 games at UK. The Wildcats were 85-26 during those years of Rick Pitino's reign as UK coach.

Their best season was 1992, when Feldhaus and his fellow seniors--Richie Farmer, John Pelphrey, and Sean Woods and junior Jamal Mashburn gave UK a 29-6 slate. That team lost 104-103 in overtime to Duke on a last-second shot by Christian Lattner in the championship game of the 1992 NCAA Regional in Philadelphia. All five jerseys have been retired, and the players are enshrined in the UK Athletic Hall of Fame.

Feldhaus played basketball five years in Japan. Along with his father and step-mother, he is the owner of the Kenton Station Golf Course, a nine-hole course in Mason County.

If I had college to do over again, I might have tried to put myself in position for a career in golf-course management. "I really like it... Mark Story Interview, 2011.

Darius Miller, 3/21/1990, 4L, (2009, 10, 11, 12). At Mason County High School, Miller averaged 19.9 points per game, grabbed 7.9 rebounds, and shot 51% in his senior year. He helped lead Mason County to the 2008 State Championship. Named 2008 Mr. Basketball, he scored more than 2000 points at Mason County.

Miller was a valuable "Sixth Man" in UK's march to its eighth NCAA championship. He was MVP of the 2011 SEC Tournament. He scored 1,248 points, good for 34th on UK's all-time list, and 487 rebounds.

Bobby Hiles (1966) – A starting guard on the freshman team, Hiles did not play on the varsity team.

Mercer (Harrodsburg)

Forest "Aggie" Sale, 6/25/1911–12/4/1985, 3L, (1931, 32, 33), played basketball at Kavanaugh High School in Lawrenceburg from 1925-1929 and returned after an All-America playing career at the University of Kentucky to coach Kavanaugh from 1933-1937. Then he moved to Harrodsburg where he became one of Kentucky's most respected coaches...He took the Pioneers to the State Tournament in 1960...That Harrodsburg team was one of two that won championships in the 20-team Central Kentucky Conference, and he was C.K.C. Coach-of-the-Year in 1960...He also served as football coach at Harrodsburg from 1946-1948...Sale played semi-pro basketball on a team with the great John Wooden while Wooden was coaching at Dayton, Ky., High School.

Sale was an All-Southeastern Conference player in the 1932-33 season, and in 1933, he was named to the Helms Athletic Foundation as the outstanding college player of the year.

Sale taught and coached basketball at Kavanaugh High School after he graduated from UK. He coached at Kavanaugh from 1933 to

1937, and he went to Harrodsburg High School as a history teacher and basketball coach in 1937.

Sale entered the Navy during World War II and achieved the rank of chief specialist.

He resumed his teaching and basketball career at Harrodsburg High. He remained basketball coach there until 1960 and retired as a teacher in 1964. After he quit coaching, Sale opened the Sale Sporting Goods Store in Harrodsburg, which he ran until about 1967. The store still bears his name. He also managed the family farm in Anderson County. In 1971, Sale, a Democrat, was elected to the Kentucky General Assembly from the 55th District. He was re-elected to the post four times. Sale served on several legislative committees, and education was one of his primary legislative interests.

In 1983, the Harrodsburg Rotary Club named Sale the Mercer County Citizen of the Year.

Remembering Aggie: *Greatness came from his simple, humble way of doing what he considered the right things...* **The Harrodsburg Herald, 1925.**

Remembering Rupp: *In January of 1933 we were playing South Carolina at Columbia. I had been eating too much and drinking too many milk shakes and had accumulated a few pounds. I was not playing as I should have been. In fact my plying was terrible. At the half, when Coach Rupp was saying a few words to us, he looked directly at me and said "Sale, I guess you have your press clippings with you tonight."* **Aggie Sale, BBM.**

Remembering Aggie: *He was a tremendous rebounder, one of the best, I think, under the basket that Kentucky ever had, really. He was a tremendous player all the way around. His junior and senior years were just tremendous. But I only had the pleasure of playing with him his sophomore year."....* **Carey Spicer, BBM**

Terry Mobley, 12/19/1943, 3L (1963, 64, 65), was All-State at Harrodsburg, where he averaged 23 ppg. He scored 568 points and 252 rebounds at UK. His last-seconds field goal gave UK an 81-79 win over Duke for the 1964 Sugar Bowl championship. Mobley is Chief Development Officer at UK. He served as UK interim athletic director for five months in 2002.

Nelson (Bardstown)

Harvey W. Mattingly, 9/26/1911–4/4/2001, Sq., (1932), snapped center, swatted home runs and pressed the roundball down-court for teams at Bardstown High School. He played for the second team of coach Adolph Rupp. However, an injury between his sophomore and junior years in college cut short his football and basketball playing days. He dropped out of sports until his senior year when he played as the regular catcher for UK's baseball team. Mattingly was a teacher and coach for six years at Park Hills Junior High in Covington.

As an infantry officer in WWII, he was wounded in action on Bouganville. He later participated in recapturing Manila in the Philippines under the command of Gen. MacArthur. Mattingly retired after 27 years with Prudential Insurance.

He also won three state basketball championships, as well as ones in golf, tennis, swimming and baseball.

Remembering MacArthur:. *Gen. MacArthur wanted to be at the front of the line. But by exposing his position like that he almost got us all killed…***Harvey Mattingly.**

Nicholas (Carlisle)

Ned Jennings, Headquarters 10/8/38–11/9/2008, 3L, (1959), 60, 61), was a 6-9 center who led Nicholas County to the 1957 State High School Tournament, the school's only appearance in the storied "Sweet Sixteen." Although his team lost, 58-55 , to Dixie Heights in the opening round–Jennings made the all-tournament team.

Jennings scored 157 points and collared 130 rebounds as a UK freshman. He underwent an appendectomy midway through the season. Then, just before his sophomore season, he received a cut in the corner of an eye. He played in only 11 games that year.

In his junior season, Jennings started 15 of 22 games, averaged 8.8 points, and was the team's second-leading rebounder. However, injuries caused him to miss three SEC games down the stretch. In a 77-72 overtime victory at Kansas, he scored 27 points and held his own against Jayhawk All-American Wayne Hightower, who had 33.

As a senior, Ned played in all of UK's 28 games, averaging 11.5 points for a team that finished 19-9. After an 8-7 start, the Cats ran off a 10-game winning streak in which Jennings got a career-high 11 field goals in an 89-68 win over Florida.

In a career limited by various ailments, Jennings managed to play in 61 games, score 548 points, and collect 448 rebounds for the Wildcats. Ned worked throughout his life in various management positions and retired from the Lexington-Fayette Urban County Government.

Oldham (LaGrange)

Robert Y. Ireland, 2/21/1894–3/15/1984, 3L, (1915, 16, 17), was second-leading scorer and captain of the 1917 Wildcat team that played an abbreviated (4-6) wartime schedule. He was a retired civil engineer who worked for the Navy.

Bart N. Peak, 1/3/1894–2/27/1981, 1L, (1917). Peak was a native of Bedford in Trimble County who played basketball and football (1915) at Kentucky State College (now the University of Kentucky). He enlisted in the army in 1917 and rose to the rank of second lieutenant.

Peak attended the YMCA graduate school at Vanderbilt University and became a YMCA secretary. Later he was named general secretary of UK's YMCA, a position he held for 37 years. In 1930, he received a law degree from UK, but he never entered private practice. As a Fayette County judge from 1958 to 1966, Peak helped establish a home for delinquent children. He transformed a former tuberculosis hospital into the Julius Marks Home for the elderly.

Scott County (Georgetown)

Jared Carter, 9/20/1986, 4L, (2002, 03, 04, 05), was an All-State selection in 2005 after guiding Scott County to a 27-4 record and the 32nd District title. He set a state record with 200 blocks that year. Carter played sparingly during his UK career.

Shelby (Shelbyville)

Mike Casey, Simpsonville. 3/26/1948–4/9/2009, 3L, (1968, 69, 71), was UK's 13th all-time scorer, with 1,535 points. A Kentucky "Mr. Basketball" in 1966, he led his Shelby County High School team to the state championship.

Casey was UK's leading scorer as a sophomore of the 1967-68 season. He averaged 20.1 points per game and led the team in field-goal and free-throw percentages. His sophomore year successes led to an appearance on the cover of Sports Illustrated. He was named All-SEC three times and All-NCAA Mideast Regional in 1968.

He averaged 19.1 points during his junior year.

Casey sat out the 1969-70 season with a broken leg received in a car accident . He returned for the 1970-71 season. Casey was second-leading scorer (17.0) to Tom Porter (17.8) on a team that finished 22-6 and was an SEC champion (16-2).

Casey was inducted into the Kentucky Athletic Hall of Fame at a ceremony in Louisville.

The late Mr. Casey retired from Balfour, a company that makes class rings and graduation items.

Remembering Gillispie: *I just don't think he knows what it means to coach at UK. I hate to say it, but a change has to be made and soon, or we're going to lose what UK is all about. Ask (Richie)*

Farmer, or (John) Pelphrey, or (Deron) Feldhous what it means to play at Kentucky. Ask them what that (Kentucky) across their chest means. Somehow we've got to let that go. If we lost a game, we came out fighting mad; we weren't going to lose two in a row. I think he's in over his head. I think he has no clue as to what's going on in... **Mike Casey, Sea of Blue.**

Remembering Mike Casey: I *was attending an NCAA meeting in New York when summoned to a long distance telephone call. It was Coach Rupp. We just lost the NCAA, he said, Mike Casey got his leg crushed in an auto accident...***Russell Rice.**

Charles Hurt, 3/28/1961, 3L, (1980, 81, 82, 83), played on Wildcat teams that were 87-22. They were SEC co-champs in '82 and champs in '83. He scored 786 points, 496 rebounds and 104 assists at UK. Hurt is an Army M/Sgt.

William C. Harrison, Bagdad, 12/12/1892–6l/16/1936, 4L, (1912), lettered one year in basketball and three in football at UK. He was graduated from Kentucky State University and attended Southern Baptist Theological Seminary, Louisville, where he earned his doctorate of philosophy.

The Foreign Mission Board of the Southern Baptist Convention sent Harrison to Brazil in 1925. He taught the Old Testament and Greek in two seminaries.

Harrison was coordinator of the college at Porto Alegre, which was founded by his wife's sister and husband. He returned to Waco and taught as a visiting professor at Baylor University and Paul Quinn College.

Elmo C. Head, 9/15/1917–1/28/1971, 3L, (1937, 38, 39), was a native of Stamping Ground. During his three varsity years with UK, the Wildcats were 46-14. They won the regular SEC schedule in 1937. They were undefeated in 1938 until Florida upset them in the tournament. They won the tournament again in 1939. Head was with the Farmers & Traders Bank for 12 years. The bank appointed him president jn January, 1969.

Bill Busey, Bagdad, 10/8/1948, (1L, (1968,) was All-State at

Shelby County High,.He teamed with Mike Casey to help the Rockets post a 33-1 record en route to a state championship. He also played quarterback in football, outfielder in baseball, and dashman and broad jumper in track. Busey played three years as a reserve at UK. He is a farmer in Bagdad.

Trimble (Bedford)

JACK TINGLE

Robert Jackson Tingle, 12/30/1924– 9/22/1958, 4L, (1944, 45, 46, 47), was playing varsity basketball for Trimble High while an eighth grader. As a freshman, he was named to the all-star team of the North Central Kentucky Conference. He received that honor four straight years. In 1941 he was the sparkplug of the TCHS team that went to the final of the regional tournament, losing out by only two points to Valley High School. Again in 1942, the team went into the quarter finals of the regional, dropping out in a game with Williamstown - an outfit with 6-foot-8 Arnold Risen who later was an All-American at Ohio State. In 1943, Tingle's last year, the TCHS Blue Demons won their first North Central Kentucky Conference Championship. Tingle scored 948 points on UK teams that were 103-11. He became one of only three players in the University's history to be named to the All-Star team of the Southeastern Conference four years in a single sport, or otherwise. The other players similarly named were Wallace "Wah Wah" Jones and Ralph Beard.

In the four years that Tingle played with Kentucky, the Wildcats won the Southeastern title each year. He was an All-American selectee.

Remembering Tingle: *One of our battlers always fighting and always in there–an all-round basketball player.* **Adolph Rupp, BBM.**

211

Woodford (Versailles)

Ernest O. Jefferson, 4/19/1917–9/23/1972, Sq., (1928), was a starter with the 1937 Midway State Basketball championship team. He was a member of the University of Kentucky 1937-38 freshman basketball team and the 1938-39 varsity basketball team. He pitched baseball with the local Versailles team from high school days and the University of Kentucky baseball team through his freshman and sophomore years, later joining the St. Louis Cardinals professional team where he set records as a pitcher and batter.

A veteran of World War II, he saw action in the European Theatre. He was wounded on several occasions, resulting in his inability to finish his career as a major league baseball player. He was a railroad engineer for the Seaboard Coastline Railroad, Waycross, Georgia, for more than 30 years.

Paul W. Noel, Midway, 8/17/1924–11/16/2005, 1L, (1943), was an All-State basketball player at Midway High School. He was coached by Ed Diddle in a Kentucky-Indiana all-star game. Noel was a forward on the UK basketball team in 1943. He dropped out of UK after a year on the team because his tenant farmer became ill and Noel was needed to help out on the farm.

Several years later, Diddle paved the way for the 6-foot 4-inch Noel to play for the New York Knicks (1948, 1949 and 1950) and the Royals (1951 and 1952).

In later years the two men teamed up together working for a wholesale drug company.

Noel officiated at Kentucky high school basketball games after he left the pros. He ran Corner Drug Store in Versailles for several years, selling the business in the mid-1980s. He was a member of the Versailles City Council before he became mayor. Noel was a member of the Woodford County Chamber of Commerce Hall of Fame.

Remembering Paul Noel: *If I would say one thing about Paul W. Noel, it would be if I had to go to war. I would certainly want him on my side; it comes from the heart...***Ralph Beard, 2005.**

Wilbur Schu, 12/18/1922–11/6/1980, (3L, 1944, 45, 46). Two bad knees and holes in an ear drum kept him out of World War II . Schu played on UK teams that were 69-8. They won   three SEC championships and the school's first NIT championship. He was one of coach Adolph Rupp's 1944 Beardless Wonders, a team that also was referred to as the "Five F Formula - Four 4-Fs and a Freshman" - because four of its members were ineligible for the draft and one was a freshman.

Schu was named on the All-Southeastern Conference second teams of 1944 and 1945, and to Pic magazine's second team. Schu also played football at UK.

Remembering Schu: *Every time that we'd go into Madison Square Garden, the organist would play "Shoo Shoo Baby."...* **Ralph Beard, BBM.**

Cats *"Take It"* On Radio Quiz

Remembering $64 Question: *Kentucky's Wildcats, who took the first two objectives on their current eastern basketball tour, Wyoming and Temple, appeared to be in good form for their third quest - a victory over Long Island tonight - when Wilbur Schu, regular forward from Versailles, answered a $128 question on the "Take It or Leave It" radio program in New York last night.*

The Cats filled their jeans at the quiz show when Phil Baker, the master of ceremonies, decided to double the usual $64 award for the last question.

Kenton (Dutch) Campbell, second-string center from Newark Ohio, was called out of the audience to read the questions after Schu had stated the team's business in New York, and the audience was rooting for the Wildcats all the way.

*After Schu had given all of the answers correctly, Baker announced that each of the two Kentucky participants would receive $64. Schu and Campbell then announced they would split the money with their teammates. ..**The Lexington Herald.***

Joseph Daniel Chandler, 10/17/1933–4/27/2004, 1L, (1955), was a member of UK's undefeated 1954 Wildcats. After serving in the Army, he pursued a career as a well-known casino executive in Las Vegas and Lake Tahoe. He and Vern Hatton authored a book, *"Rupp From Both Ends of the Bench"*.

Chandler was involved in one of the better on-court battles in the Coliseum. It occurred after Alabama substitute Jim Brogan dared Dan Chandler to cross the center line while the teams were warming up. The two reserves squared off in a melee that involved several players on both sides before police restored order. Kentucky won the game, 66-52.

Paul "Sonny" Corum, 7/6/1935, Sq., (1955), was a native of Midway who played high school ball at Darlington Prep School in Rome. Ga. He earned All-Mid South for two successive seasons. As a sophomore at UK, he played on the 1955 team that finished 23-3 after losing to Marquette and defeating Penn State in the Mideast Regional.

Bo Lanter, 9/4/59, 3L, (1980, 81, 82), played prep ball at Woodford County High, where he averaged 19 ppg. Lanter was twice All-CKC and All-District.. He transferred to UK from Midwestern State University in Texas. Lanter played in 41 games for UK. The Wildcats were SEC champs all three years and went to the Final Four in '84.

Chapter XVIII
Pennyroyal Section

The Pennyroyal, largest of Kentucky's geographical divisions, abuts all the others: the Eastern Coal Field, the Bluegrass, along its grinding fringe of the Knobs, the Western Coal Field, and the Jackson purchase–as well as northern Tennessee and southern Indiana and Illinois.

The Pennyroyal extends across 35 of the state's 120 counties:

Barren (Glasgow)

Brandon Stockton, 6/25/1994, 4L, (2003, 04, 05, 06), was 2002 Kentucky "Mr. Basketball". He made All-State at Glasgow High and was Gatorade "Player of the Year" in Kentucky. Stockton is Glasgow's leading scorer with 2,674 points.

Stockton was one of four captains on the 2006 UK team. The Wildcats were SEC champs his first three years at UK.

Caldwell (Princeton)

Harold L. Amoss, Cobb, 9/8/1886, Sq., (1904), earned a letter on UK's second basketball team in 1904. He was a physician in Greenwich, Conn. for 23 years and was a professor of medicine at Duke University. Amoss was a major in the Army Medical Corps.

Casey (Liberty)

Don P. Branson, Yosemite, 6/18/1882–2/19/1979, 2L, (1905, 06). There are no stats available for Branson's two varsity years as a Wildcat. However, he was a freshman in 1903 and perhaps among the students that started the sport at UK. He also lettered two years in football.

Crittenden (Marion)

C. T. "Turkey" Hughes, 2L, (1924, 25). In high school, in Todd County, Hughes lettered in football, basketball and baseball. Although not a member of the track team, he was sent to the state meet in Lexington. He finished second and was offered a scholarship at U.K. There he earned letters in football, basketball, baseball and track (for a total of 13 letters) becoming the first four-letter man in U.K.'s history.

He coached five sports over the years. Hughes also served 27 years as chairman of the Department of Health and Physical Education. He was baseball coach at Eastern for 30 years. The school's baseball diamond is named the Turkey Hughes Field.

One of his best basketball teams was the 1930-31 squad. That team included the Carr Creek boys who took their small school to the Kentucky basketball state finals and then on to the national finals. (See "Coaches)

Remembering "Turkey": *There are various versions of how he became "Turkey." The one I like had him doing some broken field running–and an observer was reported to say "look at that boy run. He runs just like a turkey!".*

He was a fine gentleman, an important part of Madison's (athletic) heritage and I am glad I knew him... **Fred Engle Register columnist.**

Fleming (Flemingsburg)

Wendell Clay Evans, 3/8/34–8/7/2000, Sq., (1954), saw action in seven games as a sub on UK's undefeated 1954 season. Then he transferred to Morehead. Evans was a retired agency manager for State Farm Insurance and a former teacher, basketball coach and school administrator in the Fleming County school system.

Kenton (Covington)

Milerd J. "Andy" Anderson, 11/25/13, 3L, (1934, 35, 36), was an All-State guard in 1931 with the Covington Holmes basketball team that advanced to state tournament semi-finals. Anderson played two years of football and four years of basketball atUK.. He was captain of the 1937 basketball team. Anderson was general agent for the National Life Insurance Company of Vermont and for the Berkshire Life Insurance Company. He was elected Lexington city commissioner in 1947 as a candidate on the City Ticket headed by Tom Mooney.

Mickey Rouse, Ludlow, 5/11/1918–4/14/2012), 3L, (1938, 39, 40), was UK team captain in 1940. He scored 363 points in 56 games. Rouse was the first Wildcat to have his jersey retired.

Remembering Mickey: *When asked why he retired Mickey's jersey, Rupp replied, "Leadership."*...**Russell Rice, 1970.**

Remembering Rupp: *We were leading Tennessee by two points in the closing minute when Lee Huber and I went up for rebound under the UT basket. Huber accidently tipped the ball in to tie the score and send the game overtime. Adolph said, "God, now you're making it for them." Keith Farnsley hit a long hook and we beat them 36-34 in two OT's, which was all that saved us...* **Mickey Rouse, 2005.**

Taylor (Campbellsville)

Merion Haskins, 5/13/55, 3L (1975, 76, 77), was All-State at Taylor County High, which he led to an 87-21 four-year record. He played in three high school all-star games. Haskins was UK co-captain with Larry Johnson in 1977. He was a member of UK's Final Four in 1975.

Warren (Bowling Green)

Josh Carrier, 1/30/1983), 4L, (2006, 07, 08, 09), was Kentucky's 2001 Mr. Basketball. He averaged 23.7 points and 5.0 rebounds in his senior season, while leading Bowling Green to a 23-6 record ... Played in the 2001 Derby Festival All-Star game ... Closed out his career as the all-time leading scorer at Bowling Green with 1,955 points ... Also holds the school record for single-game scoring with 53 points ... Averaged 23.8 ppg while shooting 45 percent as a junior ... Was named Honorable-Mention All-American by Street & Smith's in the fall of 2000 ... Earned first-team All-State honors from the Louisville Courier-Journal and the Lexington Herald-Leader as a junior ... Father, Darrel, was an All-American at Western Kentucky and had an outstanding career in the ABA ... Carrier scored 110 points in five seasons at UK.

Jason Lathrem, 11/12,1L, (1996), averaged 22 ppg during his senior year at Greenwood High. He led the Gators to the championship of the Bluegrass Tournament in Louisville. They also won the 4th Region crown. He was the Region Player of the Year, earning second team All-State honors. He played on UK's 1996 NCAA championship team.

Wayne (Monticello)

Derrill W. Hart, Pisgah, 12/12/1892–6/16/1936, 1911, 12, 16), was second-leading scorer on UK's undefeated 1912 team, and leading scorer (13.3) on the 1916 team that finished 8-6.

Hart taught school for four years as a member of the faculty of Lexington High school. He obtained a master's degree from the University in 1916. The same year he enlisted in the navy as an apprentice seaman and two years later was commissioned an ensign.

At the close of the war, he became connected with the Doubleday Page Company, New York, publishing the Garden Magazine, later the American Home. From 1919 to 1934 he was associated with various horticultural publications and in 1934 he became editor of the garden section of the New York Sun. He later became advertising manager of the Flower Grower.

Chapter XIX
Western Coal Fields Section

The Western Coal Field region of Kentucky forms a compact, almost circular area south of the Ohio River in western Kentucky. It stretches across all of nine counties–Butler, Daviess, Graves, Hancock, Henderson, McLean, Muhlenberg, Ohio, Union, and Webster– and segments of at least eight others–Breckinridge, Christian, Crittenden, Edmonson, Grayson, Hardin, Hopkins, Logan, and Todd.

Breckinridge

Butler

Christian (Hopkinsville)

George Atkins, 7/10/1941, Sq., (1963). During three varsity years at Hopkinsville High, Atkins scored 1,621 points. His high point was 40 and he went over 30 ppg 12 times. He scored 27 against the Tennessee freshmen; however, Atkins played sparingly at UK.

Atkins is a former director of public relations for Humana Corporation. He has served as state auditor, secretary of cabinet, secretary of finance, and state auditors for public accounts.

Tommy Porter, Gracey, 10/17/1945, 3L (1966, 67, 68), was All-State and All-America at Christian County High. He scored 1,212 points in a three-year career. Porter was a member of the 1966 "Rupp's Runts" team that lost to Texas Western in the NCAA championship game.

Ravi Moss, 6/21/1984, 4L, (2003, 04, 05, 06), averaged 21.0 ppg at University Heights Academy, earning second-team All-State honors. He was "Player of the Year" in Western Kentucky. He played sparingly as a freshman at UK, but later contributed significantly in several close games. He played on the 1996 NCAA Championship team.

Crittenden (Marion)

Ercel B. Little, Tolu, 8/14/1908–10/15/1987 (1931, 32), played on Rupp's first two teams at UK. Born in Livingston County, he was a retired assistant principal at Madisonville North Hopkins High School and a former principal of Crittenden County High School.

Daviess (Owensboro)

Arville R. Hickerson, 11/23/1906–9/26/85, Sq., (1926). Hickerson saw action as a reserve in four games for the 1926 Wildcats, who were 15-9. He was a retired manager for the purchasing and stores department of Louisville Gas & Electric Co. He was an Army veteran of WWI.

Wm. Wayne Foust, 10/19/1903–9/13/1989), played one season of basketball and also played baseball at UK. He was the retired owner and operator of Green River Hatcheries and a former principal of Daviess County High School. In 1927, two years after beginning work as a science teacher and basketball coach at DCHS, he was elected principal, a position he held until 1941, when he resigned to go into business on a full-time basis.

During World War II, he was chairman of USO drives and participated in several war bond drives.

Bobby Watson, 3/12/1930, 3L, (1950, 51, 52). Watson was an All-SEC, both regular season and tournament, in 1952. He scored 1,001 points in three years at UK.). Watson coached Owensboro to state basketball titles in 1972 and '80. He is now a real estate agent in Owensboro.

Cliff Hagan, 12/9/1931, 3L, (1951, 52, 54), led Owensboro to the 1949 state basketball championship. The Red Devils defeated Lafayette 65-47 in the final with Hagan breaking the single game scoring record by pouring in 41 points. His play in that game is still regarded by many as the finest all-around performance in the history of the tournament. He broke all scoring records at Owensboro, averaging 27.5 points his last semester. Hagan was a three time first-team all-state performer.

. In the fall of 1952, a point shaving scandal involving three Kentucky players over a four-year period forced Kentucky to forfeit its upcoming season, the senior year of Hagan, Frank Ramsey and Lou Tsioropoulos. The suspension of the season made Kentucky's basketball team, in effect, the first college sports team to get the "death penalty."

Hagan, Ramsey and Tsioropoulos all graduated from Kentucky in 1953 and, as a result, became eligible for the NBA Draft. All three players were selected by the Boston Celtics–Ramsey in the first round, Hagan in the third and Tsioropoulos in the seventh. All three also returned to play at Kentucky despite graduating. In Kentucky's opening game that season, an 86-59 victory over Temple on December 5, 1953, Hagan scored what was a school single-game record of 51 points; this performance would not be surpassed until 1970. After finishing the regular season (one in which Hagan averaged 24.0 points per game) with a perfect 25-0 record and a #1 ranking in the Associated Press. Kentucky had been offered a bid into the NCAA Tournament However, then-existing NCAA rules prohibited graduate students from participating in post-season play; they declined the bid because their participation would have forced them to play without Hagan, Ramsey and Tsioropoulos, thus jeopardizing their perfect season.

Hagan scored 1,475 points at UK; he grabbed 1035 rebounds, which placed him second, three fewer than Ramsey. In 1952 and 1954 he was named both All-American and First Team All-SEC. His uniform number 6 is retired by the University of Kentucky.

Hagan played his entire 10-year NBA career (1956–1966) with the St. Louis Hawks. He was also a player-coach for the Dallas Chaparrals in the first two-plus years of the American Basketball Association's existence (1967–1970).

He served several years as UK's athletic director.

Remembering Hagan: *When I was a freshman and all we did* *was practice, as we were suspended that year. We were scrimmaging Memphis State and beating them but not as much as we should have been doing. They were a real scrappy bunch and were giving Hagan a hard time on the boards. Coach Rupp had men from Chicago visiting him that day, and he had invited them out to watch us practice. Our play did not improve much. Coach Rupp blew his whistle and turned to the men in the stands and said, "You fellows from Chicago have heard of our great Cliff Hagan. Cliff, come over here where they can see you. I'm sure they couldn't tell which one you were the way you were playing," and Cliff took a bow...* **Hugh Coy, BBM.**

Remembering State Tournament: T*he final game In Louisville marked the saddest day of my life. High School basketball was so great for me. It was the end of my world. I cried...* **Cliff Hagan, BBM.**

Bill Bibb, 1L, (1954), earned All-State honors at Owensboro, where he also played baseball. He played in 16 games during UK's undefeated season in 1954; then he transferred to Kentucky Wesleyan, during the '55 season after UK lost to Georgia Tech.

Randy Embry, 7/9/1943, 3L, (1963/64/65). Kentucky's Mr. Basketball in 1961, Embry enjoyed a highly successful career as a player and coach. He led Owensboro's basketball team to a 1960 state tournament appearance and the baseball team to back-to-back state berths in 1960 and 1961. Later as a baseball coach Embry led Daviess County to the 1971 State championship, and as boys basketball coach at Owensboro, his teams won 12 district and eight regional titles from 1981-99. At UK, he scored 393 points in 66 games. He was team captain in 1965.

Wayne Chapman, 15/15/1945, Fr., (1966). Chapman transferred to Western after his freshman year at UK.

He is the father of former NBA player Rex Chapman. He is now a scout for the NBA's Denver Nuggets.

Rex Chapman, 10/11/67, 2 (1987, 88). At Apollo High, Chapman was the 1986 Gatorade Player of the Year in Kentucky. In addition to All-State honors, he was Parade, Scholastic Coach, and Mc Donald's All-America. He was All-SEC during his freshman and sophomore years. At UK. Chapman amassed a total of 1,073 points and 220 assists in only two years at Kentucky before opting to enter the NBA Draft. He played 12 years a pro. In 2006, Chapman accepted the position of vice president of player personnel with the Denver Nuggets.

Graves (Mayfield)

Adrian "Odie" Smith, 10/6/1936, 2 (1957, 58). After starring at Farmington High, Smith attended Northeast Junior College in Mississippi. He was a member of UK's 1958 NCAA championship team. Smith scored 518 points in two years UK. He was a member of the undefeated U.S. men's basketball team that won the gold medal in the 1960 Olympics and was inducted into the Naismith Memorial Basketball Hall of Fame on August 13, 2010.

Smith's professional career highlights included his surprising winning of the 1966 NBA All-Star Game MVP in which he scored 24 points in 26 minutes of play (assisted, literally, by his regular-season teammate Oscar Robertson), and his league- leading free throw percentage of 90.3% in the 1966-67 season.

After eleven seasons of playing professional basketball Smith entered the banking industry, where he is a Commercial Relationship Manager for Cincinnati-based Fifth Third Bank.

Grayson (Leitchfield)

Jim Dinwiddie, 5/1/1948–2/7/2012, 3L, (1969, 70, 71), was a 6-4 guard who played for the Wildcats under Adolph Rupp for three seasons, from 1968 to 1971, scoring 277 points in 72 games over his career. He played on teams that were 71-13 regular season and 49-5 in the SEC, winning three conference championships. Dinwiddie was an attorney in Leitchfield.

Hancock (Lewisport)

Edward Patrick Kelly, Hawesville, 9/14/1948, 1L, (1905), was a member of UK's third basketball team in 1905. He graduated from the law school of the University of Kentucky in the class of 1906, returning to Hancock County, where he began the practice of law. For a few terms he was also Principal of Beechmont High School. At the time of his death he was serving his third term as county attorney of Hancock County.

Lewis Berkley Davis, 10/27/1911–6/20/1997, 1L, (1934). Davis was born in Lewisport and earned a degree in electrical engineering from the University of Kentucky in 1934. He was a member of the 1934 team that set a national record with 23 consecutive wins.

Later in 1934, Davis joined the Ken-Rad Tube and Lamp Corp. in Owensboro as an engineer. When General Electric bought Ken-Rad in 1945, Davis was named manager of operations.

In 1956, he became general manager of the company's electronic components division with its headquarters in Owensboro. overseeing plants in Syracuse, Auburn and Schenectady, N.Y., Tell City, Ind., and Anniston, Ala. He was elected vice president of G.E. in 1960. At one time, the General Electric plant here employed 6,700 people.

Hardin (Elizabethtown)

Antwain Barbour, 6/27/1982, 2L, (2003, 04). Named All-State and MVP after leading Elizabethtown to the KHSAA title in 2000. The Wildcats were SEC champs in 20002 and overall SEC champs in 2004.

Wendell Lyons, Vine Grove, 12/17/52 (Fr. 1970-71). Lyons was All-State at North Hardin High. He played in three games as a freshman at UK.

Eddie Mason, Sq., (1959), was All-State at Elizabethtown High, where he was selected as the district's "Most Outstanding

Player". He was second leading scorer (176 points, 18.7 avg.) on the 1959 UK freshman team.

Henderson (Henderson)

James M. Server, 5/16/1894–6/18/1964, 2L, (1915, 16). His teams were 15-11.

Hopkins (Madisonville)

Neville Earl Stone, 7/31/1886–10/16/1940, 1L, (1908). Stone played on the 1908 UK team that was 9-6. He was a well-known highway and bridge construction contractor.

Vincent Depaul Splane 11/30/1921–10/24/1989, 1L, (1942). Born in Paintsville, Splane spent most of his life in Middleburg. He played on the 1942 UK team that was 17-6 (8-1 SEC). They lost to Dartmouth47-28 in UK's first NCAA Tournament appearance. Splane was an Army Air Corps veteran and a lifetime member of American Dental, Florida Dental and Clay County Dental Associations.

Remembering Rupp: *The Coach Rupp of thirty years ago was a different man than the Coach Rupp of today. I say this in regard to his temperament, not to his desire to win or his desire for perfection. Sarcasm was a trait he had developed to a razor's edge and when it came to a caustic remark, he knew no master. His temper control went out the windows of the old Alumni Gym on more than one occasion. I remember several instances where I was on the receiving end and received the full brunt of one of his broadsides.*

We were playing Georgia Tech in Atlanta. The game was close, and Moore, a guard for Tech, had already scored 18 points when Adolph sent me in to guard him. I promptly fouled him on a shot which went in and he made the free throw awarded also. Adolph took me out pronto, and when I reached the sidelines to confront him, his face was purple with rage and that blood vessel in his fore-

*head was pulsating wildly. He screamed at me, "Splane, what the...
is the matter with you? Have you gone crazy?"...* **Vince Splane,
BBM, 19765.**

Frank Ramsey, 7/13/31, (1951, 52, 54), played for Madisonville High School, leading the Maroons to consecutive State Tournament berths in 1948 and 1949. An All-State basketball performer
for two seasons, Ramsey was also an All-State baseball selection in
1949, and a four-year member of the Maroon football squad. Frank
Ramsey made various All-SEC and All-America teams while scoring 1,344 points, 13th on UK's all-time list. He also pulled down
1,030 rebounds and dished out 275 assists at UK.

Ramsey was later inducted into the Naismith Basketball Hall of
Fame in Springfield, Massachusetts. Served as 1st. Lt. in Army and
was drafted #5 Overall in the 1st Round of the 1953 NBA Draft by
Boston.

Remembering the Tornado: O*n Nov. 15, 2005, threatening
weather outside Ramsey's home in a community adjacent to the
Madisonville Country Club sent the Basketball Hall of Famer into
a closet in his bedroom for refuge. There he rode out what proved to
be a tornado.*

*"I expected to walk out of that closet and be standing in my
bedroom, maybe with a hole in my ceiling," Ramsey said. "Instead,
when I walked out, I was standing completely outside and my house
was 50-feet away, broken into pieces.* **Frank Ramsey, 2005.**

Travis Ford, 12/29/1969, 3L, (1992, 93, 94), was a Parade
All-American at North Hopkins High. He transferred to UK after
a freshman year at Missouri. At UK, he served as a team captain in
1994. He scored 951 points, 428 assists, and 124 steals in 100 games
at UK. Ford was All-SEC, both regular season and academic. He
also was an NCAA All-Regional player. Ford currently is the head
coach at Oklahoma State.

Gary Gamble, Earlington, 3/28/1946, 3L, (1976, 77, 78),
scored 169 points at UK. He played on Wildcat teams that were
76-16. They were 30-2 in 1978 with a national championship over

Duke 88-84 in the Final Four. Gamble is a real estate dealer in Tennessee.

Skip McCaw, Sq., (1990). An all-conference and honorable mention all-state at North Hopkins High, McCaw averaged 13 points and seven rebounds. He led his team to a 26-6 record and a berth in the state playoffs his senior year. McCaw played six games as a Wildcat.

Jon Hood, 5/9/1991, 2L, (2010, 2011), averaged 29.4 points, 12.9 rebounds, and 3.1 blocked shots his senior season at Madisonville High. In 1909, he was named "Mr. Basketball," and Gatorade "Player of the "Year" in Kentucky. Hood scored 13 points in the 1909 Wazoo Kentucky Derby Festival Basketball Classic. He was held out due to an injury in 2012 after limited action his first two years at UK.

Muhlenberg (Drakesboro)

Roger Newman, 5/4/1938, 1L, (1961), averaged 26.1 as a senior at Green County High. He played in several high school all-star games. He served as captain of the 1956 Kentucky-Indiana game. Newman was a starting forward on the 1961 UK team that was 19-9, losing to Ohio State 88-74 in the Mideast Regional in Louisville. Newman is an engineer in Lake Forest, Ill.

Reggie Warford, 9/15/1954, 1L, (1976), scored 1,940 points at Drakesboro High. He was second team All-state. Warford played in UK's 1975 UK's NCAA championship game. He also played in the East-West All-Star game. He once hit 50 straight free throws in game at UK.

Patrick Sparks, Central City, 2L, (2005, 06). Sparks was the leading scorer (31.4 ppg) in Kentucky as a senior at Muhlenberg North High school. His 2,653 points, 607 rebounds, 657 assists, and 409 steals are a school record.

Sparks was All-SEC In 2005. He played on UK teams that were 90-28, winning SEC championships in the process.

Ohio (Beaver Dam)

Marshall Barnes, 3/2/1897–12/16/1985, Sq., (1923), was a reserve on the 1923 UK basketball team that finished 13-10. He was a former president of Beaver Dam Deposit Bank and former vice president of Owensboro Deposit Bank.

Todd

Union (Morganfield)

Fred Cowan, 4/23/58, 4L, (1978, 79, 80, 81). Cowan led Union County High to its first regional championship. He became its first All-State selection. He averaged 23.6 ppg, 13.3 rpg in leading his team to a 28-4 record. Cowan played in several all-star games. He was a member of UK's 1978 NCAA champions. Cowan scored 975 points and 489 rebounds as a Wildcat. He was All-NCAA Regional in 1979-80. After playing professional basketball, Cowan became an entrepreneur in Madisonville.

Polk L. Threlkeld, Waverly, 8/18/86–12/15/1958, Sq., (1909, 10), played fullback on the football team, was a member of the basketball team and was a three-letter man on the track team at UK. A retired civil engineer, he formerly was head of the Right-of-Way Department of Zone B of the Kentucky Department of Highways.

Larry Johnson, 11/28/54, 4L, (1974, 75, 76, 77). Johnson averaged 16 points, 10 rebounds, and 10 assists a game his senior year at Union County High. He played in the Kentucky East-West and Kentucky-Indiana All-Star games.

Johnson was co-captain of the Wildcats his senior year. He scored a career total of 856 points, 390 rebounds, and 319 assists. The Wildcats were NIT champs in 1976, SEC champs in 1977 and SEC and national champs in 1978.

Dwayne Casey, 4/17/1957, 4L, (1976, 77, 78, 79), graduated from Union County High School in 1975. At the University of Kentucky Casey had a career average of 1.3 points and 0.6 assists per game. He served as team captain during his senior year. He graduated from the University of Kentucky with a degree in business administration in 1979. Casey has subsequently served as follows: 1994-2005, Seattle Supersonics (assistant), 2005-2007, Minnesota Timberwolves; 2008, 2011, Dallas Mavericks, and 2011-present, Toronto Raptors.

Chapter XX
Purchase Section

The Jackson Purchase came into the commonwealth as an extension of Christian County with Old Wadesboro designated as its capital and land office. Over time, it was divided into eight counties, as follows with their seats of government.

Ballard (Wickliffe)

Kenny Rollins, 7/14/1923, 3L, (1943, 47, 48), was All-SEC and All-SEC Tournament. He was captain of the 1947 Wildcats, and the 1948 "Fabulous Five" team that won SEC, National and Olympic events. He scored 684 points in 98 games at UK.

Remembering the Tryout: *To say that I was coming back to a great big surprise would be an understatement because when I saw all the ballplayers that walked on that floor on the first time that fall, I said to myself, Kenny you've come to the wrong place...***Kenny Rollins BBM, 1976.**

Fulton (Hickman)

Hickman (Clinton)

Harold Ross, 3/25/1936, 3L, (1956, 57, 58). An All-State performer, Ross was the state's leading scorer in 1954. He earned three letters, playing in 24 games for UK. Ross was a member of UK's 1958 NCAA champions.

Samuel Harper, 11/27/1943–3/7/1999, 2L, (1963, 64). Harper played on UK teams that were 37-15 during his two varsity years. They were SEC co-champions in '62 and UKIT champs in both years. Sam E. owned Harper's Pharmacy in Danville.

Graves (Mayfield)

Leo Brewer, 7/9/1889–11/3/1965, 1L, (1907, 08), joined UK Basketball in 1908; the only records available listing him as a manager was in that year. He spent 40 years on the law faculty of the University of Texas, but returned to San Antonio in 1928 to resume private practice.

McCracken (Paducah)

Lawrence S. Burnham, 8/25/1900–2/9/1985, 4L, (1919, 20, 22, 23), was a native of Paducah, formerly of Lexington, who earned four basketball letters at UK. The Wildcats were 44-31 during those years.

Stan Key, Hazel, 2/2/50, (1970, 71, 72). Key set a school scoring record with 53 points against South Marshall and scored 2, 100 points at Calloway County High. He was a unanimous All-State choice. Key also lettered four years in baseball.

Clyde C. Cooper, Brooksville, 10/10/25–3/15) 1L, 1995, (1945). Cooper was a member of the 1943-44 Brooksville High School basketball team, which went undefeated in regular season. He played on UK teams for Adolph Rupp at the University of Kentucky and in 1948-49 played for the Nashville Volunteers semi-pro basketball team. In 1950, he coached the YMCA team of Kankakee, Ill. to the national title.

Marshall (Calvert City)

James L. King, Sharpe, 1/24/20, 3L, (1940, 41, 42), played center three years for Wildcat teams that were SEC (Reg. &T.) and Sugar Bowl champs his sophomore year, and SEC champs in both events in 1942 when they lost to Dartmouth in the Final Four. King was leading scorer in 1941. He was a two-time All-SEC (second team). 2nd. Lt. King was killed February 24, 1944, near Gotha, Germany, when the B-24 on which he was co-pilot was shot down.

Joseph B. Holland, Benton, 9/26/1924–9/18/2010, 3L, (1946, 47, 48). Though a World War II stint in the Navy came first, Holland arrived at UK after graduating from Benton High School in Kentucky. He was the high school team's captain and led it to second place in the state tournament. He scored 504 points in 105 games with the Wildcats, making All-SEC and All-Tournament in 1947. He also ran track.

At UK, he was a reserve on the Fabulous Five's 1947-48 championship team. Holland was drafted in 1948 by Baltimore and in 1949, he joined Fabulous Five members Alex Groza, Cliff Barker, Ralph Beard and Wallace "Wah Wah" Jones in forming the Indianapolis Olympians of the NBA. It was the only time in the history of professional basketball that five players from one school joined a pro team together and the only time the players themselves owned the team. Holland later became a car dealer, owning Joe Holland Chevrolet in Charleston, W.Va. During his 50 years of work in the industry, he also bought Bill Gatton's Friendship Chevrolet on High Street in Lexington and turned it into Joe Holland Chevrolet. He later moved the dealership to New Circle Road and sold it to Rod Hatfield in 2002.

Remembering Joe Holland: *To me, he was a giant back then. He was kind of a fortress on the floor and was very strong, very physical...***Joe B. Hall.**

Remembering Rupp: *We thought ours was a great team with good size and all other attributes that it takes to make a good team. Some of us were saying there probably wouldn't be another like that team because of the WWII bringing it together, etc. Coach Rupp made a very wise statement to this effect: There will be in years to come, and I will probably have them here, men that will jump higher and shoot better than even this great team...***Joe Holland, 1974.**

Pat Doyle, 4/1/1941, 1L, (1963) Doyle was a two-time All-District and All-Region player at North Marshall. He helped the Jets to the 1959 Boys' State Basketball title while earning MVP honors. In addition, Doyle was named "Mr. Basketball" that same year. Doyle played sparingly in three varsity years at UK, lettering in '63.

Chapter XXI
Coaches

A good coach can win with good players. A bad coach can not win with good players. A good coach can not win with bad players... **Adolph Rupp.**

John "Sonny" Allen led Coach Bob Laughlin's Breckinridge Training School to the 1946 state championship. Two other Eagles, Frank Fraley and Don Battson, joined Allen on the All-State Tournament team. Allen was Kentucky's "Star of Stars" in the 1946 Kentucky-Indiana All-Star game. He also was Most Valuable Player in the 1946 16th Regional Tournament. Allen was an outstanding coach at Breckinridge, leading his 1963 team to the State Tournament. His basketball record was 175-100 and his baseball record was 225-25. He was director of athletics at Breckinridge from 1953 to 1963.

Stan Arnzen–Known as the "finest player to wear the Red and Black" of Newport High School, Arnzen excelled in baseball and basketball...He would later return to his alma mater for a highly successful tenure as basketball coach...His teams never had a losing record in 21 years, winning 452 games while losing only 158... Twelve of his basketball squads had 20 or more wins...Coach Arnzen took five teams to the Sweet Sixteen, with his 1954 team advancing to the title game before losing to Inez...Perhaps the greatest tribute to this man's teaching was the fact that at one time, six of his former players held head coaching positions in the northern Kentucky area.

Jimmy Bazzell - An outstanding high school basketball player at Central High School in Clinton, he carried over his dedication and hard work as a player to his coaching career...His teams were noted for being well prepared and fundamentally sound...Coach Bazzell had a career record of 417 wins and 89 losses, and his teams made six Sweet Sixteen® basketball tournament appearances...He was a longtime active member of the Kentucky High School Coaches Association and served as a coach of many high school all-star teams, and later served Allen County as a distinguished high school administrator.

Walter Brugh played all sports at Paintsville High. He made the varsity football team while in the eighth grade. Paintsville won the Big Sandy Conference football championship during his four years. Brugh won All-Conference honors three years. His life's work during 39 years at Paintsville was coaching football, golf, baseball, track and assisting in basketball.

John Burr was a consistent winner as basketball coach at Adair County and always a regional threat…He was respected as a gentleman on the bench, and certainly for his coaching ability….His Indians finished fourth in the 1954 State Tournament and came back even stronger the next year, battling to the championship game before falling to a Johnny Cox-led Hazard team 74-66…Ralph Shearer and Terry Randall were the stars of his strongest teams…His 26 Adair County teams won 568 while losing just 232 and captured 3 regional tournaments.

Ralph Carlisle led Kavanaugh to two straight state tournament appearances in basketball…As Lafayette's coach for 16 years, he guided the Generals to three state championships, in 1950, 1953, and 1957, as well as the runner-up slot in 1949…He was All-State pretourney in 1932 and All-State Tournament in 1933…At Lafayette he was a two-time Coach-of-the-Year and was Coach-of-the-Decade.

"Copper" John Campbell was All-State at Hindman in 1939. He coached Wayland for 11 years, winning four district and three regional titles. His 1956 squad, featuring Kelly Coleman, set many State Tournament records.

Ernie Chattin was an All-State player for Ashland High in both football and basketball. He served as captain in both sports. Chattin coached at Prichard High in Grayson before returning to Ashland High. He officiated both football and basketball for 33 years and was an assigning secretary. He also was on the KHSAA State Track

Committee for 20 years. Chattin attended 55 consecutive Sweet Sixteen tournaments.

Charles Combs was successful basketball coach at Hartford, Vicco, Mayfield and Daviess County. He led Hartford to three State Tournament appearances and amassed a 479-234 coaching record in 39 seasons.

Jim Conner was a coaching legend in Northern Kentucky. Jim Connor got his start at Newport Catholic High School...His baseball teams captured three state championships, winning 16 districts and 12 regionals...During his 16 years at Catholic, his basketball teams won 339 and lost 144...Three of his teams reached the Sweet Sixteen...They also won 10 district titles...He also served two colleges as basketball coach, Bellarmine in Louisville and Thomas More in his native Northern Kentucky...He also coached at Boone County from 1970-1979 and served that school as assistant principal.

Morton Combs made the winning basket for Hazard against Male High in the 1932 state championship game. He also played football and baseball for Hazard. As a coach, his Carr Creek team won the 1956 state basketball championship. He coached the Kentucky All-Stars against Indiana in 1964.

Pearl Combs began his coaching career at Vicco. His Hindman teams earned berths in six Sweet Sixteens. They made the championship game in 1939 before losing to Brooksville, and took home the big trophy in 1943 by defeating St. Xavier. Combs had a career coaching record of 761 wins and 320 losses.

George Conley–This former Ashland Tomcat is one of the few distnguished Kentuckians to both coach and officiate in the Boys' State Tournament. His Ashland basketball teams won 114 games while losing only 39 from 1949-54. The 1953 squad won the 16th Region and appeared in the Sweet 16. Conley officiated numerous state tournaments.

Warren Harding Cooper was the star of Brooksville's 1939 state championship team. He earned All-Tournament honors in 1939 and in 1940 coached Dilce Combs in the 1954 state tournament.

Cooper officiated in four state tournaments during his 36 years as a referee.

Woody Crum was a multi-sport letterman at Jenkins High School and 1947 All-State basketball player. Over the course of a 37-year high school coaching career, he won 527 games. Crum began his coaching career at Mays Lick High School, before moving to Maysville high School in 1951 as assistant basketball coach. During a nine-year tenure at Maysville, Crum guided his team to three Sweet 16 appearances. As a head baseball coach, his Daviess County High School won a state championship in 1958.In 1962 Crum coached the Kentucky All-Stars. He then spent six years as head basketball coach at Lawrence Central in Indianapolis, making one trip to the Indiana state tournament. Returning to Kentucky in 1970, Crum served as head basketball coach for eight years at Harrison County High School in Cynthiana.

Bowman "Bo" Davenport qualified for the Hall of Fame, as an All-State player who led his Bowling Green team to the 1943 State Tournament and as a coach who led Edmonson County to the state championship in 1976…Edmonson County beat Betsy Layne 77-72, Harrison County 61-57, Shelby County 53-52 and Christian County 74-52 in the final…Edmonson broke a seven- year reign by larger schools…He taught and coached 32 years, winning 526 and losing 432. All of those years were with small schools, Clarkson, Grayson County and Edmonson County…He also officiated basketball for 20 years…In addition to being a basketball star at Bowling Green High, he also played football and baseball, winning nine letters in all…He was All-District and All-Regional three years and made third team All-State the year before he collected first-team honors.

Carl Deaton compiled a 397-301 career record as basketball coach at Green County. His 1976 squad advanced to the Boys' State Basketball Tournament. His Dragons track team captured several regional championships.

Nick Denes was an All-State guard for Garrett (Ind.) High School. His Corbin Redhounds won the KHSAA basketball championship in 1936, beating Nebo 24-18 in the final game. Corbin had three All-Tournament players, Marion Cluggish, Stan Cluggish and William Asher. Moving to Louisville, Denes coached Male High to several state track championships and also won state football championships.

Ralph Dorsey was an all-state tournament basketball player at Horse Cave, where his 1933 and 1934 teams were unbeaten during the regular season...His '33 team lost in the finals to Ashland...As a coach, he led Caverna to a third place state tournament finish in 1953...His 1962 Caverna baseball team won the state championship...An eight-year Board of Control member, he was President in 1968-69 of both the Board of Control and the Kentucky High School Coaches Association.

Paul Dotson was an all-state football selection in 1963. He represented Belfry as an East/West All-Star... Later, he coached football, baseball and track, but it was in girls' basketball where he found his fame. He won 276 games while losing just 68 and guided his 1984 squad to a state runner-up finish...His teams were 60th District champs nine consecutive years...As a basketball official, he worked the Boys' Sweet Sixteen, and as the Belfry athletic director, was the founder of a group that raised $500,000 to build Belfry's modern athletic complex.

Tom Ellis–The man they called "Big Daddy", "Mr. Bulldog" and "Coach", was one of the last in Kentucky to coach football, baseball and basketball at the same time. As a player, he lettered for four years in basketball and baseball at Calhoun, leading his roundball team to the state tournament. Recruited by Ed Diddle to play football at Western, he played in the first football game he ever saw...As a coach, he recorded a 608-184 mark in basketball and a 203-98-6 record in football, serving as the headman at both Bardstown and Covington Holmes...His 1941 Bardstown team was unscored upon and his Tigers posted five undefeated seasons...At Holmes, his '46 pigskin team was awarded the mythical state title and later, he took two Bulldog basketball teams to the Sweet 16.

Jack Fultz coached three Olive Hill teams to the State Tournament. He also served as principal at Olive Hill for three years, after five years as assistant and 18 years as a teacher and coach. He was principal at West Carter High for six years. Fultz served as commissioner of the Eastern Kentucky Athletic Conference.

Joe Gilley–The highlight of Gilley's distinguished coaching career at Harlan High came in 1944 when his team won the state basketball championship, defeating Dayton 40-28.

Lyman Ginger played high school football for Henderson Bassett. He started his coaching career at Bath County High School before moving to Winchester High where he coached football, basketball and track. Ginger continued his career as a basketball coach at University High in Lexington. He was Rupp's unofficial assistant coach during WW-II.

Denzil Halbert served as the head basketball, baseball, track and golf coach at Martin from 1947-72. He recorded a 528-331 basketball coaching record, taking his 1965 team to the Sweet 16. He served as athletic director for 13 years at Allen Central and the Floyd County school system before retiring in 1985 with 38 years of total service.

Joe B. Hall starred in basketball and football at Cynthiana. He played for Adolph Rupp at UK before transferring to Sewanee midway of his sophomore year. He coached UK from 1972 to 1985. Hall previously coached at Shepherdsville High School, and Regis University and Central Missouri State University before returning to UK in 1965 to serve as an assistant coach under Adolph Rupp.

In the 1978 NCAA Tournament, he coached the Wildcats to their fifth NCAA Men's Division I Basketball Championship. He was named National Coach of the Year in 1978 and Southeastern Conference Coach of the Year on four different occasions. His record at UK was 297 - 100, and 373-156 over his career.

Along with the 1978 title, Hall also guided Kentucky to a runner-up finish to UCLA in the 1975 NCAA tournament (which included an upset of heavily-favored and previously undefeated Indiana in a regional final), a Final Four appearance in the 1984 NCAA Tournament (losing to eventual champion Georgetown), and an NIT championship in 1976. He won 8 Southeastern Conference regular season championships and one Southeastern Conference tournament championship (1984).

Joe Harper earned three baseball and four basketball letters, and was named all-district, all-region, and second team All-State as a senior at London High. He took Monticello teams to the Sweet 16 six times, advancing to the quarterfinals twice, the semi-finals twice, and losing the championship game to Flaget in 1960.

Bill Harrell was a native of Belfry who starred in basketball at Kentucky Wesleyan. He coached high school and college teams to 596 victories. His 1966 Shelby County team, led by Mike Casey, had a No. 1 ranking and a 29-1 record going into the KHAA tournament. Casey scored 20 points and the Thoroughbreds defeated Louisville Male in the championship game. Harrell was a two-time Kentucky Coach of the Year. He later led Muncie Central to Indiana state championships in 1978 and 1979.

Willie Hendrickson coached basketball at Lone Jack, Middlesboro and Bell County. His Bell County team made two Sweet 16 appearances, including a semifinal finish in 1956 and a quarterfinal finish in 1960.

Jack Hicks–This gentleman coach is a testimony that "courage, perseverance and dedication" can lead to success...In 22 years of coaching baseball, his teams won 20 district championships...They made 15 trips to the State Tournament, playing in eight title games and winning four state championships...He had a coaching record of 606 wins with 196 losses...Forty-two of his players earned college scholarships with 11 going on to play professional baseball... Jack has been a manager of several KHSAA tournaments in the Owensboro area, always willing to give of his time and efforts.

Holbert Hodges–A basketball coaching legend at Lily, Hazel Green and London, Hodges coached teams to three Sweet 16 Basketball Tournament appearances.

Ted Hornback and his Sonora teammates were forced to play nearly all their home games on outdoor courts until he and others were able to build a gymnasium for the school thanks to scrap lumber from old barracks at Ft. Knox. After playing for Ed Diddle at Western from 1925-29, he began his FFF coaching career at Corinth where, in just his first season, he led his team to a state championship, defeating Kavanaugh 22-20 in the final at Alumni Gym in Lexington. He later returned to Western as an assistant coach in basketball and the head coach of the men's tennis teams.

C. T. "Turkey" Hughes coached five sports over the years. He also served 27 years as chairman of Eastern's Department of Health and Physical Education. He was baseball coach at Eastern for 30 years. The school's diamond is named the Turkey Hughes Field. One of his best basketball teams was the 1930-31 squad. That team included the Carr Creek boys who took their small school to the Kentucky basketball state finals and then on to the national in Chicago.

Maurice Jackson began his coaching career at Cropper High School in the 1930s. He coached at Lexington's Bryan Station High School beginning in 1936. His Bryan Station team won 32 of 33 games that school year and gave eventual state champion Midway its only loss.

Jackson became Lafayette's first basketball coach in 1939, when the school first opened. The Generals' 1942 state championship was the first for a Fayette County school since 1924, when the old Lexington High School won it. He also was Lafayette's athletic director.

Soon after the Lafayette state championship, Jackson joined the Army Air Corps. He left the military as a captain in 1946. Later he was a training officer, working with disabled veterans, for the Veterans Administration. During this time he also coached basketball and baseball at the old University High School. Later came a stint as head basketball coach at Clark County High School.

Paul Jenkins was the coach at high schools in Ashland and Louisville both in Kentucky, in Portsmouth, Ohio and at Vero Beach

High School.

During this period, his football teams won 165 games, lost 29 and tied 6. Included among those victories were nine state championships in Kentucky. At St. Petersburg, his teams won 21 and lost 25.

In Kentucky, he was twice named "Coach of the Year," and he coached the state's all-star football and basketball teams and was a member of the American Coaches football rules committee. He also won three state basketball championships, as well as ones in golf, tennis, swimming and baseball.

Ellis Johnson played baseball and football during a tour as a naval fighter pilot... When a knee injury stopped him from playing football, he became coach of the Iowa Preflight station baseball team.

He began his high school coaching career at Williamson, W.Va... Johnson spent a year as an assistant at Ashland. His next stop was Morehead, where he coached basketball, football, baseball, and track and was director of physical education between 1936 and 1953. He coached nine Eagle basketball All-Americans.

Johnson still is Morehead's all-time winningest coach in football, with a 54-44-10 mark. He retired from coaching in 1953 and went into the insurance business. He came out of retirement to head the Marshall team in 1963 and retired from coaching again in 1969. Later, he was involved in cable television promotion in Huntington.

Harry Johnson earned 12 varsity letters in four sports at Fleming-Neon. He was an All-State football honoree in 1957 and an outstanding basketball star. Johnson coached many sports at Tates Creek. He worked as a basketball official for 20 years and an umpire in baseball for 14 years.

Bain "Tiny" Jones was a native of Kuttawa in Lyon County. He coached all sports at Mount Sterling for more than 30 years. Jones also coached at two other Kentucky schools, Dayton for three years and Bourbon County for one year, before returning to Mount Sterling. His basketball Trojans reached the Sweet Sixteen in 1930,

1935, 1942 and 1943.

Charles "Junie" Jones, Jr. earned 10 letters at DuPont Manual in football, basketball, track and baseball…As an all-stater in football, he led his team to an undefeated season and a state title in 1936, scoring two touchdowns in a 27-0 win over Male on Thanksgiving Day. After earning All-SEC honors in 1942 at Kentucky, he began a coaching career that took him to stops at Pikeville, St. Xavier, Manual, Atherton and Ft. Knox…His most outstanding achievement came when he led the Ft. Knox girls' basketball team to an undefeated regular season and a berth in the 1977 sweet Sixteen… He officiated high school basketball for several years.

Bobby Keith coached Clay County, led by Richie Farmer, to a state championship in 1987 and runner-up positions in 1985 and 1988. His teams won 767 victories and only 124 losses. They won 14 regionals.

Charley Lampley–This native of Possum Trot started his playing career on a dirt court…He was an outstanding basketball player at Sharpe…He began his coaching career as a high school senior, coaching a one-room grade school to the county championship…Lampley had a career coaching record of 436 wins and 218 losses, and guided North Marshall to the State Tournament on two occasions…The 1959 team won it all, defeating Manual in the title game…After 21 years of coaching, he became an outstanding school administrator.

Bob Laughlin coached Breckinridge Training, led by Sonny Allen, to the 1946 KHSAA championship. He coached nine years at Morehead State, leading the Eagles to three OVC championships. They named him league Coach of the Year in 1961.

Lawrence L. McGinnis coached three different schools to State Tournament berths. His 1936 Hartford team reached the State Tournament, as did his Daviess County teams in 1942 and 1943. He coached Owensboro to 247 victories against 142 losses. They participated in seven State Tournaments; he was athletics director until 1975. One of his former players, Bobby Watson, succeeded him as coach and captured two State Tournament championships.

Marvin Meredith was an outstanding athlete at Catlettsburg. At Russell he had a 677-205 coaching record, including three trips to the Sweet 16.

Ed Miracle starred as a football player at Middlesboro and for 36 years he was an athletic director and coach. He coached four sports at Lynch. His basketball teams won more than 300 games and seven district championships. His Lynch and Madison Central football teams won more than 200 games. He coached the East All-Stars in 1961 and 1972, and was Class A Coach of the Year in 1970.

Letcher Norton played basketball at Clark County High in 1930-31. He coached basketball at Trapp High in Clark County and in Charleston, Ind. Then he returned to Winchester and spent 14 years as Clark County coach. Norton retired with an overall record of 603-140. That included a string of 39 straight wins. His 1951 Cardinals won the state championship after finishing second the previous year.

Patrick M. Payne was the only coach to win state basketball championships in both boys' and girls' tournaments. His 1932 Hazard boys' team won the title by defeating Male in the final, 15-13, when Morton Combs scored the winning goal. Payne's 1930 Hazard girls also won the state championship. He also was an outstanding football coach at Hazard. Payne later coached basketball at Manual.

Gene Pendleton was a standout basketball player at Monticello. He led the Trojans to three consecutive trips to the Sweet 16, including a runner-up finish in 1960. He scored 2,010 career points, including a single-game high of 40. Pendleton went on to play four years of college basketball, first at Tennessee and the final three at Murray State.

James H. Phillips played for a Tolu team that reached the state finals in 1931, losing to Manual 34-23...The year before Tolu was beaten by state champion Corinth 26-25 in the semifinals...As a coach, he took Clinton Central to the 1941 State Tournament. His Central teams went to the region nine times between 1945 and 1956.

Ray Pigman–After a tour in the Navy during World War II Pigman returned to Whitesburg High as basketball and football coach and athletic director. Fifteen years after leading the Yellow jackets to the Sweet 16 as a player, he coached the basketball team (33-4) to fourth place in the 1951 State Tournament. From 1956 to 1959, Pigman served as athletics director, assistant principal and basketball coach at Trimble County. He retired in 1978 as principal of Southeastern Elementary and Junior High in Hanover, Ind.

Sam Potter coached at Lynch for 10 years. His teams won 76, lost just 19, and tied six games. His football teams of 1951-1953 won 30 consecutive regular season games. He was runner-up for The Courier-Journal's Coach-of-the-Year award in 1952, and won it the following year. Potter was coach of the East All-Stars that upset the highly favored West, led by Heisman Trophy winner Paul Hornung. Potter retired from coaching and served as principal and superintendent at Lynch, and retired again as superintendent of Shelbyville Independent Schools.

Don Richardson was a longtime baseball and basketball coach from Madison Central. He Coached the Indians to over 950 wins on the baseball diamond and 350 wins on the basketball hardwood… His 1982 baseball squad finished a perfect 40-0 en route to capturing the State Championship…Coached the boys basketball squad to a State Tournament appearance in 1987.

Goebel Ritter played basketball, football and golf for Madison High in Richmond. He took Hazard to four Sweet 16s, winning the championship in 1955. His star player, the great Johnny Cox, scored 32 points for Ritter's Bulldogs in their 74-66 championship victory over Adair County. His State Tournament record was 7-3. In addition to his 10 years at Hazard, Ritter coached one year at Fleming-Neon and four years at Whitesburg. He officiated for 18 years, serving as a referee for three state tournaments.

Aggie Sale–After an All-America playing career at the University of Kentucky he coached Kavanaugh from 1933-1937…Then he moved to Harrodsburg where he became one of Kentucky's most respected coaches...He took the Pioneers to the State Tournament in 1960...That Harrodsburg team was one of two that won championships in the 20-team Central Kentucky Conference, and he was C.K.C. Coach-of-the-Year in 1960...He also served as football coach at Harrodsburg from 1946-1948...

Roscoe Shackelford averaged 17.3 points per game during four years at Hazard High. He led the Bulldogs to the state tournament in 1953. Shackelford coached Dilce Combs before returning to Hazard in 1962-63. In 11 years there, he was 324-66, leading the Bulldogs to four trips to the state tournament. Shackelford served as Hazard's athletic director from 1964-82. He later spent five years as superintendent of Hazard City Schools.

Guy Strong coached Kentucky Wesleyan to the 1966 NCAA Division II title, then had successful Division I stints at Eastern Kentucky and Oklahoma State. He coached high school ball at Louisville Male, Richmond Madison, and Clark County. After retiring from coaching in 2001, Strong served as Director of Pupil Personnel for Clark County Schools. He is a member of Dawahare's.

Charles "Jock" Sutherland took teams from three different schools to Kentucky's state high school basketball tournament (the Sweet Sixteen): Gallatin County in 1959, Harrison County in 1966, and Lexington Lafayette in 1979. After his Lafayette team won the state tournament in 1979 Sutherland retired from coaching, and for twenty years worked as a color man for WHAS (Louisville, KY) sports broadcasts.

Mark McCoy Tarry–When little Brewers High School began practice in 1947, 35 of the 70 boys enrolled in the school reported to Coach Tarry...The team had lost only two games while winning 34 during the previous season and had finished as runner-up to Maysville in the State Tournament...During the 1947-48 season, the colorful and dynamic Tarry led the Redmen to a 36-0 record, including a championship game revenge victory, 55-48 over Maysville...That team finished the year as the Number 1-ranked team in America... No team since Brewers has finished as an undefeated state champion...Tarry's ten-year record at Brewers was 247-47, a winning percentage of 83.7.

Oran C. Teater played football, track and basketball for Paintsville High in the late 1930s. After World War II, he returned to his alma mater and coached all sports. Teater reorganized the Big Sandy Conference to include all sports and was active in organizing girls' sports. He retired in 1978 as superintendent of Paintsville schools.

J.W. "Spider" Thurman was an all-state tailback for Benham High in Harlan County. He also was a member of the undefeated (25-0) 1935-36 Benham basketball team, which a county quarantine prevented from playing in the state tournament. Thurman started the basketball tradition at Clay County High School, a tradition that reached its zenith when one of his players, Bobby Keith, coached the Tigers to the 1987 KHSAA championship.

John Bill Trivette played basketball and baseball for Pikeville College Academy from 1932-1935. He played briefly for Rupp at UK. Trivette was the basketball coach at Pikeville High for 16 years. He is commonly referred to as an inventor of the full court zone press. His Pikeville High teams won 427 games and lost 126 between 1944 and 1960. Trivette was Kentucky's coach of the year in 1957 when his team had a record of 32-4 and finished third in the State Tournament.

Wendell Wallen–The highly successful basketball coach at Johnson Central and Meade Memorial had a career mark of 385-178. He guided three teams to the Sweet 16.

Russell Williamson–During Williamson's tenure (1929-1948) as basketball coach at Inez, the Indians won eight regionals and a state title (1941). Inez placed four of his players on the All-Tournament teams.

Fairce O. Woods was an amazing basketball player for Garrett High in Floyd County, a high scorer despite his 5-4 height. In 14 years at Breathitt County, Woods coached six regional champions, five consecutively from 1958-62. His Breathitt teams won 389 games while losing only 81.

John Wooden coached two years at Dayton High School in Kentucky. His first year at Dayton marked the only time he had a losing record (6–11) as a coach. After Dayton, he returned to Indiana, teaching English and coaching basketball at South Bend Central High School until entering the Armed Forces. His high school coaching record over 11 years, two at Dayton and nine at Central, was 218–42.

Wooden coached two years at Indiana State before coaching UCLA from 1948-75. His Bruin teams compiled a slate of 620-147. His overall college coaching record was 664-162. That included a record 88 in a row and 10 NCAA championships in 12 years. Prior to his last game, a 92-85 win over UK in 1975 in San Diego, he announced his retirement.

Chapter XXII
Ladies Return

It was fall of 1974 when women's basketball at the University of Kentucky finally reached varsity status, and sighs of "It's about time," were heard throughout a state that prides itself on its great basketball tradition.

But women's basketball was not making its debut on campus, as many thought; Instead, it was making an exciting return after disappearing exactly 50 years before.

The first organized basketball team on campus was the women's team. Nine years after their return in 1974, UK set a then national record for attendance at a women's collegiate game (10,622 vs. Old Dominion in Memorial Coliseum on Feb. 5, 1983).

Any history of women's basketball at UK would be sorely lacking without mention of the exciting years of the "Early Era," a period that spanned 21 years, from the first collegiate game on Feb. 21, 1903, until the last on March 5, 1924.

That is when University President Frank L. McVey, in an interview with the Kentucky Kernel, said basketball had proven to be a strenuous sport for boys and therefore was too strenuous for girls. He said it was also undesirable to have the University girls traveling over the state and throughout the South in order to take part in intercollegiate sports.

"The trips are very expensive because of the necessity of proper chaperonage and provision," he said. "Some very irritating consequences have developed in the past as a result of Intercollegiate games."

The prevailing attitude (among men) was that women were too frail, both physically and mentally, for the rigors of the game.

McVey's attitude, combined with inadequate facilities and general mores of the time, all helped contribute to the demise of women's basketball, which was abolished when the University Senate passed a bill to that effect in the beginning of the 1924-25 school year.

But the women had experienced some exciting years that would never be forgotten. Their first game ever came 15 days after their male counterparts made history by participating in the first collegiate game involving a basketball team from the University of Kentucky (then known as Kentucky State College). The UK (KSC) men faced Georgetown College on the State College gym floor in Barker Hall, where spectators sat on a circular mezzanine track containing three rows of chairs.

On the following day, girls at State College, under Coach Jane Todd Watson, engaged in a match basketball game at the gym. Twelve days later, a large crowd attended another match game between the girls, and an upcoming game between the KSC girls and Kentucky University. The girls were taking attention away from a game between the boys at those two institutions.

The State boys lost their game, 42-2, but the girls, playing before 500 spectators the following day, defeated the KU girls 16-10 in the first intercollegiate game between girls' basketball teams in Lexington.

The following year, the State girls won both of their scheduled games, 14-10 over Georgetown, and 28-1 over the Jessamine Female Institution. Meanwhile, the boys compiled a 1-4 record that season.

After the 1904 season, the Kentuckian yearbook gave the girls an "All Hail," noting, "Successful from the start - two years ago - basketball as played by girls caught not only the student, but the public favor as well, and every game played drew an enthusiastic house which packed the standing room to the doors-an appreciative crowd of fellows-mad, riotously mad, over contests abounding in snappy spectacular play."

The yearbook also devoted a full page to an article written by a male student about the Georgetown game. The author referred to the girls as "fair Amazons ... presented to our penetrating stare devoid of all unnecessary weight and curves, and bravely facing the front in skirts barely reaching the ankle. Very barely."

He wrote how the porters rushed onto the gym floor after the game and made haste "to remove from the vulgar gaze of the public,

basketfuls of various articles consisting chiefly of buttons, beautiful sleeve buttons and other buttons, hairpins, pins and other pins, vari-colored ribbons and the unknown scattered remains of much cherished voodoo strings."

That same year a student named Herman Scholtz dressed as a girl and traveled to Georgetown with the State co-eds, obviously with their connivance. The heavily veiled Scholtz watched much of the spirited contest, which was forbidden to all males except those in an official capacity, before some girls noticed his feet and started giggling. Ejected from the gym, Scholtz had to be punished, but the faculty was at a loss since none of the 180 specific rules covered the incident. They gave Scholtz a general reprimand.

While the chauvinistic write-ups were undoubtedly reflective of the general attitude of the times, the progress of women's basketball at Kentucky was slowed primarily because of inadequate facilities. There were too many organizations to be accommodated in one building. There also was lack of practice time, substandard coaching and the fact that intercollegiate games were difficult to arrange because few schools had organized teams.

The boys faced similar road blocks, which the administration refused to place in the same category as the men's program.

What was hailed as a major development in women's basketball at the University occurred in 1910, when the co-eds were withdrawn from the women's program, run by Helen 0. Stout, and allied with the Athletics Association. The merger compelled the boys to share practice time and coaching with the girls. The girls lost their first game that year, but won the final eight on their schedule.

Over the next 14 years, the girls would have such fine coaches as:

Dr. John J. Tigert, a former football and basketball star and team captain at Vanderbilt who attended Oxford on a Rhodes Scholarship. Tigert eventually became president of the University of Florida and U.S. Commissioner of Education.

William Tuttle, former UK basketball team captain and football star (1911-14) whose six touchdowns and 43 points against Maryville in 1914 are still UK records.

Jim Park, former UK baseball, track and basketball star and football team captain whose five touchdowns-rushing against Earlham-represent another UK record. Park eventually played major league baseball. He had the dubious honor of delivering the first homerun pitch to a young Boston pitcher/pinch hitter named George Herman "Babe" Ruth.

Sarah Blanding, former star on the New Haven Normal School Gymnasium team, who coached the KSC girls three years and then became player-captain in 1923. Blanding served as president of Vassar College.

A.B. "Happy" Chandler, who coached the team to a 7-3 record in 1922-23 with Blanding as his star player. Chandler, of course, would become two-time governor of Kentucky, U.S. Senator and Baseball Commissioner.

Coach of the last UK girls' teams of that era (1924) was Bart Peak, a UK football (1915) and basketball (1917) letterman who served many years as a YMCA career official.

After retirement, Peak became a Fayette County judge. He became noted for such punishment of juvenile offenders as making them kiss their parents.

That 1924 team swept its 10-game schedule and claimed not only the championship of Kentucky, but the championship of the

South, since Peabody and Chattanooga were among its victims.

But it was 50 years before UK sponsored a women's varsity bas-ketball team again. Since then the sport has flourished.

The first coach of the modern era was Assistant Athletics Direc-tor Sue Feamster, who guided the 1974-75 squad to a 16-9 record. The following year Feamster, who is credited with nicknaming the team "Lady Kats", directed the squad to a 13-12 record before giv-ing over the coaching reins to Debbie Yow, who compiled a 79-40 record in four seasons from 1976 through 1980.

Yow's previous experience had been in the high school ranks in her native North Carolina. She adjusted to collegiate coaching quickly, however, and guided the Lady Kats to a 19-7 record her first year. After a 23-12 season in 1977-78, she suffered through a dismal 13-16 "rebuilding" year, but was meanwhile recruiting an awesome group of athletes that included Valerie Still, Lea Wise and Patty Jo Hedges.

A 66-64 win over UT in 1979 was a bright spot for Yow, who compiled a 79-40 record during four years at UK. Kentucky had two outstanding young players coming back in Liz Lukschu and Maria Donhoff. Lukschu, a strong 6-4 center, would eventually en-ter the record books as Kentucky's second all-time scorer (she now ranks third) with 1,488 career points. Donhoff, a 6-0 forward and a classmate to Lukschu, now ranks fourth on the all-time list with 1,187 points.

What really brightened the ho-rizon was the incoming freshman class of 1979-80. Five very talented young ladies joined the team squad in the fall of 1979 and brought with them dreams of unlimited glory. Two would eventually leave the University before their playing ca-reers were over, but the three remaining–Patty Jo Hedges, Lea Wise

Valerie Still at Joseph-Beth book signing session.

and Valerie Still–became the best class of players in Lady Kat history.

By their junior year, the exciting black-haired Hedges and blond bomber Wise were generally regarded as the best guard combination in the country. Both were 5-foot-7. Hedges had dazzling quickness and leaping ability. She was also an excellent ball-handler.

Wise was an excellent defensive player who was primarily known for her outside shooting. Her best game was a 15 for 16 performance against Illinois in a 1982 NCAA playoff game. The Cats won, 88-80.

That freshman class helped vault the Lady Kats into the top 20 and into the national playoffs with a 24-5 record. During her four years at UK, Still scored more points than any other basketball player, male or female, with 2,763 points and 1,525 rebounds. She was a three-time consensus All-American. At one point she led the nation in scoring and rebounding before finishing second in both categories (24.8 ppg) and 14.3 rpg).

Still led the Kats to their highest national ranking (4th) in '83 and helped UK roll up a 30-game home court winning streak from 1980-82. In 1983, she led the sixth-ranked Kats to an 80-66 upset of powerhouse Old Dominion before a record crowd of 10,622 in Memorial Coliseum.

Still surpassed Pam Browning's all-time Lady Kat scoring mark midway of her junior season. She ripped past Dan Issel's career Wildcat scoring mark of 2,763 points just three games into her senior season.

In 1982 the Cats captured the SEC Tournament for the first time in school history with an 80-74 win over Tennessee. Following the game, the huge home crowd stormed the court in a celebration that lasted nearly 30 minutes The 1981-82 squad won the Southeastern Conference Championship Title and reached the quarter-finals of NCAA play before losing to eventual national champion Louisiana Tech on the Lady Techster's home floor. The 1984 Lady Kats were ranked fourth in the nation but fell to Indiana in the first round of the

NCAA tournament.

Terry Hall coached the Ladies from 1980-87, compiling a 138-66 record. Their best season was in 1982-83, when they set the single-game attendance record and were ranked as high as fourth nationally twice during the season.

Records are not available on the individual talents in the Early Era, but since the modern era began several players have performed up to standards that should immortalize them in Lady Kat basketball history.

Pam Browning was a little ahead of her time. The Lady Kats had a 71-40 record with her as starting center from 1974-78. She led the team in scoring and rebounding three times. Her poorest year was her senior season, when she was honored as a pre-season All-American, but was slowed with nagging injuries and averaged only 11.8 points a game.

Browning is in the Lady Kat record books for best scoring average in a season (25.5 in 1976-77), best rebounding average in a season (16.8 in 1974-75), most free throws made and most free throws attempted in a season (196-263 in 1976-77), most free throws made in a game (13 vs. Eastern Ky. in 1976-77) and most field goal attempts in a game (29 vs. Central Missouri in 1976-77). She currently is the second all-time leading scorer in Lady Kat history with 1,598 career points.

After Browning's departure, UK suffered through the aforementioned 13-16 campaign that would have been a total disaster had the Lady Kats not upset second-ranked Tennessee 66-64 before 7,000 fans in Memorial Coliseum. The attendance got a big boost when the much-anticipated game between the two schools' men's teams later that evening was canceled because of snow.

Still was a remarkable young lady who arrived on campus skinny and timid but left as the all¬ time leading scorer–male or female–in UK history. She chose UK because her older brother, Art, was a UK All¬-American football player (he later was an All-Pro lineman for the Kansas City Chiefs). Her impact was felt immediately. She averaged 22 points and 14 rebounds as she, Hedges and Wise all started and helped reverse the Lady Kats 13-16 record to a 24-5 mark their freshman season.

The talented trio of Hedges, Still and Wise led Kentucky to a 96-24 record over four seasons. In 1982, they advanced to the final game of the Midwest Regional before losing to eventual National Champion Louisiana Tech on the Techsters' home floor. And in 1983, their senior year, they were ranked fourth twice during a season that was highlighted by a stunning 80-66 upset over then-No.4 Old Dominion before a record 10,662 fans in Memorial Coliseum.

Still and Hedges own all but two of the career statistical marks for the Lady Kats. Still is in the books for most points, best scoring average, best rebounding average, most field goals attempted and made, most free throws attempted and made and most rebounds. Hedges, as mentioned before, owns the steals and assists marks.

The other two records are held by Lukschu (best field goal percentage) and Lisa Collins (free throw percentage), who completed her career in 1984.

Collins was a three-and-a-half year starter who toiled in the shadows of the three stars in the class ahead of her. And since UK was set at guards with Wise and Hedges, she was forced to learn a new position of small forward. At only 5-10, she was regularly dwarfed by the opposition, and would venture out to 15 or 20 feet to shoot the ball, which was her forte (she had a career shooting percentage of 51). In her final game as a Lady Kat, Collins set an SEC Tournament record by hitting all 10 of her field goal attempts against LSU. She ranks as eighth on the all-time list with 952 career points.

When Terry Hall arrived at Kentucky in 1980, the Lady Kats were coming off their most successful season ever and beginning to gain national respect. They had been ranked in the Top 20 throughout the 1979-80 season and had finished the year with a 24-5 record and a berth in the AIAW National playoffs.

But the season was just a hint of the great things to come under Hall's guidance. The Lady Kats had gone far beyond respectability and into the perennial role of national contender. They had been ranked in the top 20 every week and averaged 24 wins per season since Hall's arrival.

In her first year at UK, Hall's Cats went 25-6, winning the Kentucky Women's Intercollegiate Conference and reaching the final round of 16 in the AIAW National tournament. Hall was named the KWIC Coach of the Year that season.

In 1982 and again in 1983, they were considered among the top contenders for the NCAA Championship. The 1981-82 squad won the Southeastern Conference Championship and reached the quarter-finals of NCAA play before losing to eventual national champion Louisiana Tech on the Lady Techster's home floor. The Cats ranked fourth in the nation but fell to Indiana in the first round of the NCAA tournament.

Some Important Names

Brenda Hughes officiated her first basketball game in ballet shoes, but later became a pioneer for both African-Americans and women in basketball officiating...After "making do" with the shoes, she was the first female and the first African-American to represent the Bluegrass Basketball Association in the 10th and 11th Regions. Her professional achievements as an official, both on and off the court, provided her with the credentials to officiate numerous post-season games including a remarkable five Girls' Sweet Sixteen State Tournaments in her outstanding career.

B. Joan Mitchell - Joan Mitchell has been a leader in girls' sports statewide all of her adult life...She coached basketball, volleyball and softball...She helped initiate girls' sports in Northern Kentucky and was instrumental in founding the Northern Kentucky High School Girls' Coaches Association...She helped to get girls' sports accepted into the Northern Kentucky Athletic Conference... She helped to push for non-principals to be members of the Board of Control and backed the movement that brought women members to the Board...She has officiated and directed various state events and serves as executive secretary for the K.G.S.A...She was instrumental in getting volleyball and softball accepted as sanctioned sports by the KHSAA.

Bunny Daugherty–A leader and pioneer in girls' sports in Kentucky, Bunny Daugherty has been an athletic director and coach for 41 years...She has coached basketball 40 years, field hockey and volleyball 37 years, track 25 years, tennis and golf 25 years, and swimming and gymnastics 10 years...It was at Sacred Heart Academy in Louisville where she became known statewide when her team won the State Basketball Tournament in 1976...It was the second season after the Kentucky High School Athletic Association resumed girls' basketball in 1975...In the championship game, Sacred Heart turned back defending champion Butler of Jefferson County 68-55 behind the 20 points of Missy Brown, who earned All-Tournament honors...Bunny was founder and is still director of the Girls' Louisville Invitational Basketball Tournament and also of the Apple Field Hockey Tournament...She was Coach-of-the-Year for basketball in 1976...Her motto: "Kids plus Sports equal Fun!".

Roy Bowling–Girls' basketball was resumed at the high school level in 1974-75 and it didn't take long for coach Bowling and his Laurel County teams to become synonymous with success in Kentucky...Butler and Sacred Heart won the first two championships, but Laurel County started a three-year domination with a victory in the 1977 tournament, followed by championships in 1978 and 1979...Coach Bowling made Laurel County a regional contender each year and the Lady Cardinals won the state championship again in 1987...His 15 Laurel County teams won 403 games while losing only 61, and captured 12 district, 8 regional, and 4 state titles.

Sharon Garland–This Laurel County star owns a record that probably will never be broken as she was the high scorer in the championship game for three consecutive state champions...As a sophomore in 1977, she scored 15 points to lead coach Roy Bowling's Lady Cardinals to a 48-46 victory over Paris...The next year she scored 21 as Laurel beat Breathitt County 63-48...She capped her senior year with 15 points as Laurel defeated Lafayette 43-36. Sharon was a three-year All-Stater.

Donna L. J. Murphy–This Newport High School star helped give girls' basketball its rightful place alongside the boys' competition as her fluid moves, leaping ability, and patented left hand jump shot led her teammates to many victories...In 1975, she dazzled the crowds at the Girls' State Tournament with her two-game totals of 67 points and 50 rebounds, a performance that resulted in her selection as the Most Valuable Player of the tournament...She was the first recipient of the Joe Billy Mansfield Award for athletic and academic achievement, and was the first winner of Kentucky's "Miss Basketball" Award...Her senior year, she averaged 35 points and 20 rebounds in basketball, and was the state high jump champion in track in 1974.

Lea Wise-Prewitt–An All-America girls' basketball star for Lafayette High School in Lexington, helped the Lady Generals to two Sweet 16 State Basketball Tournament appearances, including the state title in 1979...Continues to be involved with girls' basketball, working on the Kentucky Utilities/KHSAA Statewide Basketball Radio Network.

Former UK star **Patty Jo Hedges-Ward** is named girls' basketball coach at Lexington Catholic. Patty Jo Hedges-Ward has played for the WNBA; University of Kentucky, Professionally in Europe and as a member of the American Team that won gold in the Pan Am games. She is regarded as one of the best teachers of basketball in the Nation.

1977–Lady Kat starting center Pam Browning became an All-American and compiled 1,598 points in her collegiate career. She ranks as the third-leading scorer at UK to this day.

1979–The Lady Kats upset second-ranked Tennessee, 66-64, before 4,500 fans in Memorial Coliseum. The attendance got a big boost when the much-anticipated game between the school's men's teams later that evening was canceled because of snow. Memorial

Coliseum hosted the largest crowd ever to attend a women's college basketball game in 1983.

1980–Terry Hall became the third head coach of the Lady Kats

1982–Lea Wise hit 15-of-16 outside shots against Illinois in an NCAA playoff game, helping the Cats win 88-80. Wise, a Lexington product, also led the team in autograph and photo requests because of her flashy and productive court play and her resemblance to actress Farrah Fawcett.

1982–The Cats captured the SEC Tournament title for the first time in school history with an 80-74 victory over Tennessee. Following the game, the huge home crowd stormed the court in a celebration that lasted nearly 30 minutes.

1983–With the talented trio of Hedges, Still and Wise, Kentucky ranked fourth twice during the 82-83 season and broke the national record for attendance at a women's collegiate game when 10,622 fans saw the Cats defeat Old Dominion.80-66, in Memorial Coliseum on Feb. 5, 1983.

1986–The university names Sharon Fanning as the fourth coach of the Lady Kats.

1987–The three-point goal is introduced to the women's game, proving to be an integral part of Kentucky basketball history for years to come.

1990–Under third¬ year coach Sharon Fanning, UK compiled a 23-8 record, edged into the top 25, and won three tournament titles, including an 85-76 come-from-behind victory over Toledo in the NWIT Championship.

1991–One year after winning the NWIT, UK made its first NCAA appearance since 1985-86.

1991–UK scores one of the biggest upsets in the program's history with a 67-66 victory over intrastate rival and eventual NCAA runner-up Western Kentucky in Bowling Green.

1999–UK celebrates 25 years of varsity women's basketball.

2000–Shantia Owens becomes the first player from UK to be taken in the WNBA draft, selected 53rd by the Phoenix Mercury.

2000–Tiffany Wait broke a school record for most games played with 122, also surpassing Jodie Whitaker on the Kats' all-time scoring list with 1,445 points.

2001–The Lady Kats took a summer tour of France and Switzerland and returned home with an unblemished 5-0 record.

2003–Valerie Still's jersey is retired at halftime of the UK-Alabama game at Memorial Coliseum, marking the first time in school history that a woman's jersey was retired.

2003–After 18 seasons as an assistant coach at Tennessee, Mickie DeMoss is named the sixth head coach of the UK women's basketball team.

2003–Within months of her hire, Mickie DeMoss and her staff hit the recruiting trail and signed one of the most highly touted recruiting classes in school history. Many dubbed the 6th-ranked class as the "Fab Five".

2003–Coach Mickie DeMoss earned her first win as the head coach at Kentucky as the Lady Kats downed IPFW, 79-59, on Nov. 21, 2003.

2004–Kentucky celebrates 100 years of varsity men's basketball.

2004–Junior Sara Potts broke the school record for most three-pointers made in a career (190) and single game (7).

2004–Senior and Kentucky native Selia,"SeSe", Helm ended her UK career etched in the record took in three different categories: scoring (5th), rebounding (8th) and field goals (3rd).

2004–Enthusiasm generated by the hiring of the wildly popular Mickie DeMoss, combined with a brilliant and well-funded marketing plan, resulted in a staggering fan craze. Kentucky fans bought tickets at an unprecedented rate. UK ranked No.1 nationally in increased attendance (3,488 more than the fans witnessed UK vs. No. 1 Tennessee).

2004–Sara Potts' 27 points help UK rally from a 17-point deficit to defeat Oregon State, 73-70, in the opening game of the Paradise Jam in St. Thomas, Virgin Islands.

2005–Freshman center Sarah Elliott scored a team-high 15 points to lead UK to a 71-63 win over 18th-ranked Georgia in Rupp Arena. It was UK Hoops' first win over a ranked opponent in five seasons and the first under second-year coach Mickie DeMoss. Elliott was named SEC Freshman of the Week after that performance, the first freshman to receive the honor in Lady Kat history.

2005–UK Coach Mickie DeMoss makes her first return to Thompson-Boling Arena in Knoxville, Tenn., where she first made a name for herself as a coach. DeMoss is presented with a glass vase by UT Coach Pat Summitt before a standing ovation.

2005–UK made its first postseason appearance since the 1998-99 season with a berth in the Sportsview.tv Women's National Invitation Tournament. The Lady Kats were rewarded for their spectacular attendance with a host site throughout the tournament. The Kats made their longest postseason run in school history, advancing to the semifinals of the WNIT before falling to West Virginia in double overtime.

2005–Sara Potts sank a jumper with 35 seconds remaining and fellow senior Danyelle Payne picked off Xavier sharpshooter Tara Boothe in the waning seconds as the Lady Kats edged the Musketeers, 67-62, to advance to the tournament's semifinal round. Potts scored 29 of her 31 points in the final period to rally the Kats from a 14-point second-half deficit.

2005–For the second consecutive season, the Lady Kats broke the school's attendance record. A total of 90,663 fans passed through the turnstiles during the 2004-05 season, smashing the school's previous single-season attendance total of 72,553 set during the 2003-04 campaign.

2005–Sara Potts finished her career as one of the most accomplished players in school history. She ranks fourth on the all-time scoring list (1563 points) and the UK career scoring average list (13.4 ppg).The lefty was UK's leading scorer in both her junior (16.8 ppg) and senior (15.6) campaigns.

2005–Valerie Still was inducted into the charter class in the newly created UK Athletics Hall of Fame. She was the only female of the 88 inductees.

2005–Kentucky began the season 8-0 for its best start since the 980-91 campaign. During that stretch the Lady Kats defeated Indiana State and Hofstra to win the 2005 Pepperdine Thanksgiving Classic. It was UK's first regular season tournament title since winning the Dartmouth Big Sky Classic in 2000.

2006–DeMoss piloted a team that went from winning a combined 20 games in the two years prior to her arrival in 2003 to a record-breaking regular season that included the most wins (22) since 1989-90. They also had the most conference wins in school history (nine), the highest conference finish (fourth) in 23 years, an appearance in the SEC Tournament semifinals for seven years, and UK's first NCAA bid in seven years. They were seeded highest (fifth) since 1983.

2006–DeMoss was named the SEC Coach of the Year by the SEC coaches and the AP. It was the first Coach of the Year honor in Lady Kat history.

2006–Kentucky became just the fourth unranked team in the history of NCAA women's basketball to knock off a No. 1 team when the Kats defeated top-ranked Tennessee 66-63, on Jan. 26, 2006–Junior Pfeiffer led the Kats in scoring with 16 points, including 7-of-7 free-throws. Pfeiffer nailed the game-winning free-throws with 14.8 seconds remaining and junior Nastassia Alcius added two charity shots in the waning seconds of the game to ice the victory. It was Kentucky's first win over the Lady Vols in 20 years.

2006–After defeating Ole Miss on the road and taking a 66-63 win over top-ranked Tennessee a game later, the Kats appeared in the top 25 national polls for the first time in 13 years. The Lady Kats were ranked 21st in The Associated Press and 23rd in the USA Today/ESPN Coaches Poll for one week. UK's No. 21 ranking marked the highest ranking in the AP poll since receiving a No.19 position on Feb. 10, 1985.

2006–Sophomore Samantha Mahoney and freshman Carly

Ormerod were named to the All-Southeastern Conference team. Mahoney was named to the second team, while Ormerod was named to the all-freshman team.

2006–Kentucky's record-breaking season came to an end with a heartbreaking loss to No. 16/17 and fourth-seeded Michigan State, 67-63, in the NCAA second round. The Kats defeated UT-Chattanooga in the first round, 69-59.

2006–Kentucky once again set season ticket records as 4,803 season tickets were sold for the 2005-06 campaign. The Lady Kats ranked 20th in the nation and third in the SEC in average attendance with 5,161 fans per game.

2007–Kentucky advanced to postseason play for the third consecutive seasons (one NCAA Tournament and two WNIT) for the first time in school history and captured back-to-back 20-win seasons for the first time since the 1989-90 and 1990-91 teams accomplished the feat. Kentucky senior Jennifer Humphrey and juniors Sarah Elliott and Samantha Mahoney each were named to the All-Southeastern Conference teams. Elliott and Mahoney were named to the second team by the league coaches and Elliott also received second-team honors from The Associated Press. Humphrey and Mahoney were named honorable mention by the AP.

2007–During halftime of the UK vs. Ole Miss game on Jan. 17, a special ceremony took place as 571 fallen soldiers from Kentucky were honored.

Since its completion in 1950, Memorial Coliseum has borne the names of thousands of Kentucky's war dead. But the lists of names -framed and hung on the walls of the ramps along two sides of the coliseum - had not been updated since the end of the Vietnam War. Their names were added to those of their predecessors during the ceremony. A season-high 7,565 fans and family members of the fallen soldiers witnessed the special event in Memorial Coliseum.

2007–The Lady Kats participated in their third straight postseason tournament with a third-round finish in the postseason WNIT. UK defeated Oakland and Ball State on the road before falling to

Wisconsin on the Badgers' home court 67-61. Kats were 14th nationally in the AP poll.

2007–After four seasons at the helm, Mickie DeMoss resigned April 11 as head coach. She compiled an overall record of 71-56 at Kentucky, including a 20-14 mark during the 2006-07 season.

2008–With Kentucky's impressive come-from¬ behind victory over No. 17/14 Georgia in Athens, Ga., on Jan. 31 the Lady Kats charted their first win over the Lady Dawgs since 2005, their first win in Athens since 1994 and their first win over a ranked SEC opponent on the road since 1986. It also marked UK's first win over any ranked opponent on the road since 1997.

2008–Kentucky charted eight wins during regular season Southeastern Conference play, marking the second-most league wins in school history. In his first season as head coach of the Wildcats, Matthew Mitchell's eight SEC wins were the most conference wins by a first-year head coach in UK Hoops history.

2008–A school-record five Lady Kats earned postseason SEC honors. Samantha Mahoney and Sarah Elliott were named to the second team, Victoria Dunlap and Amber Smith were selected to the All-Freshman Team and Chelsea Chowning was named the SEC Scholar Athlete of the Year. Elliott and Mahoney also were named honorable mention All-SEC by The Associated Press.

2008–The Lady Kats participated in a school¬ record fourth consecutive postseason tournament with a quarter finals finish in the postseason WNIT.

UK received a first-round bye and defeated Middle Tennessee and James Madison in Memorial Coliseum before narrowly falling to eventual champion Marquette in the quarterfinals in Lexington.

2008–Seniors Sarah Elliott and Samantha Mahoney played in 132 career games, breaking the school record of 129 games set by Jennifer Humphrey from 2003-07.

2008–Senior center Sarah Elliott became UK's all¬ time leading blocker. She holds the school record for blocks in a game (6), season (56), and career (195).

2008–UK ranked in the nation's top 25 and the SEC's top four in average attendance for the fifth consecutive season. The Cats were 23rd nationally and fourth in the SEC, averaging 4,765 fans per game.

2008–Kentucky saw a season-high attendance of 8,335 vs. No. 9 LSU in Rupp Arena on Jan. 27. It marked the fifth-largest crowd to see a women's game in Rupp Arena and was the seventh-largest crowd overall at UK.

2008–Matthew Mitchell hired new assistant coaches Kyra Elzy and Matt lnsell to replace Niya Butts (now the head coach at Arizona) and Vonn Read.

2010–UK won the Lady Eagle Thanksgiving Classic title in Hattiesburg, Miss., for its 28th regular¬ season tournament title in school history. The Cats defeated host-team Southern Miss in the championship game. Sophomore A'dia Mathies was elected the MVP while freshman Kastine Evans was named to the All-Classic team.

2011–Victoria Dunlap ended her career ranked in the top 10 of 14 career lists, including No. 1 in all¬ time games played and started (133) and No.2 all¬ time in scoring (1,846), rebounding (1,099), blocks (178), steals (307), free-throws made (445) and free¬ throws attempted (714).

2011–Victoria Dunlap was the 11th overall pick in the WNBA Draft as she was selected in the first round by the Washington Mystics. She became the highest draft pick in school history and the first UK player taken in the draft since Shantia Owens in 2000.

2011–The Kats ranked 26th nationally and led the SEC in steals per game (11.0). UK charted double-digit steals in 20-of-34 games and were 17-3 when doing so. Victoria Dunlap led the way, ranking 17th nationally and topping the SEC with 3.1 steals per game.

2011–The Kats ranked fifth nationally and led the SEC in turnover margin at +7.6. UK forced a league¬ high 24.0 turnovers per game while only turning it over 16.4 times per game. The Kats averaged 24.4 points per game off turnovers compared to the opponents'

13.3 ppg.

2011–The Lady Kats charted their second straight 20-win season, marking the first time UK accomplished that feat since the 2005-06 and 2006-07 seasons.

2011–Kentucky finished 11th nationally in average attendance according to the official attendance rankings kept by the NCAA. It marked UK's highest ranking since leading the nation in attendance in 1982-83.

2011–UK finished second in the SEC regular season and was runner-up in the SEC Tournament for the second straight season.

2011–The Wildcats made their school record seventh consecutive postseason appearance second-round finish in the NCAA Tournament. It marked UK's first back-to-back NCAA since the 1982-83 seasons.

2011–The Kats finished No. 17 in the final AP poll & No.16 in final USA Today/ESPN coaches' poll. It marked the highest final AP ranking since the Wildcats finished 11th in 1983.

2012- The Lady Kats completed one of the best seasons in program history in 2011-2012. They won their first regular season SEC title since 1982. They tied the school record for victories (28-7) in a season. Thirteen of those victories (13-3) set a record for conference wins.

Advancing to the Elite Eight of the Kingston Region, they lost to Connecticut, 80-65 , failing for the second time in three seasons to advance any further. Samari Walker led UK scorers with 14 points and five rebounds, which earned her All-Regional honors.

The league coaches and the Associated Press named UK's A'dia Mathies SEC Player of the Year. She also made All-Conference, the All-SEC defensive team, and the SEC All-Tournament team.

The U.S. Basketball Writers named her All-America; only one other Lady Kat, Valerie Still, has been so honored.

The Associated Press named UK coach Matthew Mitchell SEC Coach of the Year. He also won the award in 2010.

"We have to keep showing up and keep knocking on the door,"

Matthews said. "At some point in time, we'll get there."

Bookshelf Bibliographic Note

A 22"x39" three-tiered bookshelf in my office contains more than 100 books about Kentucky basketball. This does not include UK media guides dating back to 1945.

The list begins with Greg Stanley's Before *Big Blue, University of Kentucky Press, 1995,* which chronicles the early history of organized sports at the University of Kentucky. Stanley covers the half-century (1890-1940) when football ruled the athletic department.

An autographed copy (*"I hope that you enjoy every page of this book–To a real friend, Adolph F. Rupp"*) of Rupp's **Championship Basketball** occupies a place of honor. It is mostly an Xs and Os publication that delves into passing, shooting, dribbling, and other intricacies of the game.

Rupp was a poetry buff, along with many other pursuits, so it was natural for him to preface the book with the following:

> *A mighty monarch in the day of old*
> *Made offer of high honors, wealth, and gold*
> *To one who should produce in form concise*
> *A precept soothing in his hours forlorn,*
> *Yet one that in his prosperous days would warn,*
> *Many the maxim sent the King, men say,*
> *The one he chose..."This too shall pass away!"*

Abraham Lincoln followed the same philosophy, Rupp said, and what was good enough for "Honest Abe" was good enough for him; however, many years after the fact Rupp still had nightmares of his "Runts" losing to Texas Western in the 1966 NCAA championship game.

In 1979, Harry Lancaster penned *Adolph Rupp As I Knew Him,* with Cawood Ledford. The only memorial thing about this paperback is Lancaster crediting Rupp with a racist remark after UK president John W. Oswald ordered Rupp to recruit black players:

"Harry, that son of a bitch is ordering me to get some n-----s in here. What am I going to do? He's the boss."

That same year, Simon & Schuster published Frank Fitzpatrick's *And The Walls Came Tumbling Down: Kentucky, Texas Western, and the Game that Changed American Sports.* That picked up where Lancaster left off and further darkened the image of Rupp as a modern day Simon Legree.

Two valuable books in our collection are UK Professor Bert Nelli's The Kentucky Tradition and Tom Wallace's The Kentucky Basketball Encyclopedia. Both are lengthy chronicles of the Wildcat basketball program. Nelli takes a more academic approach while Wallace gives us many facts and figures that are most valuable to researchers.

Lonnie Wheeler's "Blue Yonder" is a look into the Wildcat phenomena, which Rick Pitino, in association with Dick "Hoops" Weiss, also covers in *Full Court Pressure: A Year in Kentucky Basketball.* The setting for Pitino's book is the 1991/92 season, when the Wildcats lost a heartbreaker to Duke in the NCAA Regional final.

A copy of Pitino's earlier book, *Born to Coach: A Season with the New York Knicks,* with Bill Reynolds, contains a front cover notice: "with an update that answers the question why I went to KY." It boils down to a clash of personalities between Pitino and the Knicks general manager.

Jim Host was the most productive publisher of UK books, with at least 10 to his credit. His stable of authors includes such well-known Kentucky sports personalities as Cawood Ledford and John McGill, both deceased; Billy Reed, Oscar Combs, Mike Embry and Tom Wallace. Former UK sports information directors Chris Cameron and Brooks Downing and former assistant basketball coach and former athletic directors Harry Lancaster and C.M. Newton also contributed to Host's mixture.

Billy Reed is an award-winning journalist who has been covering sports in Kentucky since 1959. A native of Mt. Sterling, he is a 1966 graduate of Transylvania University, which awarded him a distinguished alumni award in 1980. Reed has worked for the *Lexington Herald-Leader, the Courier-Journal, and Sports Illustrated.* He has many works to his credit.

Cawood Ledford, legendary "Voice of the Wildcats", was working on his seventh book for Host when he died of cancer in 2001.

Tom Wallace once served as editor of Cawood on Kentucky. He is a former columnist for *The Cats' Pause*.

Jamie H. Vaught has written four books containing interviews with players, coaches and others associated with the UK basketball program. He spent 13 years as a columnist for The Cats' Pause and currently works for *The Daily News* in Middlesboro. Jamie is an associate professor of accounting at Southeast Community College.

Kentucky's two major newspapers, *The Courier-Journal and The Herald-Leader,* have been major contributors to the list of UK publications, especially in coverage of championships won or nearly won. They are included in the following list of books on our basketball shelf:

CHAMPIONSHIP BASKETBALL, by Adolph F. Rupp, Prentice-Hall, 1948.

THE RUPP YEARS, by Tevis Laudeman, the Courier-Journal, 1972.

BASKETBALL: The Dream Game In Kentucky, by Dave Kindred, Data Courier, Inc., 1976.

KENTUCKY BASKETBALL'S BIG BLUE MACHINE, by Russell Rice, Strode Publishers, Huntsville, Ala., 1976.

A YEAR AT THE TOP, by John McGill and Walt Johnson, photography by Walt Johnson, Jim Host and Associates Inc., 1978.

BASKETBALL IN THE BLUE GRASS STATE: The Championship Teams, by Mike Embry, Leisure Press, New York, 1983.

MARCH MADNESS: The Kentucky High School Basketball Tournament, by Mike Embry, Icarus Press, South Bend, 1985.

RICK PITINO: Born to Coach, A Season with the New York

Knicks, with Bill Reynolds, New American Library, New York, 1988.

ADOLPH RUPP AS I KNEW HIM, by Harry Lancaster, with Cawood Ledford. 1979.

BASKETBALL PITINO STYLE, with Cawood Ledford, by Chris Cameron, Host Communications, Inc., 1990.

THE MAKING OF CHAMPIONS: Kentucky Basketball 1979-1980, by Oscar Combs, Photography by Bill Straus and Alen Malott, Lexington Productions, Inc.

MACY, by Kyle Macy as told to Cawood Ledford, Lexington Productions, Inc., 1980.

BIG BLUE MANIA: Kentucky Basketball 1981-82, by Oscar Combs, Lexington Productions, Inc., 1982.

FULL-COURT PRESSURE: A Year in Kentucky Basketball, by Rick Pitino, Hyperion, New York, 1992.

THE LIVES OF RILEY, by Mark Heisler, Macmillan USA, 1984, by Greg Stanley, University of Kentucky Press, 1995.

THE CARR CREEK LEGACY by Don Miller. Vantage Press. 1995.

HEART OF BLUE, by Cawood Ledford, Host Communications, Inc. 1995.

THE LEGACY AND THE GLORY, Greatest moments in Kentucky Basketball History, edited by Mike Bynum, Ad Craft, 1995.

THE OFFICIAL UNIVERSITY OF KENTUCKY BASKETBALL BOOK, by Randall S. Baron and Russell Rice, Devyn Press, 1986.

UNTOUCHABLE: THE CROWNING OF THE COMMONWEALTH, Host Communications, Inc., 1996.

GO BIG BLUE: Relive Kentucky's Memorial 1995-96 Season, by the staff of the Lexington Herald-Leader, Lexington Herald-Leader Co., 1996.

JOURNEY TO GREATNESS: The 1995-96 Kentucky Wildcats' National Championship, edited by Francis J. Fitzgerald, Ad Craft. 1996.

A YEAR WITH THE CATS: From Breathitt County to the White

House, by Dave Kindred, Jim Host & Associates Inc., 1997.

A LEGACY OF CHAMPIONS, Edited by Mike Bynum, Epic Sports, Masters Press, Indianapolis, 1997.

BLUE GRIT: A Review of Kentucky's Courageous 1996-97 Season, by the staff of the Lexington Herald-Leader, the Lexington Herald Co., 1997.

COMEBACK CATS: The 1997-98 Kentucky Wildcats' Unforgettable National Championship Season, edited by Mike Bynum, from the Sports Pages of the Courier-Journal.

BLUE YONDER, by Lonnie Wheeler, Orange Fraser Press, Inc., Wilmingham, Ohio, 1998.

A DREAM COME TRUE, by Cameron Mills & Brooks Downing, Addax Publishing Group, Lenexa, Kansas, 1998.

CATS UP CLOSE: Champions of Kentucky Basketball, by Jamie H. Vaught, McClanahan Publishing House, Kuttawa, Ky., 1999.

NEWTON'S LAWS, The C.M. Newton Story as told to Billy Reed, Host Communications, Inc., 2000.

BARON OF THE BLUEGRASS: Winning Words of Wisdom by and about ADOLPH Rupp, Legendary Kentucky Basketball Coach, by Mike Embry, Towle House Publishing Co., Nashville, 2000.

BASKETBALL IN THE BLUE GRASS: The Championship Teams, by Mike Embry, Leisure Press, New York, 1983.

MARCH MADNESS: The Kentucky High School Basketball Tournament, by Mike Embry., Icarus Press, South Bend, Ind. 1985.

THE KENTUCKY BASKETBALL ENCYCLOPEDIA, by Tom Wallace

100 YEARS OF KENTUCKY BASKETBALL: University of Kentucky, Publishers Mitch Barnhart (UK) & Host Communications.

KRAZY ABOUT KENTUCKY: Big Blue Hoops, by Jamie H. Vaught, Wasteland Press, Louisville, 2003.

BIG BLUE: 100 Years of Kentucky Wildcats Basketball, by Michael Bradley, Sporting News, 2002.

UK 100: A CENTURY OF BASKETBALL: A commemorative publication by the Lexington Herald-Leader sports staff.

BASKETBALL CENTURY OF CHAMPIONS, by TCP staff members, edited by Darrell Bird, the Cats' Pause, 2002.

TALES FROM THE KENTUCKY HARDWOOD: A Collection of the Greatest Kentucky Basketball Stories Ever Told, by Denny Trease, Sports Publishing LLC, 2002.

HEART OF A CHAMPION, By Jeff Sheppard and Tom Wallace, Addax Publishing Group, Lenexa, KS, 1998.

THE WILDCAT LEGENCY,: A Pictorial History of Kentucky Basketball, by Russell Rice, JCP Corp. of Virginia, Virginia Beach, Va., 1982.

KENTUCKY'S BASKETBALL BARON, by Russell Rice, Saga-more Publishing, Champaign, Ill., 1994.

FIRST CATS: Amazing Origins of the UK Sports Tradition, by Tom Stephens, Oakleaf Publishing, Inc., 2006.

AND THE WALLS CAME TUMBLING DOWN: Kentucky, Texas Western, and the Game that Changed American Sports, by Frank Fitzpatrick 2006.

Born to Coach: A Season with the New York Knicks, by Rick Pitino, with Dick "Hoops" Weiss.

THE KENTUCKY BASKETBALL VAULT; A History of UK Basketball, by Russell Rice, Whitman Publishers, LCC, 2009.

KHSAA SWEET SIXTEEN: Boys' Tournament History and Record Book, edited by John McGill, first published in 1982.

BOUNCE BACK, by John Calipari, Simon & Schuster, 2010, 304 pages.

BEYOND A DREAM: A Mother's Courage a Family's Fight, a Son's Determination, by Mark Krebs with Dr. James Conrad Gerner, Beyond a Dream Publishing, 2010.

Throughout my career as a newspaperman (1951–1967), a sports publicist (1967–1989), an author, and a quarter-century as a columnist for *The Cats' Pause,* I interviewed a myriad of UK athletes, past and present. My articles in TCP alone numbered more than one thousand. They were a basic research tool for this book.

Unless otherwise indicated, all pictures in this book are from University of Kentucky Media Relations, or the Russell Rice collection.